G000152786

Restoring
FINE CHINA

Restoring

FINE CHINA

Muriel White

B. T. Batsford Ltd, London

Acknowledgements
I am greatly indebted to many people who have
helped in one way or another with the
preparation of this book. I especially wish to
thank the following who have helped in finding
ceramics to illustrate techniques: Hart and
Rosenberg, Mr L. D. W. Buckle, and Miss J.
Day. My thanks are due to Royal Worcester
Spode Ltd for permission to reproduce the
photographs at Figs 2–8 and to Copydex Ltd
who supplied the photograph for Fig 84. Also, to
the many students whose problems have led to
interesting solutions as well as traumatic
moments. Above all, to my family, who have
provided practical help as well as moral support.

For Jeremy White, photographer
and
Sarah White, illustrator

First published 1981
© Muriel White 1981

All rights reserved. No part of this publication
may be reproduced in any form or by any means
without permission from the Publishers

ISBN 0 7134 1837 0

Printed in Great Britain
by Robert Maclehose Ltd
Glasgow, Scotland
for the publishers,
B. T. Batsford Ltd,
4 Fitzhardinge Street, London W1H OAH

Contents

A suitable occupation?
Cost
Costing
Accepting commissions
Reference library
Training

Colour photographs

1·Introduction to China Restoration

The aim of this book is to supply a source of reference and information for the conscientious student who wishes to reach a professional standard. The emphasis is on restoring fine quality china, which includes earthenware, stoneware, bone china and porcelain. The methods described will not enable odds and ends to be patched up quickly and cheaply in order to make them more saleable. Nor is it intended that they should be used on domestic china. Apart from hygienic considerations, the cost in both time and materials make restoration impractical except on valuable articles. It would probably be cheaper to buy a new tea set than to replace one cup handle. It is not suggested that these methods should be used on rare museum pieces, for which there is quite a different code of practice and a different range of materials.

Just as much thought and attention to ethical considerations must go into a commercial repair as the museum restorers bestow on their work. The restoration of china is not without its critics, who feel that all repairs should be clearly obvious. But I would argue that a figure with two good arms rather than stumps, or a dish without a network of black cracks, is more aesthetically pleasing. This objection to restoration is seldom applied to a chair with three legs or a clock that does not tick. Any repair should be carried out with honesty, confining the work to the damaged area only, without rejuvenation elsewhere. It must also be clearly understood that 'restored' does not mean 'in mint condition'. Over-restoration and poorly finished work is to blame for much of the objection and resistance to restoration.

China restoring is interesting, absorbing, rewarding and always varied. If two damaged objects are identical, it would be rare indeed to find them broken in exactly the same way. Restoring anything that is irreplaceable is a great responsibility. The student must be willing and able to devote time to practice under expert tuition. The theory of repairing ceramics does not automatically provide the skill needed to bond accurately, model exactly or paint difficult subjects. It is an exacting but worthwhile training.

Although it may seem that the pitfalls and difficulties have been over-stressed to discourage the student, it must be remembered that they are the accumulated problems of many years and several hundred students. It does not follow that every student will encounter every problem. Experience is knowing how to avoid the pitfalls, learning is discovering how to get out of them. With practice most students can achieve neat repairs to minor chips and small breaks on plain china. However, if the ability to model accurately and draw well has to be acquired before anything more complicated can be tackled, the student must be prepared for further study and practice.

The materials to be used and basic methods of working are explained in preference to describing specific jobs which may never be encountered. Each restoration is an individual case around which these techniques are adapted. Recommendations are given in the light of experience, not as theoretical answers to hypothetical questions. An understanding of the underlying principles will enable the restorer to know which tasks to avoid and which can be completed successfully. It is important to know, also, which should be referred to another profession. China mending methods should not be applied to repairing other materials. Each has its own methods and disciplines needing specific study and thorough understanding. A great deal of unintentional damage can be caused by dabbling. For instance, although the methods described can be safely applied to Parian ware they are not intended for marble, which it imitates. If what is taken for

Fig. 1 An old repair. The handle has been riveted and laced into position

marble turns out to be alabaster which, although similar in appearance, is soluble in water, the inaccurate identification would lead to disaster.

Before using new or alternative materials precise specifications should be obtained from the manufacturer. If only vague answers can be obtained about durability, hardness, heat tolerance and resistance to chemicals, it is imperative that exhaustive independent tests are carried out before accepting optimistic claims. No method which is irreversible without damage to the object should ever be used. In the future better methods of restoration will become available or subsequent owners may prefer unrestored pieces.

There is a long history of repair to ceramic objects. In the middle of the seventeenth century the Chinese were observed stitching together broken pieces of porcelain with copper wire. There is a European porcelain model, made about a hundred years later, of a repairer with a riveted bowl. The potters naturally saw the repairers as a threat to future business. This led to a long dispute which was eventually settled by the pottery sellers doing the repairs. By 1900 many firms were advertising their services in the national press and riveting was a service offered by many ironmongers and china shops.

The Victorians were particularly addicted to refurbishing and mending, which is made abundantly clear by the suggestions and recipes in the cookery books and encyclopaedias of the period.

Freshly gathered snail slime is one suggestion for repairing china. Although no instructions are given for its harvesting or application. Grated Suffolk cheese beaten with quick lime is a recipe in another Victorian book. Everyone made an attempt to stick china pieces together again, often with great success. The chief difficulty was the solubility of the materials used. The marketing of epoxy resin adhesives has improved methods of restoration. With the skilful use of the right materials, repairs are long lasting and inconspicuous.

To understand the nature of pots it is as well to know something of their manufacture. There are many books on the subject, covering both general methods of manufacture or devoted to the history of one particular factory. Additionally, many modern firms arrange tours of their potworks and maintain excellent museums for public use.

In simple terms, china is clay which, after shaping, is irreversibly changed into an insoluble, rigid form by submission to very high temperatures. The type of body resulting from this process depends on the composition of the clay and the firing temperature used. Refinements and improvements in techniques have been introduced over the centuries, but the basic principle of a clay body covered by an impervious glass-like skin is unchanged. The origins of transforming dry clay into useful vessels is not recorded.

The potter's craft developed slowly through the centuries until three main classes of ware emerged. At the lowest temperatures porous earthenware is produced. By varying the ingredients firing at higher temperatures becomes possible and stoneware and porcelain are made. The greater heat fuses the materials to give a vitrified non-porous body. Ceramic articles, both useful or decorative, can be formed by hand modelling, casting in a mould or by being shaped with the aid of a wheel or lathe. This is done while the clay is in a damp, plastic state. It must be completely dried out before firing. The earliest form of decoration was done by incising or impressing the clay before it was fired.

Decoration can also be applied to the surface with a different coloured clay or slip. The article can be given an outer skin of glaze, which is similar in composition to glass, either to make it

Fig. 2 Making plates on a modern potter's wheel

Fig. 3 Cleaning up a casting before assembling into a group

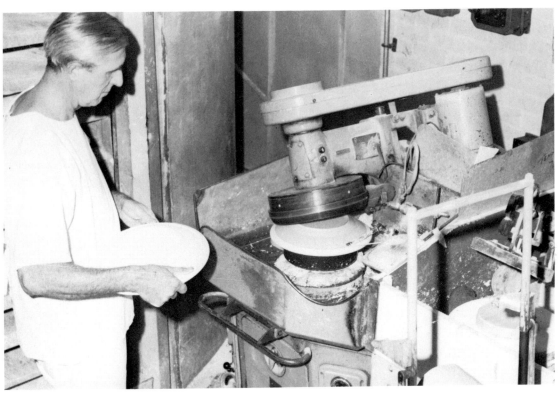

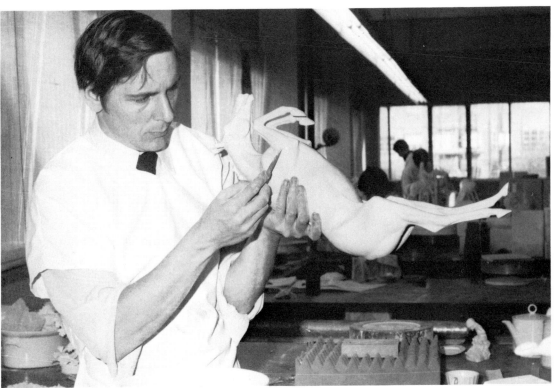

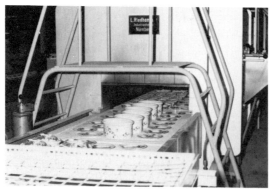

Fig. 4 Porcelain entering a modern kiln on a conveyor belt

Fig. 5 Preparing a figure group for the kiln. The group on the left has been fired and shows the amount of shrinkage which takes place

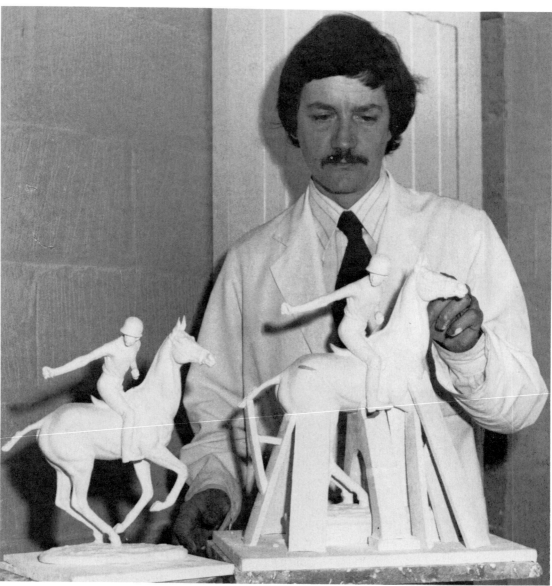

Fig. 6 Painting a limited edition group

Fig. 8 Gilding a vase

Fig. 7 Decorating a plate

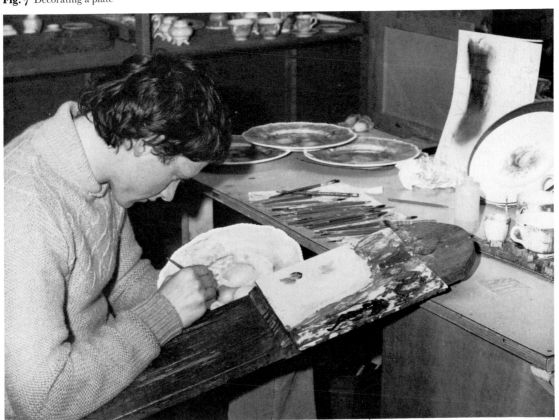

watertight or for decoration. The glaze can be either transparent or opaque according to the materials used in its manufacture. Metal oxides are added to the glaze to give a range of colours. The enamel colours used for decorating china are made by virtifying glaze and oxides together in a crucible. The resulting glass-like mass is ground to a powder and mixed to a paste with a suitable medium then painted on the surface of the china. Once applied the enamels are fired in a kiln to fuse them to the glaze, making them durable and fadeless. High fired ceramics are not decorated with artist's pigments which would burn away at kiln temperatures. When engraving techniques were developed transfer prints were used to apply the decorations to the china using powdered oxides to produce the colour.

The firing temperatures for the different types of ware and decoration are as follows:

1300°C and over (2340°F)	Porcelain
1250°C (2280°F) 1100°C (2020°F)	} Stoneware
1100°C (2020°F) 950°C (1740°F)	} Earthenware
950°C (1740°F) 750°C (1380°F)	} Enamel colours, depending on oxides used
700°C (1300°F)	Gold

High fired ceramics had been exported from the far east for several centuries before suitable clay deposits were discovered in Europe in the early eighteenth century. Oriental porcelain was the envy of the western world and experiments to imitate it led to great improvements in all types of pottery manufacture. The oriental influence on style and decoration has been continuous. As skill in clay refinement and kiln management increased it became possible to manufacture lighter and finer wares more cheaply. Throughout the nineteenth century china manufacturers produced a mass of wares to suit many markets. This was a time of accelerating expansion of the

Fig. 9 Tin glaze earthenware decorated with oxide. The worn glaze at the edges is typical of the ware and should not be repaired

Fig. 10 English hand painted enamel decoration

Fig. 11 English transfer printing

Fig. 12 Chinese hand painted enamel decoration

industry and a multitude of pastes and glazes, decorations and objects were produced to satisfy the demand. The trade in pottery goods was worldwide: oriental porcelains still travelled to Europe and the United States, and clay was exported from America to the United Kingdom for manufacture. At the same time Europe sent quantities of earthenware, creamware and bone china to meet the demand in the United States and Australia. Much of it was decorated with blue transfer prints depicting local scenes. Fortunes were made and lost in developing new processes for manufacturing and decorating china.

The history of ceramics is a long and fascinating one; it is also a very necessary study for the china restorer. When remodelling a missing cup handle or an arm, for instance, it is necessary to know the exact type of replacement needed. The restorer needs to know at least the country of origin and the period as a starting point for research. The beginner should disregard personal preferences at first and acquire a wide general knowledge of types of ware, shape and style of decoration in relation to their period and place of origin. From this background further study can advance into more specialised fields. Excellent illustrations can be found in the larger auctioneers' catalogues and specialist magazines. These can be most useful for study and for supplying details of design needed when replacing missing areas. Most museums have far more exhibits than space in which to display them, and articles in store can usually be inspected by prior arrangement. An enquiry to the curator of a museum known to have a collection of ceramics will frequently be most helpful in tracing a suitable pattern to copy. Return postage for a reply should always be enclosed. Useful books and publications are listed at the end of Chapter 10.

As well as the theory, the practical side of restoration must be considered. The intending restorer needs something to practise on and somewhere to work, as well as adequate tools and materials. Beginners are usually over-anxious to start restoring and do not allow enough time for learning the essentials of the job. It will save many disappointments and anxieties if the difficulties and snags are fully explored on practice pieces before embarking on complicated repairs. Very little will be learnt by doing a difficult or too advanced repair badly. It is better to learn the feel of the materials and master the use of a few good tools rather than to change techniques constantly in an attempt to find something easier. It is the skill of the hand behind the tool which counts; regrettably there are no magic wands. Nor are there any trade secrets to spy out; the only trick for good restoration is to ensure that each stage is perfectly done before proceeding further.

A few interesting but not valuable pieces should be found to start on. This may involve a little expense but this is better than the worry of learning on other peoples' china, even when the owner declares that anything is better than the

way it looks now. It is much better to wait awhile until you are proficient so that all types of repairs can be undertaken with confidence. Once a reputation for inferior, substandard repairs has been gained it will be difficult to live it down.

To get the best practice, find items with simple breaks – those which are in no more than three pieces. Getting even a few pieces in alignment is not as simple as it seems. Surface chips and small pieces missing from plate edges or teapot spouts will provide excellent experience in handling filling composition in a simple way. Pieces of china which have been previously mended will give practice in taking apart and cleaning old repairs as well as in re-bonding them. If figures are available, choose ones with damaged drapery or bocage (closely clustered flowers and foliage) and leave broken limbs until a little experience at modelling has been gained. Cups without handles are most useful in providing practice for free hand modelling and painting. Piecing together badly shattered bowls and dishes is difficult and time consuming even for the experienced repairer; it is much better to use the time available doing a variety of simple breaks. Avoid acquiring a stack of old, discoloured plates with long cracks. There is always a plentiful supply of these, but long cracks, especially on plain china, need the expert use of an airbrush. A stack of plates is very useful when experimenting with painting and colour matching but choose sound ones which can be used as a permanent reference. Very large articles should be avoided unless a heating cabinet and a turntable of suitable size are available. Large *jardinières*, oriental vases and carp bowls weigh up to 25 kg ($\frac{1}{2}$ cwt) so the restorer must be capable of manipulating heavy weights while working on such items. Doing a minor repair to an already restored object can also present problems. Unless it is certain that the materials originally used can be safely submitted to further treatment, previous repairs should first be removed entirely. If they are extensive this may involve more work than a small additional repair warrants. As well as a good selection of breakages, a variety of types of china is advisable, so that applying various textures may be tried out. Try to obtain jasper and bisque as well as glazed china, enamelled as well as printed decoration. Practice time is never wasted.

The materials and tools needed for each stage of the work are listed and discussed at the beginning of each chapter. Suggestions for organising the working space will be found in the final chapter. Advice on making tools and caring for them is also included. If the requirements seem excessive, it must be pointed out that this book is intended as a reference for serious study. It is as well to realise at the outset that the cost of equipment, tools and materials plus the time needed for restoring the china make it unsuitable just as a hobby for anyone who is unable to devote more than the odd half hour at weekends for training. China restoration is a combination of several difficult crafts. The restorer needs ability in modelling, painting and drawing plus a little knowledge of chemistry to be able to handle materials skilfully and responsibly. The restorer has a responsibility to the china being repaired and to its future owners, so must never be intimidated into doing a quick, cheap cover-up job. Contrary to popular belief restoring is not just a blob of plaster covered with a lick of paint taking ten minutes at the most. All but the most minor repairs will take many hours of work, compared with which the cost of materials is a small proportion of the total cost. Many people consider doing their own repairs as an economy measure, but unless a large quantity of china is in need of attention the cost of the necessary equipment could outweigh any saving. Apart from possible damage to the article, failed attempts at repairs can be very costly in the long run. If professional advice has to be sought the time spent in removing previous repairs would be an additional cost.

Anyone wishing to commission a restorer's services should first ask to see some examples of recent work so that the standard of workmanship can be judged. Make sure, also, that there is a clear understanding of the restorer's intentions and establish a maximum price for the work. The work is highly skilled and time consuming, so a reasonable fee must be expected. The various aspects of the costs involved in restoration will be discussed in the last chapter.

The purpose of the book will have been fulfilled if through its assistance the student is encouraged to aim for a higher standard of workmanship and a sounder knowledge of reputable methods and materials.

Fig. 13 Suitable items for practising cleaning and bonding. The china should be varied and interesting but, to begin with, not valuable

Fig. 14 Suitable pieces for the beginner to practise modelling and moulding. The damage should be as varied as possible

2 ⊹ Cleaning and Preparation

China has been considered precious enough to mend for many generations. Repairs range from the silver encasing of oriental porcelain to the lead sleeve on a humble earthenware teapot spout. Many methods have been used to hold the fragments together and ingenious ways found to make new pieces. China has been sewn together with wire, riveted and stuck. New pieces have been engineered from metal, wood, plaster, gelatine and fibreglass; anything that would hold a shape. A decision has to be taken as to whether these repairs are to be removed altogether and redone with modern materials, or if they are to be considered as part of the object's history and should remain. Whatever the conclusion the china will need to be cleaned.

Before plunging into the practicalities of restoration the job must be assessed and a programme of treatment decided upon. The china should be scrutinised carefully, preferably under magnification, for hidden damage or weaknesses caused by fine cracks. Be prepared to find more damage than anticipated, especially when dealing with items that have been previously restored. When an arm on a figure has been entirely repainted it is uncertain whether it is a single break, whether the whole arm has been replaced or only a finger damaged. It is not unknown for the colour of ornamental china to be changed to fit the decor. This is usually done by a previous owner with nail varnish, or something similar, and comes off with ease.

Most often, china to be mended is dirty, stained and held together with liberal quantities of an unknown brown substance or a mass of metal work. These must all be removed and solvents stronger than water will frequently be needed, plus a few tools to deal with the metal. No cleaning method is universally safe, so the china mender must be prepared to halt operations at any moment. Never leave a piece to soak for hours unattended, even in clean water. Inspect for any change every few minutes to begin with and then, if no harm is apparent, every half hour.

Materials and tools

Detergent (Lissapol NDB or mild domestic washing up liquid); for cleaning china

De-ionised water or purified water; used for cleaning china

Domestic abrasive powder (Ajax, Vim); used occasionally for obstinate dirt

Barrier cream (Rosalex No. 9, Kerodex 71); used to protect hands from solvents

Methylated spirits (denatured alcohol); a solvent for grease

Acetone and Cellulose thinners; solvents for shellac and cellulose glues

Paraffin (Kerosene); a solvent for bitumen and pitch

Water soluble paint stripper (Nitromors green label); a solvent for most modern adhesives

Oxalic acid crystals; inkstain remover

Rust remover (Jenolite, Naval Jelly); rust and iron stain removers

Dental steriliser (Steradent); lime deposit remover

Sepiolite or hydrated magnesium silicate; used to make stain removing poultices

Dismantling lubricant (WD40, Plus-gas); for releasing rusted nuts and bolts

Chlorine bleach (Parazone, Brobat); bleach for vegetable stains

Biological bleaching powder (Biotex); bleach for protein stains

Hydrogen peroxide 100 volume; for removing dirt and stains

Butyl protective gloves; for protecting the hands from chemicals

Bowls and containers; for washing and bleaching solutions

Brushes; for cleaning china
Probes or potters' pins; for removing rivets
Tension files (Abrafile); for cutting lacings
Soldering iron; for melting solder
Scalpel, pliers, forceps; for removing rivets
Magnifying glass or spectacles; for close inspection of work
Cotton wool and clean rag; for swabbing and cleaning

A non-ionic detergent at a 1% dilution in de-ionised water should be used for washing broken china. A mild domestic washing up liquid may be used on non-porous china provided it is without additional hand protectors and perfumes.

De-ionised water should always be used for washing or soaking low fired earthenware. Tap water contains dissolved chemicals which are capable of reacting with china where the glaze is cracked or missing. The reaction is visible as a furry white crystaline deposit which will constantly reappear after you have removed it. Apparatus is available to de-ionise tap water but it is expensive. Purified water can be purchased in small quantities from a pharmacist.

A little abrasive cleaning powder can be used on chips to remove stubborn dirt which does not respond to simple washing.

Barrier cream should always be applied to the hands before washing china or handling solvents. Its protective effect usually lasts about four hours. Apply only as much as the skin will absorb otherwise the hands will become so slippery in water that the china will be at risk. Protective gloves can also be used but they should be made of a material that will not be affected by chemicals.

The solvents listed will be needed to deal with adhesives that do not dissolve in water. Their use and application is detailed in the text. They should not be used indiscriminately; water should always be the first choice. They must always be used with care.

Bleaches should not be used as a matter of course, only if they are really needed, and then sparingly. Gold can be adversely affected by solvents and bleaches so its reaction should always be tested before immersing gold decoration in either.

Fig. 15 The result of washing low fired earthenware in tap water

Fig. 16 Cleaning tools. Cotton swab sticks, tooth brushes, spout brush, bottle brush and penknife

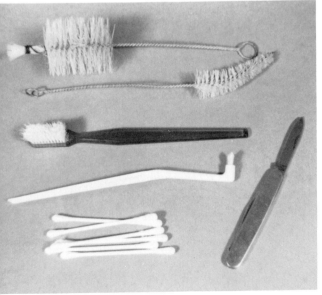

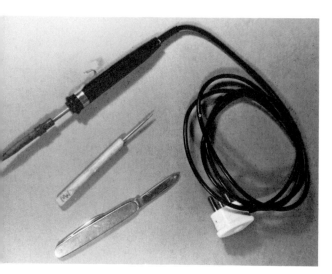

Fig. 17 Tools for removing rivets and lacings. Soldering iron, probe and penknife

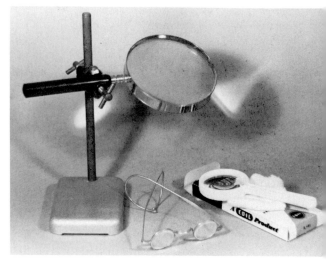

Fig. 18 A good magnifying lens is essential for close inspection of the work

Bowls and containers will be needed in a variety of shapes and sizes to accommodate the china while washing and soaking. Preferably these should be made of plastic, which will help to avoid chipping the china. Suitable receptacles can often be found among containers sold for use in refrigerators.

A collection of brushes of all descriptions is needed to clean dirty edges and crevices. Toothbrushes, hard and soft, angled and straight, are useful, as are bottle and spout brushes with flexible wire handles which can be bent to reach into otherwise inaccessible corners. It is handy to have both the long and short bristle kinds. Use soft paint brushes for delicate flower and figure groups. Orange sticks or bamboo splints are useful for getting into small nooks.

A few tools will be necessary for removing rivets and lacings. They should be small in scale and clean, never blunt or rusty. Probes will be needed for digging plaster out of rivet and lacing holes, and scalpels or a thin bladed penknife for cutting and scraping. Tension files are thin round files intended to be used in a sawframe but which can be used as a hand tool for cutting through metal. They are made with a soft core and can be bent to accommodate curved surfaces. The thinnest grades should be used.

An electric soldering iron will be needed for melting away the solder covering lacings. It should be a small, 15 watt iron.

Small pliers and forceps are useful for pulling out difficult rivets and lacings and for gripping small fragments of metal.

Some form of magnification is required for close inspection as the work progresses. Magnifying spectacles are most useful as they leave the hands and bench free. An optician will supply the most suitable type for the individual.

A plentiful supply of rag is always needed, not only to clean tools and hands but to cope with spills. It should be clean, absorbent and fluff free.

Cotton wool will be needed to make swabs.

Warning: Although many of the chemicals are regarded as normal household commodities they should be handled and stored with care. Always use them in a well ventilated place away from children, pets and food. Most of the chemicals are toxic, flammable or explosive so they must be clearly labelled and stored in a cool, safe place, preferably one which can be locked. Do not mix solvents; when combined they can produce toxic gases.

Removing adhesives

The first practical step in restoring ceramics is removing the old repairs and thoroughly cleaning the china. Unless previous repairs are extremely well done and it is certain they will be undamaged by or not harm any subsequent treatment, they must be removed before any other work starts.

The restorer is also called upon to take apart and re-do recent unsatisfactory attempts at restoration which can present problems when modern adhesives have been used.

It is a great advantage if the type of adhesive used originally is known so that the appropriate solvent can be used right away. Unfortunately this is rarely so and it is wisest to start with the mildest treatment, which is hot water, and not to use chemical solvents until this proves necessary. Many old glues give up when soaked in hot water. Tap water may not be safe for this job. De-ionised or purified water must always be used for all low fired ceramics, terra cotta, earthenware artifacts, old tiles and pottery of this type. These articles are not within the province of fine china restoration and should be treated as museum repairs. If crystals do form on earthenware which has been put into tap water they must be removed by rinsing in successive changes of de-ionised water until the crystals do not reform. High fired china is not normally affected.

Fig. 19 A miscellany removed from previous repairs

Animal or fish based adhesives

Usually, these need moisture and heat to dissolve them. A short soak in hot water for 10 minutes or so should be sufficient time to determine if the glue is softening. Further soaking in fresh hot water can be given if the glue is not soft enough for the china to come apart easily. Not only must the pieces separate but all traces of the adhesive must be removed or they will not fit together again. Some adhesives will strip off in one skin while others need to be picked off by sliding a scalpel or thin blade between the glue and china. No more than one item at a time should be placed in a bowl to soak or be cleaned in case they knock together and damage one another.

If hot water does not part the join, immersing the warmed china in a bowl of boiling water should be tried. Endeavour to separate the pieces while they are still very hot; allowing them to cool even a little will reset the glue. It is the damp heat more than the water itself which is melting the glue. Handle the pieces firmly, but do not force them apart or they may break even more. It is always worth a second attempt with a fresh supply of boiling water. Once parted, detach all the glue from the edges of the break before they get too cool. Immerse in fresh boiling water several times if necessary. A pair of thin cotton gloves inside waterproof ones will make handling very hot china possible. Take care to preserve the edges of the glaze along the break; it can easily be chipped with rough handling.

If all attempts with boiling water fail, chemical solvents must be tried. Care must be taken in handling them. They should be applied by means of a long handled paint brush or on cotton wool which is either wrapped around a short pointed stick (an orange stick is ideal) or held in a pair of forceps. Lightweight plastic gloves should be worn but choose a quality which withstands the chemicals to be used. Rubber quickly dissolves with paint stripper, leaving coloured prints on the work. The effect of the solvent on gold decoration should always be tested on a small inconspicuous area first to make sure it is unharmed.

Self adhesive tape and labels

Occasionally it is necessary to deal with self adhesive tape on china. If this has been in place a long time the adhesive will have hardened and great care must be used in removing it. Plenty of methylated spirits or acetone should be used to soften and wash away the adhesive before attempting to lift the backing away, or else chips of glaze and enamel will come with it. Yet greater care is needed when it is stuck over gold leaf, as even freshly applied self adhesive tape will pull it off.

Shellac

Late nineteenth century repairs were often done with shellac, which looks like shiny toffee. This may need several applications of methylated spirits or acetone to soften it. Both methylated spirits and acetone evaporate very quickly and are flammable. Small quantities should be decanted into a labelled screw-topped jar for bench use. The main supply should be stored safely in a cool dark cupboard. The solvents should be applied fairly liberally, a few moments allowed for penetration, and then any softened adhesive should be removed with a scalpel. This can be repeated until the join parts. The adhesive remaining along the broken edges must be completely removed before washing away the solvent, rinsing and drying.

Cellulose adhesives should be removed by the same method.

Bitumen or pitch

A hard, brittle, black substance which always seems to have been used to mend the whitest china. It will dissolve with applications of paraffin. A small object can be immersed in a shallow tin of paraffin, keeping it well away from naked flames, pilot lights etc. As the pitch dissolves into the paraffin it creates a black slurry which should not be allowed to contaminate chips or cracks in the china. Replace the paraffin as soon as it becomes dirty. Make sure the last of the ingrained pitch is removed with clean paraffin; wash, rinse and dry.

Modern epoxy resins

The instant and so called super glues come apart with the aid of water solvent paint stripper. This should be applied over the adhesive along the line of the break with a long handled paint brush kept solely for this purpose and washed immediately after each use. Keep the stripper well away from the skin and clothing. If an accident does occur wash in plenty of warm water.

The coating of solvent is left in place for approximately 20 minutes and is then removed by washing in warm water. No useful purpose is served by leaving it on longer than the stipulated time as it will dry out. Several (in some cases, many) applications will be necessary to allow the solvent to penetrate right through the join. With a large top-heavy piece of china it is advisable to cushion the object while the stripper is working. Put it in a carton well padded with screwed up paper for support in case the join parts un-expectedly. As the adhesive softens it can be scraped away with a scalpel before further application of solvent. If after eight or nine applications the join shows no sign of parting

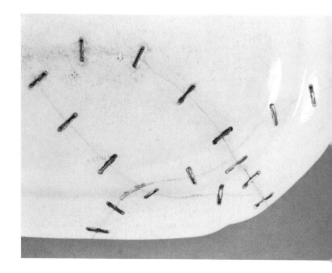

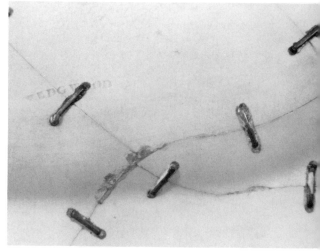

immersion in boiling water may hasten the process. The heat will expand the join and will help to part it without force.

Do not give up; the join will part eventually. A lot depends on how long and how firmly the join has been made. Once parted the china must continue to be cleared with further applications of stripper until no trace of the old adhesive remains. Because epoxy resin adhesive will be used later, at the bonding stage, it is essential that all traces of paint stripper is thoroughly removed if the new repair is to be successful.

Whatever adhesive was used originally, every scrap must be removed if the china is to be reassembled accurately again. Use a scalpel or razer blade to pick off individual flecks of glue rather than scrape indiscriminately over the whole area. Inspect frequently under a magnifying glass to make sure the edges are clean. Metal tools are liable to leave a grey mark on china, and this must always be scrubbed off. If light can be seen through the join when the edges are placed together it means that somewhere in that area a particle of old glue remains and is holding the pieces apart. When all the glue has been removed wash and rinse the pieces. If the broken edges are not discoloured and do not need bleaching, the pieces can now be stored, when dry, in a polythene bag until you are ready to start bonding. The advantage of a plastic bag is that the contents can be seen without handling the china unnecessarily.

Removing rivets

Most riveters were skilled at their craft, and where a very neat, inconspicuous job has been done it may be preferable to leave well alone. It is at least obvious which parts are still the original ones. Removing the rivets, rebonding, filling, and overpainting, however well done, could be considered as more disfiguring than a thin break line which does not obscure the original in any way.

Holes were drilled halfway through the china

Fig. 20 To prevent the china snapping at the edges, the outside rivets must be removed first

Fig. 21 A close-up of the rivets and plaster on an old repair

Fig. 22 A spout from a metal teapot used as a replacement

Fig. 23 The replacement was secured by plaster and metal braces. Careful removal was necessary to prevent further damage

exactly opposite one another. A metal wire was cut to the exact size with legs bent slightly inwards similar to a staple. The rivet was then sprung into position, tapped flat along the surface of the china and any gap in the holes filled with plaster. Where rivets have become loose, the joints blacken with dirt and the movement in the join wears away the edges. Here the rivets must be removed and the pieces of china rebonded.

The rivets should be removed by first digging out the plaster in the holes with a probe, then gently prizing the metal strap upwards with a thin knife or scalpel. A useful probe for this job can be made by inserting a stout darning needle into a piece of dowel or other suitable handle. Always remove the rivets starting from each end of the break and working towards the centre. The strain on the china if one rivet is left at the edge of an article can easily cause it to snap across at the rivet hole.

Sometimes rivets that have worked loose have been reinforced and are difficult to dig out. These may need to be sawn through with a fine tension file and the two halves pulled out separately with a pair of pliers.

Do this carefully to avoid leaving part of the rivet in the hole. Fortunately the riveter rarely used glue as well as rivets, so the pieces should come apart as soon as the rivets are out. If the pieces seem to be stuck fast it is usually only with dirt, and hot water separates them. Probe out every scrap of plaster from the holes or the new filler will not be in contact with the side or base of

the hole and will drop out. The holes and the edges of the break will be dirty so they must be washed and, if they are stained, treated with bleach. A well sharpened orange stick soaked in water and dipped into fine household abrasive will deal very effectively with dirty rivet holes. Once clean make sure all the abrasive powder is removed by plenty of rinsing. Rusty stains must be removed with the appropriate solvent. Make sure the holes are dried out properly. A twist of cotton wool around an orange stick will absorb most of the water. Any remaining moisture should be left to evaporate in a warm dry atmosphere.

Removing lacings

These consist of thin wires bound through holes completely piercing the china, with the surface neatened with solder run over the wire and into the holes. They were used where there was likely to be any strain or weight, mostly for attaching handles and knobs. Saw through the lacings with a tension file and attempt to withdraw the pieces of wire with pliers. As the solder is a soft metal try not to force it into the holes while sawing through the lacings. If the pieces do not come out easily it is necessary to melt the solder with a low wattage soldering iron. Warm the china and apply the preheated soldering iron to the metal allowing the solder to run out of the hole as it becomes molten. This may take some time on a thick object as the china will dissipate the heat. Use a cloth or forceps to hold the china if the fragments are small as they will become hot and can cause a burn. A small soldering iron of the type used for radio repairs will not be hot enough to damage the china – only the repairer!

Do not attempt to drill out rivets. The tip of a drill can reach temperatures in excess of 600°C (1110°F) which can crack the china.

The china now needs to be thoroughly cleaned and any stain removed.

Removing nuts and bolts

These were used to repair the broken sections of large urns or vases standing on plinths. A hole was drilled in the base of the vase through the stem

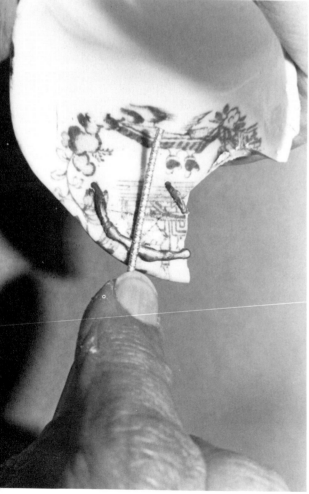

Fig. 24 More remained of the original spout than was anticipated

Fig. 25 Cutting through a lacing with a tension file

22

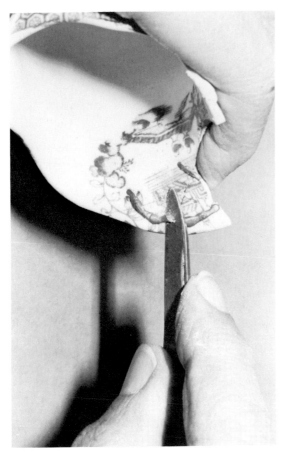

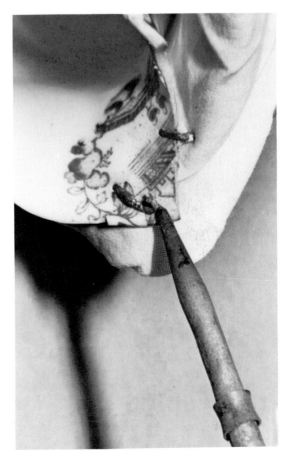

Fig. 26 Prising up the metal lacings

Fig. 27 Using a soldering iron to melt away the solder surrounding the lacing

and in the top of the plinth. The pieces were then threaded onto a bolt and a nut screwed on the end to hold the sections together. They were usually iron and normally become so rusted with cleaning that it is difficult to see how the repair is constructed. The nut can usually be freed from the bolt with applications of a dismantling lubricant. This is usually supplied in aerosol cans and is simple to use. The fluid is allowed to soak in for 10 minutes and if the nut is not loosened further applications should be made until the nut can be unscrewed. The bolt should be withdrawn carefully. The pieces usually come apart without further treatment. Filling used with metalwork is mostly plaster of Paris which will soften in water. The pieces are now ready for cleaning and stain removing.

Some large urns were originally made in sections and bolted together in the pottery. This is usually apparent as the hole is not an unglazed drilled hole but is neatly potted, smooth and probably glazed. No attempt should be made to alter this arrangement.

Removing pins and dowels

Quite often figures have joins reinforced with pins and dowels. All manner of objects are discovered inside arms and legs, from nails to rolled up newspaper. Parting the repaired breaks in figures must always be done carefully as these obstructions are not visible from the outside. In the first place the figures were made in separate moulds and the pieces assembled with thin clay slip before firing. These joins are weak spots and too much force in the wrong place will cause an additional break. Fingers and flowers are so thin that they are particularly vulnerable. Soften and scrape away the glue gradually until the pieces fall apart.

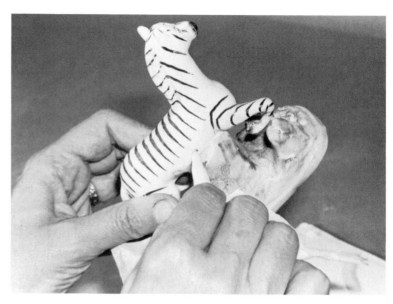

Fig. 28 Using a tissue as a wick to remove surplus water from the interior of a figure

When a wooden dowel or a roll of paper has been used to strengthen the join it will swell as soon as it gets wet. This means even more care is needed as pressure from the swelling material will tend to crack the china surrounding it. Work steadily at the job, alternately softening and scraping until all the adhesive is removed.

It has been a common practice in the past to fill figures that are badly damaged with plaster, bitumen or glue for extra strength. These must be dissolved with the appropriate solvent. All these materials must be completely removed or they will force their way out through any cracks or joins, badly staining subsequent work.

Particular attention must be given to getting all solvents and water out of figures; they are usually hollow and will hold water for days. The quickest way to dry them out is to screw the corner of a cellulose tissue (cleansing tissue) into a cylinder and insert it into the air hole, usually found in the base. This will act as a wick. The figure is shaken gently until the tissue is wet and then the process is repeated with dry tissue until no water is left inside. The figure should then be left in a warm atmosphere until all moisture has evaporated.

Cleaning

On the rare occasions when the restorer has a new, clean break to mend all that will be required is to wash the pieces in hot water and detergent using purified water for porous earthenware pieces. Dry them by draining, not wiping, so they will be free from fingermarks and fluff. Store the pieces, once they are quite dry, in a plastic bag to keep them clean until ready for further work to be done.

Breaks and chips which are ingrained with dirt should be scrubbed with a toothbrush. If warm water and detergent is insufficient to remove the marks, a little domestic abrasive powder can be used on the brush. When quite clean rinse off all detergent and abrasive, then leave to dry. China must be clean all over, inside as well as out. If only the break is cleaned any dust or dirt elsewhere on the china will be picked up on fingers or tools at a later stage. It will then be transferred to the adhesive or filler and sealed permanently into the repair.

Once all the glue, metal and old filler has been removed the china must be completely cleaned of all solvents and stains. Thorough rinsing in clean warm water will deal with the solvents; if they are not stained the pieces can be carefully dried and protected from dust until ready for further repair. Obstinate stains often remain where tannin or grease has entered the break. Cracks and chips also allow dirt to penetrate and frequently it spreads out under the glaze. If the discoloration has been there for years it may not disappear completely, but every attempt should be made to minimise these unsightly marks by bleaching. If the china has any gilding, first test on an inconspicuous place that the bleach does not harm the gold. If it does and the gold is near the area to be bleached it is better to accept the staining rather than to inflict further damage.

Bleaching will not always improve plates and dishes which are badly discoloured under crazing cracks. The cracks are minute and uneven in size and distribution, with the stain probably baked in so that total removal is extremely difficult. The bleach cannot penetrate evenly and leaves dark and light patches. This presents a worse appearance than before treatment and little can be done to remedy the situation. The risk must be considered before deciding whether to attempt bleaching. If an article is old and has had a lot of use, the discoloration is part of its history. Bleach does not remove the cause of the stain, it only lightens it. The discoloration may well return after a period of time, particularly if the object is heated.

Cleaning agents
Chlorine bleach
Stains from a vegetable source, tea or coffee for example, respond to a chlorine bleach. When the item to be treated is a hard paste, porcelain or stoneware, the china may be immersed in a 12% solution of domestic bleach and hot water. Always use bleach in a plastic or glass vessel, not metal. The stains will not disappear instantly when immersed in the bleach; some hours will usually elapse before fading is visible. However, the china must not be left without attention. To start with, an inspection every 10 minutes should be made to ensure that the bleach is not harming the article in any way. This period can be increased if the bleaching is even but items should never be left overnight without attention. Tannin staining the glaze inside teacups can be removed by soaking in bleach. A little domestic abrasive used gently may be needed to help. Never use the abrasive on gold. Gold leaf can become encrusted with tannin, sometimes to the extent that it is unrecognisable as gold. When soaked in detergent and water at the usual dilution tannin will usually soften sufficiently to be removed with cotton wool wound round an orange stick. The application of a foam silver cleaner will remove obstinate tarnishing. Test on an inconspicuous area first.

If the body of the china is soft and porous, earthenware or early creamware, immersing the whole article when the stain is only on the surface of the break can push the stain into the china. This leaves a dark line, which is not removable, a little way in from the edge. The further the bleach solution travels the further the dark line gets pushed in. It is much safer to saturate a strip of cotton wool with dilute bleach, up to 25% bleach to water, and lay this along the area to be treated. This cotton wool poultice is covered with plastic film to reduce evaporation. Constant watch must be kept to make sure all is proceeding safely; it will probably take some hours to remove the stain.

Sepiolite
For a stain that has penetrated some distance under the glaze, whether it is along broken edges or surrounding a chip, sepiolite can be used to draw it out. It is mixed to a paste with de-ionised or purified water and the mixture is then applied to the broken surface with a brush. Apply to a depth of about 3 mm ($\frac{1}{8}$ in). Allow the poultice to dry out slowly, either by putting the article into a plastic bag or covering with plastic film. When it becomes crumbly brush the sepiolite away. This process can be repeated if necessary. When as much stain as possible has been removed rinse thoroughly. For heavy staining sepiolite can be mixed with the appropriate bleach for the stain, mixing and applying it exactly as when water is used to make the poultice. This treatment can be repeated until there is no further improvement.

Hydrogen peroxide
This can be applied to stains undiluted. Either saturate cotton wool strips with peroxide or mix it with sepiolite to form a paste and apply to the stained area. The strips are left in place under plastic film for several hours; check progress frequently. When the stain stops fading the strips are removed and the area well rinsed in warm water and dried. Wear gloves or use forceps when handling peroxide. If peroxide does come into contact with skin or clothing wash immediately with plenty of warm water.

Biological or enzyme bleach
This type of bleach is used when the stains are suspected of being protein based. It is now available as a washing aid. When using a proprietary brand allow 1 tablespoon of powder to 2 l (4 pt) of warm, not hot, water. It is then used in exactly the same way as the diluted chlorine solution. In countries where its sale is not permitted for ecological reasons pepsin and acid can be used. The pharmacist will dispense a pepsin and acid solution for dissolving protein to a recognised standard formula.

Oxalic acid

Old inkwells are frequently disfigured by brown or black stains. These can be improved by immersing in a solution of 1 teaspoon oxalic acid crystals in 550 ml (1 pt) of hot water, always provided any gold is tested first. This may take some time and a careful watch must be kept throughout the operation for uneven bleaching. It will be necessary to change the solution as it becomes soiled. When the bleaching has reached a satisfactory stage rinse throughly before drying.

A container stained on the interior only can be filled with oxalic acid solution instead of being immersed. Old Staffordshire greyhound inkwells must be very well cleaned. Because of the small opening, made just large enough to hold a pen, it is difficult to remove the dried ink which has gradually built up inside, but unless it is soaked away and the china thoroughly dried when clean the residue will creep through any crazing and stain the surface.

Oxalic acid solution is toxic. Keep the crystals in a safe place.

Rust removers

Iron stains are usually caused by metal rivets and lacings oxidising, leaving brown stains in holes and across the glaze. They can be improved or removed entirely with the aid of a proprietary rust remover. Apply by brushing onto the stain. It should respond within five or ten minutes and the treatment can be repeated if necessary. Rubbing with fine steel wool will help to remove the marks but great care must be taken not to leave any strands of steel wool trapped in holes or crevices or they in turn will rust and mark the china. Most rust removers contain phosphoric acid and are intended for use on metal. They inhibit further rusting by forming a bond with the metal surface. This is not required on china so the manufacturers instructions not to wash away the product must be ignored and the china washed thoroughly in warm water. Always obey the manufacturers instructions for safe handling.

Dental steriliser

Vases and bowls which have been used to hold water will have a ring of hard lime deposit around them. Do not attempt to scrape or chip this off. There is a risk that the glaze will be scratched or chipped if the deposit is very hard. The encrustation can be removed by soaking in a solution of denture cleaner which is intended for removing various deposits. Follow the manufacturers recommendations for strength of solutions and length of time for soaking. The usual precautions of testing any gold and frequent inspection during immersion should be followed. Wash and rinse in clean water when clear of deposits. Use a liner in the object if it is to hold water in the future.

Summary

Never mix different types of bleach or solvent as a short cut or if uncertain which one to use. Use the bleaches and solvents separately and if the first one tried does not have any effect rinse thoroughly before trying another. Mixed together they may either neutralise each other or produce toxic gases. Sometimes when a stain is only partially faded leaving it in sunlight will reduce the marks still further.

Once as much of the stain as possible has been removed the china must be washed in warm water and detergent, then rinsed. This cleaning must be done very thoroughly to make sure all the solvent has been removed, or it will react unfavourably with the adhesive to be used in the repair.

When clean the article must be dried out completely. It is better to leave it to drain as this will avoid handling. Hard paste china does not absorb water but any crevices or cracks must be checked for moisture. It may be necessary to leave absorbent china like earthenware in a warm dry atmosphere for several days before all the water evaporates from beneath the glaze. Do not attempt rebonding while there is the slightest greying under the glaze adjoining the break. This indicates the presence of water. Should water be sealed into a break or left inside a figure it will boil when heated at the overpainting stage and force steam out at the weakest spot, at least spoiling a lot of work but probably forcing a joint apart.

So often many of the errors made at this stage of the work do not show up until much later, usually after a particularly satisfactory piece of painting has been done. It is essential to take extra care when cleaning to make sure that every last speck of dirt is gone. Nothing is more depressing than to find a row of brown blisters from old adhesive erupting through a perfect coat of paint. The only remedy is to start from the begining again. As the joint is obviously dirty it shouldn't be too difficult to take apart!

3᛫Bonding

Once the china has been scrupulously cleaned and is completely dry, reassembling can begin. There are numerous adhesives on the market, many making great claims for permanence and invisibility. The technology of adhesives is so advanced that it is now possible to produce indissoluble adhesives. However, their use is hazardous so they are only available under license when they can be used under laboratory conditions. No adhesive is entirely invisible. The concealment of the join depends a great deal on the close fit of the break as well as skill and accuracy in bonding, whatever the adhesive used. The final choice must be given to an adhesive which does not harm either the china or the user, is durable, heatproof and waterproof and is resistant to most chemicals with which a piece of fine china is likely to come into contact in the course of handling and cleaning.

Ceramics which are kept in a controlled, air- and moisture-proof environment, where handling and cleaning do not have to be taken into consideration, have a wider range of restoration materials available. The treatment for these museum type repairs must always be decided upon in consultation with the curator authorising the work.

Materials and tools

Epoxy resin adhesive (Araldite twin tube packs, Blue/Black tubes); for bonding

Titanium oxide; used to lighten the colour of the adhesive

Artists' dry ground colour, black; for darkening the adhesive for black ceramics only

Methylated spirit (denatured alcolhol), surgical spirit; solvent for unset epoxy resin

Palette, strong cartridge paper, heavy white drawing paper; used when mixing adhesives

Spatula, palette knife; used to mix adhesive

Orange sticks; may be used to apply adhesive

Brown paper gum strip, 2 cm (1 in) wide; for strapping china

PTFE tape; self clinging tape

Plastic modelling clay (Plasticine), white; useful supporting material which does not shrink

Boards or trays; used as stands while the adhesive is setting

Salt trays; used for propping articles at an angle until adhesive is set

Abrasive paper, glass-paper (flour), aluminium oxide paper (fine and medium); used to smooth the hardened adhesive on joins

Needle files; for smoothing adhesive

Dusting brush or blower brush; for removing dust

File card; for cleaning clogged files

Scalpel or thin bladed knife

Scissors

Barrier cream (Rosalex No. 9, Kerodex 71); to protect the skin from epoxy resin

Resin removing cream (Rosalex No. 42, Kerodex 22); to remove hardened epoxy resin from the skin

Soft, clean, fluff-free rags; for cleaning hands and tools

A variety of spring clips; these are useful for aligning edges

Dust respirator; to avoid inhaling epoxy resin dust while rubbing down

The strongest adhesive on sale to the public is epoxy resin. The quick-setting varieties of epoxy resins are unsuitable as they will not withstand the temperature required for stoving when overpainting; neither is it possible to position, accurately, several pieces of china in the short time available before setting begins. However steady the hands appear to be, the ability to hold anything rock steady, even for 30 seconds, is not very certain. It is always necessary to breathe, for one thing.

The recommended type of epoxy resin adhesive

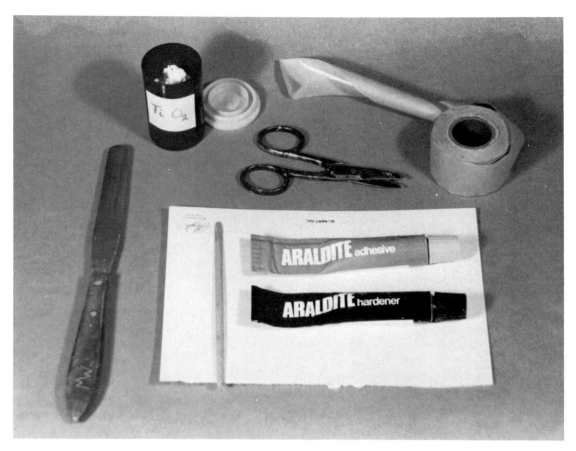

Fig. 29 Tools and materials needed for bonding

is entirely suitable for china restoration, it is easily obtainable and, provided sensible precautions are taken, safe to use. It is compatible with all the materials and methods used throughout. It is a two part adhesive mixed in equal quantities.

Titanium oxide and dry ground black pigment are the only colours used in the adhesive. Epoxy resin darkens a little in time so that mixing the adhesive with pigments to match the china in the hope of concealment results in a discoloured join after a few months.

Methylated spirit is used for keeping the fingers and tools clean. It will also dissolve epoxy resin before it has hardened. This means that it is useful for wiping off sticky finger marks, but it must be kept well away from newly bonded joins.

A palette is needed on which to mix the epoxy resin adhesive. A tile or piece of glass can be used for this purpose but it will need constant and very thorough cleaning. A piece of stiff cartridge paper is more suitable as it can be discarded after use, saving both time and cleaning materials and avoiding the risk of contaminating a later batch of

adhesive. Old greeting cards make ideal palettes. Always use a fresh, clean palette for each mix.

Spatulas or palette knives can be either metal or plastic. The metal ones are thinner and more flexible. If a plastic tool is used make sure it does not dissolve on contact with either epoxy resin or methylated spirits. A serviceable tool can be made from a strip of bamboo. It can be pared down with a knife until it is thin and then smoothed with abrasive paper. This makes an excellent spatula for applying adhesive to the china. An orange stick is useful for putting the adhesive into small gaps.

Brown paper gum strip is used for holding the broken edges of the china together while the adhesive is setting. It is applied wet and, because it shrinks as it dries, will pull the edges of the join more closely together. Do not use transparent self-adhesive tape as it relaxes and allows the china to move.

PTFE tape is a soft, elastic, self clinging strip

28

most useful for holding small fragments of china in place, for holding together broken limbs and similar awkward repairs. It will cling to the china but is not sticky.

Plastic modelling clay is invaluable for making supports and wedges. Never use coloured plastic modelling clay as this will stain the china.

A board or tray for holding newly bonded china after assembling will enable the object to be moved without placing any strain on the join. Off-cuts of chip board or hardboard will give good service provided they are flat and not warped.

A salt tray is used to steady objects that must be left at an angle for the break to remain horizontal while setting. A box or tray several inches deep and large enough to contain the object is required. Salt, not sand, is used as a filling. If a few grains do get attached to the adhesive they can soon be dissolved with a little water. Sand, once embedded in a join, is very difficult to remove. When not in use the salt must be kept dry. Left exposed to the air it will absorb moisture from the atmosphere and become unusable.

A good supply of abrasive paper is required as it must be replaced as soon as it becomes clogged or worn out. Abrasive paper consists of three major components: an abrasive mineral, a backing and a bonding agent. Aluminium oxide is a hard wearing mineral capable of penetrating almost any surface. The graded mineral is applied to backing to produce two types of coverage, open and close coat. Open coat paper does not clog as quickly as the close coat which gives a smoother finish. The grades of grit used and the nature of the coating is marked on the backing. Coarse, medium and fine open coat papers will be needed. These are used to rub down surplus adhesive. Ground glass is used for the manufacture of a fine, close coat abrasive paper termed flour paper which is used for the final smoothing. Papers coated with other abrasives, for example, crocus or wet and dry silicon paper, will discolour the joins and fillings as they shed the coating, which is red or black.

Needle files come in a variety of shapes with both pointed and blunt ends. To begin with, flat and round files are sufficient. Other shapes can be acquired as the need arises. Good quality files will outlast many cheap ones and will give more

Fig. 30 Supporting an awkward shape in a salt tray

Fig. 31 Abrasive paper. Cut into narrow strips ready for use

29

Diagram 1 Files are made in a variety of shapes

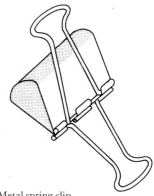

Diagram 4 Metal spring clip

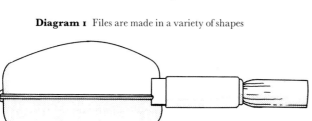

Diagram 2 Blower brush for removing dust and fluff

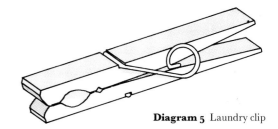

Diagram 5 Laundry clip

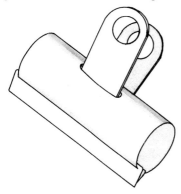

Diagram 3 Clips for holding joins. Stationers' spring clip

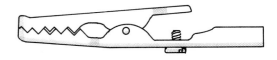

Diagram 6 Electrical crocodile clip

efficient service throughout their life. They get very clogged with swarf from the adhesive and must be kept clean by stroking on a file card. This is a fine wire mat which brushes the swarf from the teeth of the file.

A brush or blower will be needed because the rubbing down creates a dust. The surface of the china should be constantly swept with either a small bristle brush or the type used by photographers, which has bristles attached to a rubber bellows.

Scapels, razor blades, scissors and a thin bladed knife are needed repeatedly. They must be kept sharp or they will merely drag at the materials.

Spring clips will be needed to hold edge pieces in place. The types intended for use in the laundry

and office and small electrical crocodile clips can all be used.

Soft clean rag is used constantly. Make sure it is absorbent but does not shed fluff onto the work.

Warning: Epoxy resins are toxic. Materials should be prevented from coming into contact with the eyes and skin. A barrier cream should always be used before working with epoxy resin adhesive. Do not use more than the skin can absorb, however, and wipe off any excess, as the cream can form a barrier on the china, inhibiting the tenacity of adhesive and paint. Hands should be washed with soap and plenty of warm water immediately after working. Tools, not fingers, should be used for mixing and applying adhesives.

30

Methylated spirit is the solvent for cleaning hands and tools before the resin sets. If any resin should harden on the skin use a resin-removing cream following the makers' instructions. Do not attempt to pick off the adhesive or the skin will be damaged. A respirator should always be used when rubbing down as the epoxy resin dust is dangerous when inhaled.

Preparation

The bonding of all broken pieces needs exactly the same basic treatment:

the surfaces to be joined must be clinically clean;
adhesive must be applied to both surfaces to be joined;
the pieces must be pressed very firmly together;
pressure on the join must be maintained during setting;
firm support must be given until the epoxy resin is set.

The difference in techniques lies in the methods of providing pressure and support. The mender must often use ingenuity in devising equipment for this purpose.

Always rehearse the reassembly before any other preparations are started. Make sure the pieces fit together snugly, but do not handle the areas to be bonded. The adhesive will not work on grease and fingers always leave a faint greasy imprint, as many lawbreakers as well as restorers find to their cost. Have all the necessary equipment prepared for use before mixing the adhesive.

It is very convenient to stand the bonded china on a flat piece of board or a tray while the adhesive is setting. If it is necessary to move it to one side the tray can be held; then there will be no strain or movement on the china. The join needs to be held tightly in place under firm pressure during setting. If the joins are not close and rigid the pieces will slide out of alignment or the adhesive will set on each piece of china separately without bonding them together properly. Brown paper gum strip in small neat pieces will not only hold the china in place but as it is put on damp it will shrink as it dries and pull the edges together more firmly. Cut the strips in advance and fasten them in place on the china before applying the adhesive. This will avoid the difficulty of trying to locate them on the work while holding the join together. The small strips can be made in quantity quite quickly by taking a length of gum strip, folding it lengthwise with the gum side outwards and then snipping off sections about 0.5 cm ($\frac{1}{4}$ in) to 1 cm ($\frac{1}{2}$ in) wide according to the size and weight of the china. They are then folded ready for use.

Fig. 32 Gum strip hinges ready for use

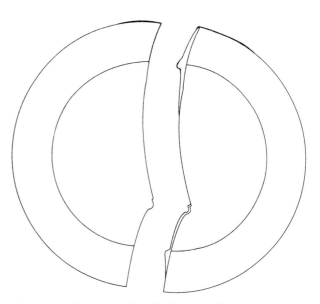

Diagram 7 Stages in bonding. The break must be thoroughly cleaned and dried

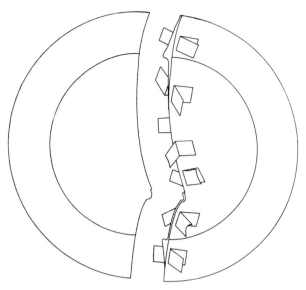

Diagram 8 The gum strip tabs in position. A row is applied to each side of one broken section

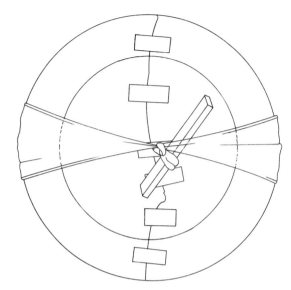

Diagram 10 A tourniquet is added for further pressure

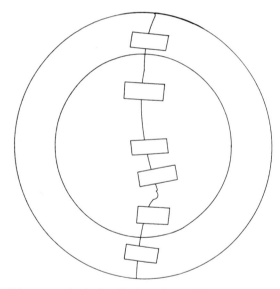

Diagram 9 Apply the adhesive and stretch the wet tabs across the join

One half of each hinge is stuck to the china and the other end left free. At this stage the hinges are attached along both sides of one piece of china only. Place the straps at about 1 cm ($\frac{1}{2}$ in) intervals along the edge of the break. This allows a gap so that the breakline can be seen when checking the join for accurate location. Position them 3 mm ($\frac{1}{8}$ in) in from the edge so they are not in the way when spreading the adhesive. Make

sure the tabs are firmly pressed in place or they will pop off as they dry out. Have these attached before the adhesive is mixed.

Do not use self adhesive tape as besides damaging gilt it stretches, as mentioned before, and allows the join to relax.

The weight of the china tends to pull the pieces of china down and out of position. This will be apparent when the pieces are tried together for fit. Wedges of plastic modelling clay to support the sagging portions can be made in advance and slid into position once the binding is across the join. Form the plastic modelling clay into the correct size for the wedge by pressing into shape on a sound section of china which is identical to the one to be supported. Dip the plastic modelling clay in water before moulding against the china to facilitate its release. Remove the plastic modelling clay carefully so that it is not pulled out of shape. Leave these supports aside until the join is bonded.

If the china to be joined is heavy a few additional, longer strips of gum strip will be required to reinforce the strapping. Alternatively, a tourniquet can be used. For this a band is passed right round the china and tightened up with the aid of a stick placed under the band and twisted. Continue twisting until the band is drum tight. A suitable band can be improvised from a strip of nylon jersey fabric or a stocking. The fabric is soft and will not damage the china. It can also be cut to any size. Use a wide band for heavy china and reduce the size for tiny items. The tourniquet must always be placed at right angles to the join otherwise tightening the band will force the break sideways.

If the article is chipped or has a piece missing, simply bond the pieces that are there, being very careful to align them accurately. The chip or hole will be filled in once the bonding has been completed.

Mixing the adhesive

The adhesive is supplied as separate tubes of adhesive and hardener which are mixed together. It is most important to use strictly equal quantities of each or the setting properties of the resin will be upset. If in doubt about the accuracy of measuring, pencil two parallel lines on the palette and squeeze sufficient from each tube to reach from one line to the other. Accurate proportions are easier to achieve if the length squeezed from each tube is at least 1 cm ($\frac{1}{2}$ in). Small blobs cannot be gauged accurately.

To help keep the mixture a lighter colour a very small quantity of titanium oxide is added. If 2 cm (1 in) has been squeezed from each tube add about a pin head of titanium. This proportion must be maintained whatever amount is prepared. Any more titanium than this will weaken the adhesive and make it too bulky for a close join. The three ingredients must be very well mixed or the join may fail. Mix with a palette knife or spatula until no streaks or bubbles are visible.

When the china for bonding is black (for example basalt ware) the epoxy resin can be mixed with a little black pigment instead of titanium oxide, which would leave a sharply contrasting break line.

Using the adhesive

Bonding a two piece break
With the gum strip tabs in place, plastic modelling clay wedges and additional straps or tourniquet ready, adhesive is spread thinly and evenly along both broken edges with a spatula. Do not use a finger which, besides being greasy, will stick to every object touched and pull out of position the pieces just assembled. It is not recommended for the restorer's skin either. The adhesive must be spread evenly, otherwise the edges of the join will be held apart by the lumps. Without close contact along the whole of the join

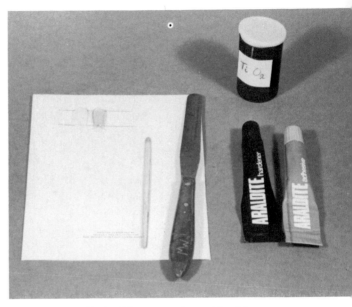

Fig. 33 Mixing adhesive. Measure equal quantities of the epoxy resin carefully

there will be air gaps and weakness in the thinly spread areas.

Do not warm the china before applying the adhesive. It will make the adhesive very liquid and insufficient will remain in position to fill the tiny chips along the edge of the break. It is quite sufficient for the china to be at normal room temperature.

Enough adhesive should be used to squeeze out into a ridge when the pieces are pressed hard together. The ridge should be the thickness of thread rather than string. Its purpose is to fill all the minute chips along the edge of the glaze. After the adhesive has been applied the loose flaps of the gum strip are wetted and the broken edges brought together and located accurately. Push the pieces together very firmly; laying them side by side is not enough to bond them. Smooth the wet flaps of gum strip across the join, stretching and pressing into place.

Do not remove the excess adhesive squeezed out of the join at this stage. The edges of the break must be tested to make sure they are flush. Run the point of a scalpel across the join. If it catches on a step in one direction the higher piece of china must be pushed down into position. Should the blade catch from each direction there is a groove not a step. Push the pieces together to make sure they are a tight fit and that the groove is not caused by a gap in the join. In all probability the

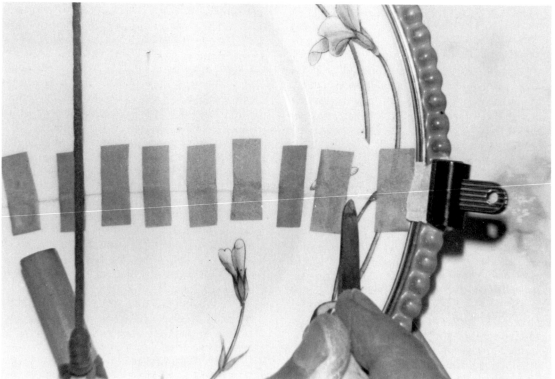

groove is the result of minute chips missing from the glaze, in which case they will be filled by the adhesive.

When one edge of a join persists in rising or dropping out of alignment it can be clipped into position with a spring laundry peg or a stationers' spring clip. Make sure the clip is doing its job and not forcing the join apart. A strip of cellulose tissue should be placed between the clip and the join. Any adhesive on the surface of the china will then stick to the tissue which is easily scraped away when the clip is removed.

Screw clamps should never be used. It is impossible to judge how much pressure is being applied; half a turn too many and the china is crushed.

Wet and position any additional strips of gum paper that are required for heavy china. Use an equal number on each side of the china otherwise as they shrink the pull will be greater on one side, tending to open the join. A tourniquet can be applied if more suitable. Make sure that it is tight enough to be effective.

Wipe any sticky marks from the surface of the china with a little methylated spirits. Keep well away from the join or else the small ridge of adhesive which is to fill the chips will be removed and epoxy resin smeared over the china.

Place the object on a tray and if plastic modelling clay is to be used put it in position making sure that the outside edges of the china are even. Make certain the join has not slipped out of alignment. Push into place if necessary and leave the adhesive to set. The china should be held firmly in place once the gum strip has stiffened but check the join once or twice during the first two hours so that any adjustment can be made before the adhesive is too hard for correction.

Epoxy resin mixture remains workable for one-and-a-half to two hours, depending on the room temperature. It will be set and strong enough to handle in 24 hours. Hardening will continue for a further 48 hours but maximum strength is not reached until cured in mild heat. As the china will be heated after painting it is not necessary to heat cure at this stage.

Apart from checking and adjusting if necessary in the first two hours the china should be left

Fig. 34 A simple join held in position with gum strip, tourniquet and spring clips

Fig. 35 Check each side of the join with the tip of a penknife for exact alignment

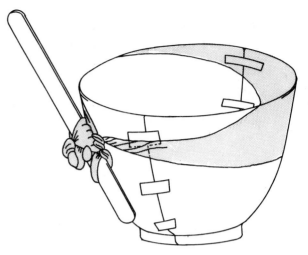

Diagram 11 Position of tourniquet for a bowl-shaped object

undisturbed for at least 24 hours. If it is necessary to move the object, pick it up on the tray. Do not hold the china so that there is any weight or strain on the join.

Bonding bowls, jugs, etc.
Additional strapping of gum strip for a deep vessel should be fixed round the outside only. Fringe one edge of the gum strip. It will then fit the slope of the sides comfortably. For a large object several strips can be applied at intervals, which will form a stiff casing when dry. When a tourniquet is needed for a bowl-shaped article it is most effective if arranged round the circumference of the bowl. This will give better pressure than one which goes over the top and under the base.

Bonding multiple breaks
Have plenty of practice with simple breaks in a variety of shapes before tackling anything more complicated. When an object is in many or even a few pieces the job takes a little more patience and time to complete. The pieces must all be bonded at the same time. Sticking a few pieces and allowing the adhesive to set before completing the job usually results in either not enough or too much space for the last few pieces. They will be out of alignment at the final edge because the adhesive between each piece takes up a small amount of space. Completely reassembling the whole item while the adhesive is soft means that the last pieces can be eased into position and then all the joins pressed carefully into place.

36

Because of the angles of some of the broken edges it is likely that certain pieces are locked out unless reassembled in the correct sequence. Rehearse the order in which the pieces are to be put together and lay them out so the sequence of working can be clearly seen.

Apply the gum strip tabs and prepare sufficient plastic modelling clay wedges to support any section which tends to sag. Additional strength will have to be given with gum strip straps. Tightening up a tourniquet usually squeezes multiple breaks out of place.

The broken pieces can be joined in pairs, chosing first the pieces which lock together positively. Allow the gum strip tabs to dry for a few minutes, which will give a measure of support. Each pair can then be added to another pair and the gum strip dried as before. This is continued until all the pieces are assembled. The greatest accuracy is needed in locating the joins, but providing the assembling is completed before the adhesive sets, slight adjustment can be made as work progresses.

When the china is finally in one piece all the breaklines must be checked for alignment. Edge pieces that rise out of position can be held in position with clips. For middle sections a small weight can be used to press downwards. Use a tissue between the weight and the china to prevent unintentional adhesion. Leave the work on a board while the epoxy resin is setting. Sometimes, particularly for a deep object, it is advisable to assemble it upside down and leave it to set in that position. The weight falling on the rim will help to hold the joins level.

Check during the first two hours that none of the joins have slipped out of line and, if necessary, adjust carefully; it is so easy to correct one piece and push aside several others.

Bonding broken edges

When it is the edge only of a plate or dish that is broken the weight of the china pulls the join apart. It will be necessary to make a support of plastic modelling clay to cradle the whole of the broken area while the adhesive is setting. Roll out a sufficient length of plastic modelling clay to span

Fig. 36 Bonding a multiple break. Have everything ready before applying the adhesive

Fig. 37 In a multiple break the pieces can first be joined in pairs. Allow the gum strip but not the adhesive to dry before joining further pairs

the broken portion and of sufficient thickness to support the weight without sagging. A thin sheet will be too flimsy and will just hang on the china. Form the support by first dipping the plastic modelling clay into cold water to prevent it sticking to the china. Press the plastic modelling clay against an identical and sound area of china to make a mould. Ease away carefully to avoid distortion. The broken pieces are now prepared and assembled exactly as before. Finally, the plastic modelling clay is put in place and pressed into position until the broken edge is fully supported. As always, the alignment is checked until the adhesive is too stiff to allow further movement. The article is left for a full 24 hours.

Bonding surface chips

This type of chip will need no support as it has its own china backing. Apply adhesive to both surfaces and press the chip firmly into position. The layer of adhesive must be thin and very even if the chip is to lie flush with the surrounding china. The flake must be held down while setting with a spring clip or a weight. Gum strip is not used on a concave surface because as it contracts while drying it will lift the chip out of position. The usual hardening time is required.

Bonding handles

The point of attachment of a cup or jug handle is very small for the weight it has to support when the article is lifted. Modern adhesives are equal to this strain but particular attention must be given to the joining operation to ensure that the quality of the repair is as good as the materials. Any free standing part like a handle needs particularly good support. If the broken member can be balanced so that the break is horizontal, with the weight falling onto the join, it will help greatly. A tray filled with salt is a good way of supporting items at various angles.

Prepare a roll of plastic modelling clay thick enough to fit under the handle across the surface of the china. Press the modelling clay onto the china, smearing it down onto the surface to hold it securely in place. Put the handle in position over the plastic modelling clay before applying any adhesive, matching the break scars carefully to check the shape of the support.

Mould the plastic modelling clay to the inside shape of the handle. Remove the handle carefully so the support is not pulled out of shape. A strap of gum strip will be required long enough to go along the length of the handle and fasten onto the main part of the item at each end. Do not have the strip too wide or it will be difficult to get it in place. This will pull the handle tightly into position while the plastic modelling clay will stop it tilting sideways. Make sure no plastic modelling clay has been picked up on the broken areas of the china or the strength of the adhesive will be impaired. Use methylated spirits to remove it if necessary.

Once the support is in place and the strap is ready, adhesive is applied to the broken areas of the china. The pieces are brought together and pressed very firmly into position. Pinch the plastic modelling clay up around the handle and stretch the wet gum strip over the top, attaching it securely along the handle and on the china above and below the handle.

The article can now be rested in the salt tray with the handle uppermost. Settle it in firmly, partially burying it if necessary to make it stable. Make sure the break is horizontal. Check that the join is in alignment until the adhesive is set and then leave undisturbed for 24 hours. Handles, whether they are on a cup, on top of a lid or on the side of a tureen can all be attached by this method.

Bonding handles which are in several pieces

This can be a very difficult job as any pressure tends to concertina the joins. PTFE tape can be used to hold the pieces in place on the supporting plastic modelling clay. This is a self clinging plastic tape, not self adhesive. It will not shrink but as it clings to most surfaces by static it will prevent the pieces from slipping out of position.

The handle must be assembled without adhesive and a pattern made for the plastic modelling clay support. Lay the broken pieces together in their correct shape on a card and draw round the inner edge carefully. Build up a plastic modelling clay support using this pattern and attach it to the china to come inside the handle. Apply adhesive to the broken pieces of handle and assemble them over the support so that the joins can be made tight enough to fit the available gap. The handle must be attached to the article at the same time. If bonded separately it will usually be too long to fit into the original space once the adhesive is added. Small pellets of soft plastic modelling clay can be added at each side of the handle to make it more secure. Leave a space clear at the joins to be able to see that they are level and in good contact with each other. The adjustment

and correct alignment of joins is tricky and will take a little time.

As soon as they are in place add a strip of PTFE tape, stretching it slightly and continuing it beyond the top and bottom of the handle. This will hold the pieces in place without force. Check for true alignment and leave in a salt tray to set. Do not move it, or the joins will be jarred out of position.

Bonding broken spouts and lips

The usual basic requirements apply to the mending of teapot spouts and jug lips. The easiest way to make the support for the broken pieces is to roll a cone of plastic modelling clay to fit inside the spout or lip. It must be long enough to protrude beyond the end of the finished spout. Insert carefully without getting the plastic modelling clay onto the broken edges. Bend the protruding end of the support downwards following the curve of the original china. Bonding then follows the normal routine. Leave the item balanced in the salt tray with the break horizontal.

Bonding knobs and heads

The main difficulty encountered when replacing these parts is that the stem or neck is usually broken at an angle. The heavy top then tends to slide down the slope of the break. Two or three balls of plastic modelling clay exactly fitting the cavity under the knob or chin will provide the necessary support. Two crossed straps of gum strip passing from the shoulder over the top and fastened on the opposite side will give the pressure to make a secure join. Unfortunately, if the join is

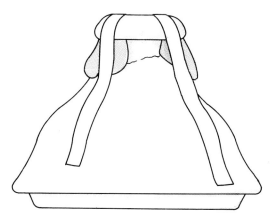

Diagram 12 Supporting a bonded knob with gum strip and pads of plastic modelling clay

Fig. 38 A head held firmly in position with gum strip tapes. The pads of plastic modelling clay prevent the head tipping out of balance

Fig. 39 This group was in many pieces. In this case free-standing pieces could be bonded separately and the group gradually reassembled

placed horizontally in the salt tray, the heavy head will be at an angle and drag on the join at one side. This particular item may not be suitable for balancing. In all other respects the method of bonding is the same as in previous cases.

Bonding limbs, wings, branches and free-standing drapery

A method has to be devised for supporting a protruding section whose weight would immediately pull it out of position. This occurs frequently with figures and branched candlesticks, for example. Plastic modelling clay can be modelled into slings and props. These must always be fashioned stoutly enough to really hold the broken member in place. A thick platform will frequently have to be built out, making a shelf for the piece to rest on. The edges of the join should always be pulled together with gum strip if possible. Even very narrow straps will be a help.

Here the salt tray is most useful for balance and support. The object can be partially buried and the salt piled up under the broken part.

When free-standing pieces have multiple breaks, provided the breaks are quite disassociated and do not run into one another, they can be bonded one at a time. For example, an arm broken at both elbow and wrist can be joined by attaching the hand to the wrist, then when quite set the lower arm can be bonded to the elbow. This will be much easier than trying to deal with all the joins at the same time.

On fingers, shepherds' crooks, musical instruments and similar tiny areas, the area of contact is so small that the join is vulnerable until the adhesive is fully cured. To make handling less hazardous the item can be cured in a perfectly clean oven for 30 minutes at a temperature of 115°C (240°F) after the 24 hour setting period. This curing is not normally necessary as a separate stage because the adhesive will be brought to maturity when stoved at the painting stage. Full instructions on stoving are contained in the chapter on painting.

Bonding open or loose cracks

When a crack which travels to the edge of a piece of china can be moved slightly, it must be sealed with epoxy resin adhesive. It will need strapping firmly with gum strip and a tourniquet, if the shape will permit it. The edges must be held level with a spring clip. Warm the china to 65°C (150°F) in an oven and while the china is still warm apply adhesive along both sides of the crack. Press in as much adhesive as possible with a spatula. If the crack has any movement open it very, very gently to allow the adhesive to enter the crack. This is one of the rare occasions when a second pair of hands can be useful. An assistant can open the crack slightly while the adhesive is pressed in. The adhesive becomes very runny on the warm china and as it cools will be sucked into the crack and the edges of the join bonded together. Strap as tightly as possible. Make sure the crack is level, clipping or weighting if necessary.

Bonding a sprung crack

Once a crack has sprung out of alignment either one side above the other or with a gap opening up, it is extremely difficult to force the edges together again. Too much force results in broken, not cracked, china. Even if the china is deliberately broken in an attempt to make a better join the china is still mis-shapen and will not fit together truly accurately. Frequently a crack is held open by loose granules of china trapped in the crack. If the crack can be opened a little and the particles blown out the fit will be much improved.

Warm the china and apply adhesive to both sides along the crack. Bring the edges together as far as possible, strapping very tightly. A great improvement can be made by filling the crack with adhesive and strapping tightly but it must be remembered that the object is held under stress. Future heavy vibration or extremes of temperature can cause the crack to run further or snap across at a right angle.

Sealing a hair crack

Epoxy resin adhesive is too thick to penetrate a crack which cannot be opened. However tightly the edges of the crack are held together it will

contain some air. This will expand and disturb any paint applied over the crack so it must be sealed before any painting is done. This is achieved with glaze medium before applying the base coats. The method is explained in Chapter 5.

Removing strappings and supports

When 24 hours have elapsed after applying the adhesive, the bindings and wedges can be removed. The plastic modelling clay can be lifted away gently and any that remains can be scraped away with a scalpel. Finally all traces are removed with methylated spirit. The gum strip must never be pulled or scraped off or else any gold beneath it will be damaged. Soak in hot water for a few minutes and it will peel away easily. Dry thoroughly. Make sure no salt remains on the china from the salt tray or it will attract moisture from the atmosphere and harm later work. Now the results of the bonding are revealed and the surplus adhesive can be dealt with.

Rubbing down the adhesive

The joins should be secure and with a fine roll of adhesive along both sides. The adhesive can be carefully abraded just flush with the surface of the china so that further filling is unnecessary along the breakline. Do not pare away with a knife or the adhesive will be dragged out of the join, leaving a fine groove which would be very difficult to fill. Always use the listed abrasives.

The abrasive papers must be cut into narrow strips, no more than 1 cm ($\frac{1}{2}$ in) wide. One end is folded over about 3 mm ($\frac{1}{8}$ in) and this small surface only is rubbed along the adhesive. Used in this way the abrasive cannot scratch the surrounding china. Start by using a medium grade aluminium oxide abrasive paper and finish with flour glasspaper. Do not continue rubbing once the surface of the china is reached or the adhesive, which is softer than the china, will be scratched out of the join, leaving a groove. When finished, the break line should be satin smooth and indistinguishable from the adjoining china.

Needle files can be used to reach awkward places, particularly on figures. Use them to abrade; do not use the tips as chisels or else lumps of adhesive will be dug out, making holes and furrows. The cutting action of the file is on the forward movement; do not use a sideways motion, which causes deep scratching. As soon as a file

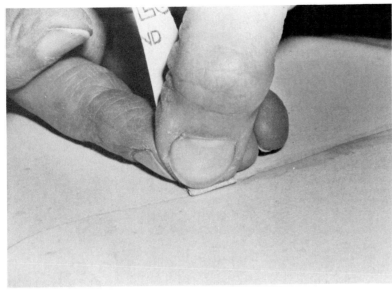

Fig. 40 Abrading excess adhesive from a join. Use a narrow strip of abrasive paper folded into a small pad

becomes clogged it must be cleaned by stroking on a file card to remove the accumulated adhesive.

If chips and rivet holes are to be filled it may be more convenient to abrade the joins when rubbing down the fillings but it is usually easier, when the join is alongside a hole, to smooth in the soft filler without the hindrance of a lump of hardened adhesive to catch the modelling tool. The abrading should be done as soon as possible once the adhesive is hard. The curing process continues for 72 hours, so if postponed for too long the rubbing down becomes progressively harder.

Faults in bonding

When joins fail to bond the cause could be one of several faults or perhaps a combination of several. The edges could have been dusty, wet or greasy or they were not held in close enough contact with each other. Whatever the cause, all the adhesive must be removed from the broken edges with paint stripper, making several applications if necessary, and the edges thoroughly cleaned and prepared for rebonding. The join must then be rebonded making sure all the rules are followed meticulously.

If adhesive remains rubbery, even after a full 24 hours have elapsed since bonding, it could be that the room temperature is too low. Allow further time for setting in a warmer place. If no further setting takes place it indicates that too great a proportion of adhesive to hardener was used when mixing the epoxy resin adhesive. The join must be

broken down and thoroughly cleaned of adhesive with paint stripper and then rebonded.

A very dark join is the result of either too much hardener to adhesive being used in the epoxy resin mixture or of insufficient titanium being added. Dirt could have been introduced into the adhesive via dirty fingers or dusty china. The only remedy for a conspicuous join is to remove the adhesive and rebond the join.

Gum strip trapped in the join can be removed by soaking in warm water. Remove the paper, when softened, with a scalpel. The hole left can be filled by running fresh adhesive into it after warming the china.

A step in the join can never be disguised. Take apart with paint stripper, remove every speck of adhesive and rebond, making sure that the join is held adequately firm. Remember to check the join after bonding while the adhesive is setting.

This second stage in repairing is very important. If the bonding is not satisfactory, take it apart as soon as possible; the newer the join the easier the adhesive is to dissolve. Unless the join is close and level with no groove or step, no amount of paint will conceal it. In fact, a coat of paint will make any irregularity more obvious. Sticking two pieces of china together seems so simple but to achieve a perfect join requires practice as well as close attention to every detail. The effort for perfection will not be wasted. Much dissatisfaction with the final results of restoration has its origin in the initial stages of the job.

41

4·Filling and Modelling

When the repair calls for the reconstruction of missing portions of china the methods of replacement can be divided into four categories. The materials and basic principles for using them are the same for all fillings and for modelling, but the restorer needs to know how to adapt them for specific jobs.

Firstly, the simple fillings required for rivet holes and surface chips. All that is needed for these is to fill the cavity with a suitable filling composition.

Secondly, the replacement of small missing areas which are wholly or partially surrounded by china, such as broken edges or pieces lost from the middle of a break. These are the simplest repairs to do and provide excellent practice in handling tools and materials.

Thirdly, the direct modelling of free standing areas such as handles or parts of figures when the missing area has to be built up by free hand modelling. This does require considerable modelling skill when replacing heads or limbs and these repairs should be tackled after experience has been gained with simple replacements.

Finally, replacement can also be done by casting the new piece in a mould. This only becomes possible where an identical object exists from which it is possible to take the pattern. This seems an ideal way to avoid free hand modelling but acquiring the identical twin is usually a problem.

Materials and tools

Epoxy resin (Araldite); a carrier and strengthener
Best quality china clay; a fine, light coloured clay in powder form
Titanium oxide; used to lighten the colour of the mixture
Artists' dry ground colour, black; for use on black ceramics
Methylated spirit (denatured alcohol); a solvent for epoxy resin, used to clean tools and hands
Modelling tools; for modelling and shaping
Orange sticks; for applying adhesive
Palette knife or spatula; for mixing adhesive and composition
Cartridge or thick drawing paper; for use as a mixing palette
Silicon non-stick parchment; for use as a modelling board
Resin remover; for removing hardened resin from the hands
Plastic modelling clay (Plasticine); to make supports and press moulds
Needle files; for shaping and smoothing hardened composition
Flour glass paper, coarse, medium and fine aluminium oxide; for smoothing and shaping hardened composition
Dust respirator; worn to prevent inhaling dust while rubbing down
Dusting brush or blower brush; to remove dust from china caused when rubbing down

Many mixtures and ready-made compounds have been used in the history of china mending and chemists will continue to devise more in the future. Epoxy resin and best quality china clay with the addition of a little titanium oxide fulfil the restorer's requirements most successfully. These requirements are, that the composition:

must be compatible with both the adhesive and the painting materials used to complete the restoration;
must be strong enough to stand up to handling and cleaning with water and mild chemicals;
does not shrink or swell when drying;
must be reasonably easy to model;
is a neutral colour which makes obliteration easier when painting over the repair;

provides a finished surface which will retain paint well.

This filling composition is not quite as hard as china but has greater impact strength. Epoxy resin provides the strength and adhesion, the china clay adds the necessary bulk and a good texture for painting, and titanium oxide is added to improve and stabilise the colour of the mixture. Too much titanium oxide, or titanium oxide used on its own without china clay, tends to cause the composition to split when heated and be too sticky to model well.

When preparing filling composition for basalt or Jackfield ware, black powdered pigment should replace the titanium oxide.

The china clay is a cream coloured powder and is purchased by the kilo. It must be stored in an airtight container and not allowed to become damp. Plaster of Paris, whiting or french chalk, either on its own or used with resin, is brittle and lacking in smoothness. Kaolin is very dark and gesso and barbola swell while drying, thus loosing their shape. They are also brittle when set.

The composition made with epoxy resin and china clay is easily modelled with small modelling tools and the detail finished, when it is set, with needle files and abrasives. To avoid repetition, the materials required and the methods used for rubbing down fillings and the final shaping with abrasives when modelling are dealt with at the end of the chapter.

A selection of small wooden modelling tools will be needed to work the composition. If metal tools are used they may leave black streaks on the china and scratch enamel decoration and gilding. Many plastic tools are unsuitable as they dissolve on contact with composition or methylated spirit. Box is the usual and preferred wood for modelling tools, having a long, straight grain and being smooth and slightly flexible. The very small sizes of tools required for china restoration can be purchased ready made, or potters' large tools can be split into narrow strips and the tips fashioned into convenient shapes. Seasoned bamboo can be split and shaped, making smooth, pliable spatulas. It will often be necessary to make a tool specially to suit a particular piece of work. Sometimes an extra long or a miniature tool will be needed. It is necessary to have a blade shaped tool for smoothing, one with a good point for indenting and a ball or blunt ended one for concave areas. Orange sticks are suitable for

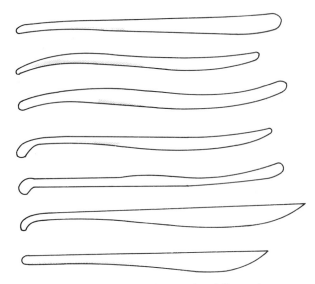

Diagram 13 Various shapes of boxwood modelling tools

pressing in small fillings but they are short grained and snap easily. Good tools help the work. Delicate modelling cannot be done with an ill made tool which is rough and clumsy. Always use modelling tools for applying and smoothing the composition. This will ensure clean hands and therefore clean china.

It is necessary to have a palette on which to mix the modelling composition. A stiff card, as described for use when bonding, which can be thrown away after use, is the most economical form of palette. A few sheets of silicon coated non-stick parchment are very useful when rolling out or flattening portions of composition for modelling.

The composition is a stiff compound which needs thorough mixing, so a good strong flexible palette knife is essential. Metal knives are the easiest to use as they are thin and flexible and are not harmed by contact with methylated spirit.

Methylated spirit, as well as cleaning fingers and tools, is used as a lubricant between tools and modelling composition. It must be used sparingly or the epoxy resin will be washed away. As soon as the tool drags at the composition dip the modelling tool into a jar of methylated spirit and shake off the excess before continuing.

Plastic modelling clay is used to make small press moulds and also for supporting the composition while it is setting.

Warning: The dust created when rubbing down

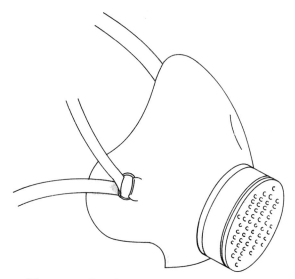

Diagram 14 A respirator, not a gauze mask, should be worn for protection from dust

should not be inhaled. A suitable respirator with an efficient dust filter should be worn. A gauze mask is inadequate.

Always apply barrier cream before starting work. The composition should be mixed with a palette knife and not handled unless absolutely necessary.

Making filling and modelling composition

Equal proportions of epoxy resin hardener and adhesive are squeezed onto the palette and mixed thoroughly. Titanium oxide is added to lighten the colour of the composition. When using 2 cm (1 in) each of hardener and adhesive add the equivalent of half a split pea of titanium oxide. This mixture is worked into sufficient china clay to form a pastry-like consistency. Use as much clay as the adhesive will hold without crumbling. It is much less messy to mix if the epoxy resin is gathered onto the palette knife and then pressed and turned into a pile of clay, don't try sprinkling the clay onto a pat of adhesive. Finally, dust the fingers with china clay and knead until quite smooth and without pockets of clay or air. Clean the fingers immediately.

It is difficult to give precise quantities when such small amounts of materials are needed unless a chemist's balance is used to weigh the ingredients. The appearance, colour and workability of the mixture and are the criteria. The composition should be a light beige matt and stiff enough to hold a solid shape, but neither crumbly nor sticky.

Use black pigment in the filling composition when repairing china which is entirely black. Mix sufficient dry ground pigment with the china clay and epoxy resin to match the surrounding china and knead thoroughly until no streaks remain. If only one surface is black the neutral beige composition should be used.

This composition remains workable for about two hours and has the same setting and hardening time as epoxy resin used alone as an adhesive. It is now ready for use either as a filler or a modelling composition. While fresh and at its softest it should be used to fill cracks, holes and small surface chips. As it becomes stiffer it is ideal for direct modelling of new handles, knobs or any missing limbs, because it will hold its shape more readily. It will stick to itself while soft but needs adhesive when applied to hardened composition or china. The usual mixture of equal quantities of epoxy resin adhesive and hardener with a little titanium oxide is used to anchor all fillings and modelling in place. To use, cut off a portion of composition. Never stretch it by pulling or tearing it away because later it will contract to its original size, causing splits to appear in the filling. *The filling composition shown in the photographs has been darkened deliberately so that it may be clearly seen.*

Using the filling composition

Filling grooves
If the bonding and rubbing down has been carefully carried out grooves should not occur. However, perfection does not come immediately. Although such a small gap is difficult to fill it must be done if a score in the surface is not to be visible through the overpainting.

Form a fine thread by rolling out a portion of freshly made composition on silicon parchment or a card dusted with clay. Do not press too hard when forming a roll of composition or it will flatten and not make an even cylinder. Apply a small amount of adhesive into the groove with a sharply pointed orange stick or a fine splinter of bamboo. Working on slightly warm, not cold, china will assist the adhesive to penetrate the groove. Lay the roll of composition along the

Fig. 41 Mixing adhesive into the china clay

Fig. 42 Kneading filling composition. Use the fingers as little as possible

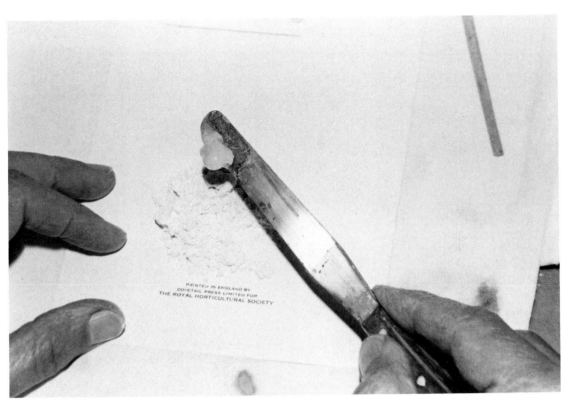

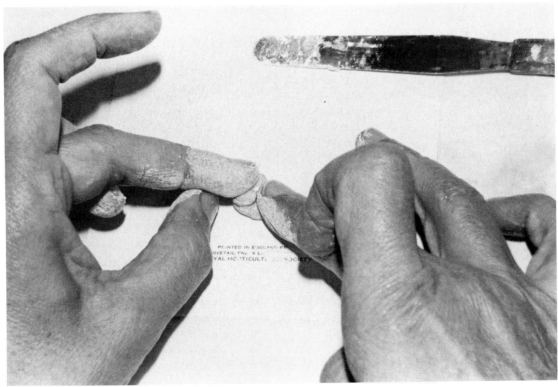

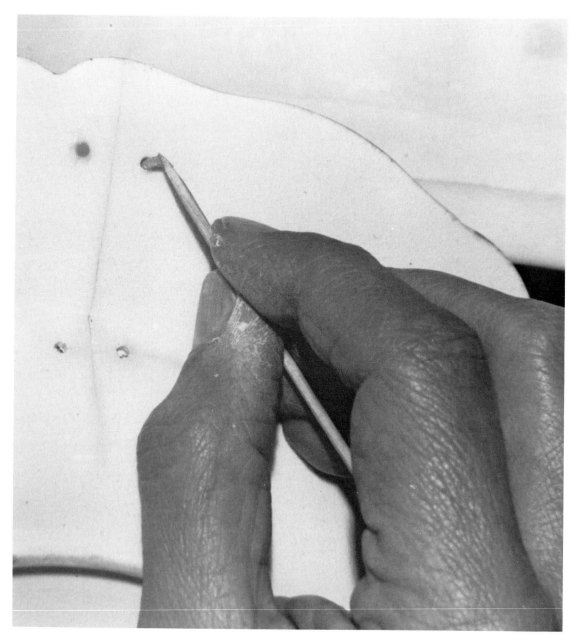

Fig. 43 Inserting a roll of filler into the base of a rivet hole

groove and press in firmly with a modelling tool. Work as much filler into the groove as possible and finally smooth the surface with the modelling tool. The tool can be lubricated with just enough methylated spirit to prevent it sticking to the filler. Clean the china of any finger marks with methylated spirit applied on a soft rag before they harden, taking care not to flood the surface and wash away the composition. Leave the filler to harden for 24 hours. Rubbing down or cutting away the surplus before it is completely dry will drag the filling out of its seating.

Filling rivet holes
The holes must of course be thoroughly clean, with no plaster dust remaining, or the filler will not stay in position. The composition should be used very fresh so that it is soft enough to press

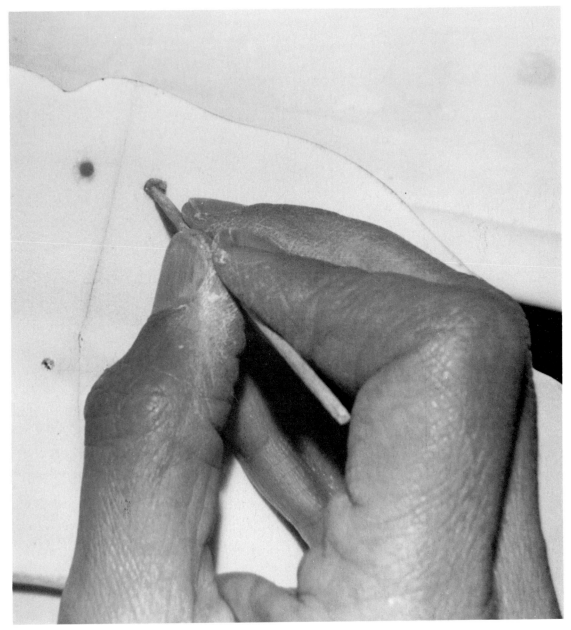

Fig. 44 Tamping in the filler. The hole on the left has been filled and smoothed off

right to the base of the smallest hole.

Apply adhesive around the sides and on the bottom of the hole with a sharpened orange stick. Roll out a cylinder of composition a little thinner than the hole it is to fill. Cut off a small portion, longer than the hole is deep, and insert it right to the base of the hole, pushing it in with a pointed stick. Make certain the filler is in good contact with the whole of the interior of the cavity. A small air pocket left at this stage will expand and find its way to the surface when heated, causing a blister every time the repair is painted.

When the rivet hole is completely full smooth the surface with a modelling tool, taking care not to drag the filler as this could leave a gap down one side of the hole. The filler should be left a little proud so that it can be rubbed down flush with the

47

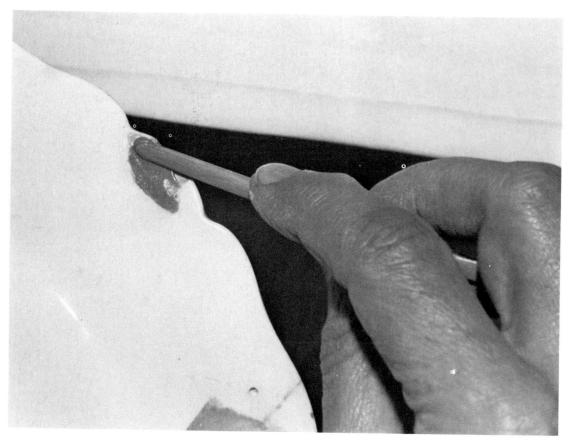

surface when hard. Do not leave too much filler protruding as rubbing down is hard work and time consuming. Clean off any finger marks.

When a rivet or lacing hole goes right through the china, one side must first be blocked off with a small piece of gum strip to prevent the filler being pushed out the other side. Once the first filling has hardened and the gum strip removed it may be necessary to add a little filler to perfect the surface which was under the gum strip. The filler on both sides of the hole should be left fractionally proud to allow for rubbing down when hard. Leave the filling to harden for 24 hours.

Filling surface chips
The filling for shallow surface chips will need adhesive to hold it in place on the china. Cover the damaged area of china with a thin, even film of adhesive making sure the edges are sufficiently coated. Press a suitably sized pellet of filler firmly into the centre of the chip, smoothing towards the edges. Coax and smooth it gently into shape; do not pull or stretch because it will contract to its

Fig. 45 Filling a shallow shell chip with composition

Fig. 46 Making a press mould with plastic modelling clay. This will support the filling for a broken rim

Fig. 47 Putting a plastic modelling clay support into position before filling with composition

original volume as it dries, pulling away from the adhesive. Make sure there are no crevices at the edges where the filler meets the surface of the china. Moisten the modelling tool slightly with methylated spirit to prevent it pulling at the filling. Do not use methylated spirit excessively or it will act as a solvent on the epoxy resin.

Any surface modelling such as scallops or fluting can be added while the composition is soft. Bring the modelling as near to the final finish as possible. Although shaping can be done with abrasives once the filling has set it is a great mistake to leave too much unwanted composition to harden. Rubbing down accounts for much of the time spent on restoration, so the better the modelling the less time is wasted with abrasives.

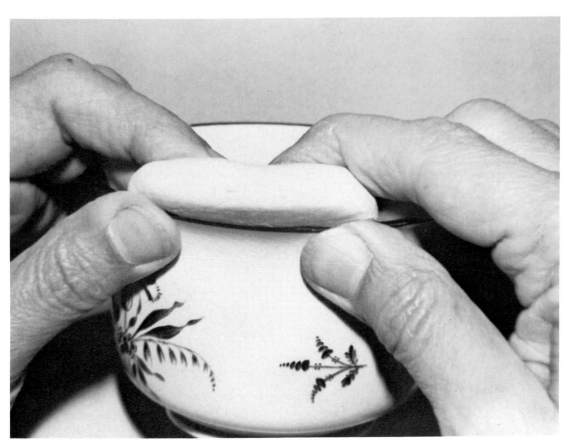

To allow the surface to be prepared for painting the filler is left very slightly proud, but only very slightly. Remove any sticky finger marks from the china before they harden and allow 24 hours setting time for the filler before preparing the surface for painting.

Filling in missing chips and holes

Epoxy resin composition used in thin sheets has little rigidity until set, and will sag under its own weight unless it has support. The most convenient material for supporting small missing pieces which have no complicated modelling is plastic modelling clay. It is pliable but will hold simple shapes and shallow relief modelling. It is quick and easy to use for the supporting backing

Fig. 48 Putting the first layer of composition into position

required for plate and bowl rims and similar items.

To form a support of the right shape knead a ball of plastic modelling clay until smooth and soft; dip it in cold water to prevent it sticking to the surface of the china. Select a sound section of the china which will act as the pattern, ensuring that any scallops or modelling match the section to be replaced. Press the plastic modelling clay firmly and steadily onto the chosen area. It must be large enough to overlap the gap to be filled and chunky enough to have sufficient strength to support the composition. Ease the plastic modelling clay away from the china without distorting

Fig. 49 The stages in building up a missing area, from the supporting plastic clay to the final surface modelling

the impression. If the plastic modelling clay is very soft through handling and a warm atmosphere it can be stiffened after the impression has been taken by chilling in a refrigerator or very cold water before being used as a support.

Apply a thin coating of adhesive to the broken edges of the gap to be filled and position the plastic modelling clay. Match up the edges and any flutes or scallops accurately. Smooth and smear the edges of the plastic modelling clay against the surface of the china a little to hold it securely in place. Do not get any plastic modelling clay on the broken edges which would prevent the

filler adhering strongly. Unless the china is very thin the gap should be filled in layers. Epoxy resin generates its own heat while setting is proceeding and too great a volume will cause overheating, resulting in strain splits. The layers should be restricted to a maximum of 6 mm ($\frac{1}{4}$ in) thickness.

Knead sufficient composition until smooth. Flatten into approximately the right shape and size to completely cover, but fill to only half the depth of the missing area. Ease it into position on the support, but without stretching it as stretched composition will contract to its original size and crack. Press the edges of the composition and china together very firmly with a modelling tool. Good continuous union right round the join is essential. Leave undisturbed for 24 hours to harden. If a subsequent layer of composition is added before the foundation filling is thoroughly hard the pressure of modelling will disturb its seating on the china and lead to cracking at the edges.

Peel away the plastic modelling clay support. Any residue can be scraped away and finally all traces are removed with methylated spirit. Any hardened filler that would protrude above the line of the final surface should be filed down at this stage. It will make the subsequent filling or modelling much easier if there are no hard lumps or ridges to catch the modelling tool. The filling now forms a rigid foundation on which to build up composition until it is level with the surface of the china.

Apply adhesive wherever fresh composition is to be added. Where a large area is to be built up model the soft composition into a sheet of suitable shape and thickness. Lay it in position; then, with a modelling tool press it firmly on the foundation making sure no air pockets remain. Check that the surface which was moulded against the plastic modelling clay is correct, adding any filler that may be necessary. Any relief modelling on the surface can be added while the composition is soft. The filling and modelling must be as close to the original shape as it is possible to make it to avoid unnecessary rubbing down. Clean away any finger marks before they become hard. Allow the filling to harden for 24 hours before a start is made on the abrading.

When the gap is situated in the bulge of a spherical object with insufficient access to provide a plastic modelling clay support, a way must be devised to hold the composition in place until it is stiff enough to hold shape without support. It is often possible to get a pad of plastic modelling clay in place with the aid of a long tool or spoon, but it is essential to be able to scrape out every scrap once the filling has hardened. A few crossed bands of gum strip manoeuvred into position will hold the foundation layer of composition sufficiently until it is dry. Once the entire filling is complete the gum strip can be washed out with water. A plastic bag inserted into the article and filled with salt will also give sufficient support. Wherever the plastic bag will contact the composition it should be brushed with liquid detergent to prevent it sticking. This salt bag will follow the contour of the china and provide adequate support for the foundation layer of composition. Whatever is used as a support must be removed before the painting and stoving stages can begin. When it is impossible to arrange the support from the inside a lattice of composition can be made separately on a piece of plastic modelling clay. This must be large enough to fit across the gap and be contoured to match the shape. Arrange a trellis work of strips of composition on the supporting plastic modelling clay and leave to harden. Final adjustments for size can be made with a file once the composition is hard. Apply adhesive to the broken edges of the china and lay the lattice in place. It can be held in place until hard with a cross of gum strip on the outside. Once this network is firmly in place the surface can be built up.

Building up teapot spouts
Building up these narrow, cone shaped areas is an adaption of the method used for filling large chips. Unless an identical duplicate is available the support has to be made without the aid of a suitable area from which to take a press mould. The exact shape to be modelled must first be established. If the whole of the tip of the spout is gone so that no clues remain for guidance, the shape and length required must be researched. If an illustration of an identical article cannot be traced, period and style must be considered when deciding on the replacement shape.

Once the shape is determined the support is made for the spout by rolling a cone of plastic modelling clay to fit the aperture of the broken spout closely and to come well beyond the final length required. This cone is inserted firmly into the existing remnants of the spout like a plug. Bend down the end gently to assume the correct curve, following on the line of the remaining portion. The shaping at the end can be marked on the plastic modelling clay with a modelling tool.

Flatten a sheet of composition large enough to completely cover the whole of the missing area but to only half the finished thickness. Apply adhesive to the broken china edges and lay the composition around the cone joining onto the remaining china firmly and shaping it against the plastic modelling clay. With a scalpel trim the tip of the spout level with the guide marks made in the cone support. When this foundation sheet is a satisfactory shape it is left to harden.

After 24 hours the cone is removed and the composition cleaned of all plastic modelling clay. The final layers can then be built up until as thick

Fig. 50 An edge ridge and tendril modelled into the surface
layer of composition

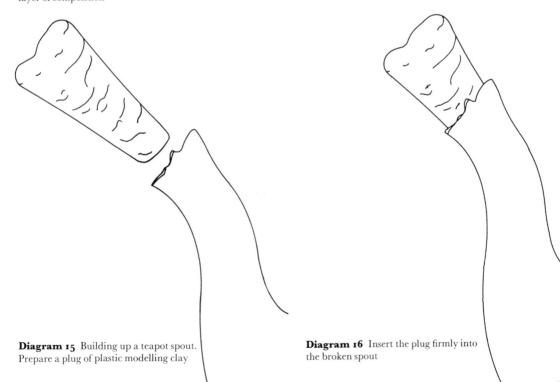

Diagram 15 Building up a teapot spout.
Prepare a plug of plastic modelling clay

Diagram 16 Insert the plug firmly into
the broken spout

53

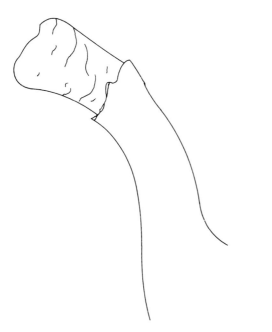

Diagram 17 Bend the plastic modelling clay into the correct curve

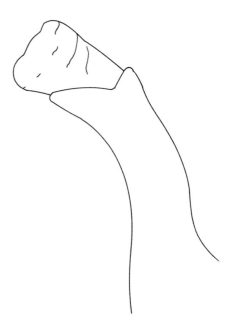

Diagram 19 Composition is added and shaped to the correct size

as required using a sheet of freshly made composition held in place with adhesive. The shaping should be done on the soft composition as exactly as possible, putting in any decorative modelling on the surface. This, again, is to avoid excessive rubbing down. Final shaping can be done with a file when the composition has hardened but this is a time consuming operation and should be kept to a minimum.

Replacing the pouring lip of a jug
Make a cone the width of the lip and lay it along the channel of the original. Fix firmly onto the surrounding china and mark on the plastic modelling clay the outer shape which the filling is to follow. Apply adhesive to the broken china and add the foundation sheet of composition to the underside only of the cone. As before, cover the entire area to be filled but to only half the final depth. Trim the edge of the composition to the correct level and shape before leaving to harden. After 24 hours remove the plastic modelling clay cone and clean the foundation layer of composition. Coat the foundation with adhesive and add freshly made composition until the thickness corresponds with the surrounding china. Add any surface modelling before the composition is allowed to harden. Final shaping and rubbing down in preparation for painting can now be done.

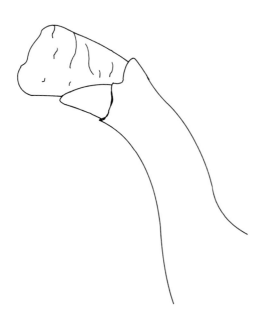

Diagram 18 The first layer of composition is added

Modelling a long narrow neck for a vase or urn

When the replacement required is straight sided, roll out a cylinder of plastic modelling clay the diameter of the inside of the neck and a little longer than needed. Insert the roll into the neck but make sure it doesn't contact the broken edge. Build up with composition in layers as before, allowing the composition to harden thoroughly between layers. For a shaped or flared opening a cone of plastic modelling clay is rolled out and inserted in the aperture, and then the exact shape is built up with plastic modelling clay on this cone. If part of the original rim remains the plastic modelling clay can be pressed against this, moved round a little way and pressed again until the entire circumference is obtained. This must be done carefully or the resulting shape will be irregular and useless. The building up of the composition in layers against the support then proceeds exactly as before.

Replacement handles and knobs

Frequently the design of these is not only exclusive to one pottery but often particular handles are only found in association with one style of knob. This means a time consuming but interesting search through books and collections to find the pattern for the replacement. Research must always be taken into consideration when assessing the time needed for a job. The replacement of a handle, whether it is for a cup, a lid or a tureen follows the same method even though the handles lie in a different position in each case. The method can also be adapted for replacing limbs or accessories on figure groups.

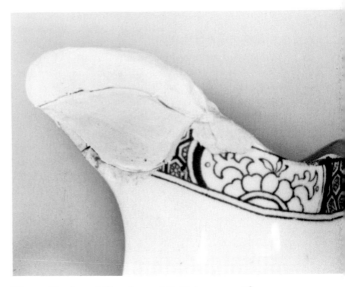

Fig. 51 Plastic modelling clay modelled into a support for a jug lip

Any free standing projecting area needs a rigid core on which to build up the modelling. Without a stiff supporting foundation or armature to work against the modelling composition is pushed from one position to another and is impossible to shape. The most suitable core is hardened composition. If wood or metal is used for this purpose every change of temperature will throw a strain on the join as the expansion rates of china, composition,

Fig. 52 Care must be taken to remodel the appropriate handle. Although similar, these handles all differ slightly. They are Spode, Hilditch and Worcester

wood and metal are different. This will eventually make the join crack, allowing damp to enter and further deterioration to take place. A further advantage of a composition foundation is that a miscalculation in the size or shape of the core does not mean that the replacement must be removed and a fresh start made. Should the core be revealed by large scale corrections it will not affect the result as the same materials have been used throughout. Modern compounds are strong enough to be used without reinforcement. It is far more often the china, not the composition, which breaks in a subsequent accident.

Making handles

When making a new handle start by drawing the proposed replacement handle to the correct size and shape. This can most easily be assessed by cutting a template of the cup shape from a stiff card and drawing the new handle shape on this. If the cup is held steady on a piece of card while a pencil line is drawn round its silhouette an accurate template can be made easily. Cut round the pencil line. Hold this pattern in position on the side of the cup while the handle is drawn to scale using the broken off handle stubs or scars as a guide for distance and thickness. With the drawing of the handle alongside the cup it soon becomes obvious if the style and proportions are right. Any adjustment at this stage is very easy, but once modelled in composition a lot of rubbing down or even starting again is a lengthy remedy.

Prepare a roll of composition as long as the handle and approximately half its finished thickness to form a core. Lay it in position on the card along the centre of the drawn handle. Leave undisturbed to harden for 24 hours, then carefully remove it from the card and check it against the cup to make sure that it is an exact fit. If it is too long adjust by filing. If it is just a little short it can be adjusted with extra filler when fixing into position.

Press a roll of plastic modelling clay under the handle space, attaching firmly to the body of the cup ready to support the core for the handle. Apply adhesive to the handle stubs and each end of the composition core. Secure a small pad of freshly made composition on the handle stubs and press the core into the pads. Draw up and smooth

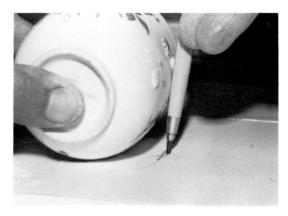

Fig. 53 Drawing around a cup to make an accurate template

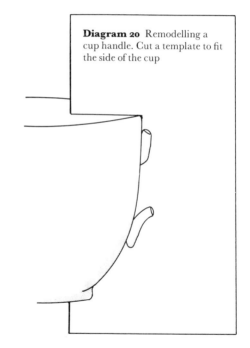

Diagram 20 Remodelling a cup handle. Cut a template to fit the side of the cup

Fig. 54 Hold the drawing of the proposed handle against the cup. If there is an error in proportion or position it will be obvious

56

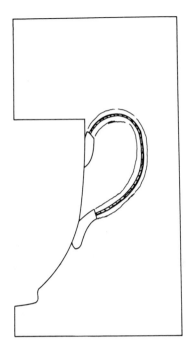

Diagram 21 Draw the proposed handle and place a roll of composition along the centre

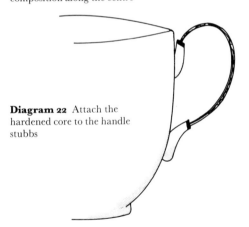

Diagram 22 Attach the hardened core to the handle stubbs

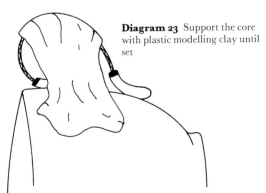

Diagram 23 Support the core with plastic modelling clay until set

Diagram 24 Build up composition to the required size and shape

the new composition round the ends of the core to ensure a good union. Make sure the handle is straight and at the correct height. Pinch the plastic modelling clay over the centre of the core keeping it away from the joins. Do not strap with gum strip or the tightening action of the shrinking paper will force the soft pad of composition out of line.

Allow 24 hours for the composition and adhesive to harden before cleaning away the plastic modelling clay. Coat the core with adhesive and build the handle to the required thickness and shape with freshly made composition. This can be applied either as small pellets or as a flattened bandage wound round the core. Whichever way is found to be easier care must be exercised not to leave any air gaps. Continually model over the whole area, fining

Fig. 55 Building up composition around the centre core of a handle

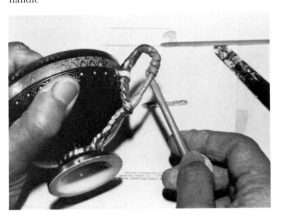

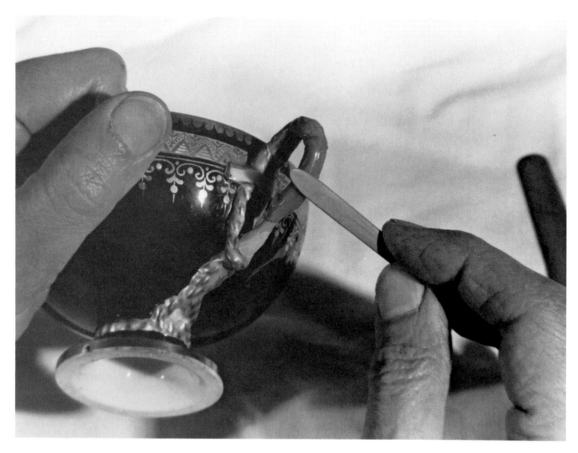

down where too thick and adding composition where it is too thin. Never completely finish off one part only or the proportions will be difficult to maintain. When no further improvement can be made to the modelling the composition is allowed to harden for 24 hours. Final shaping and refining of the surface can be done with files and abrasive strips. There must be no crevices or ridges visible at the joining points, so make sure these are either filled or rubbed smooth.

Making knobs

First make a core of composition which is as long as the knob is high and about half as thick as the narrowest part. This can be left to harden and then placed in position with adhesive and a pad of composition; alternatively, the soft composition can be added to the china immediately. Apply adhesive to the broken area. Prepare a core from composition which has been made for an hour and fix it in position with a collar of plastic modelling clay to prevent it drooping out of shape. Once the core is hard the shape can be

Fig. 56 Smoothing and shaping the composition

Diagram 25 Rub down to the final shape ready for painting

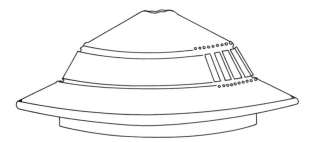

Diagram 26 Modelling a missing knob. Apply adhesive to the cleaned break

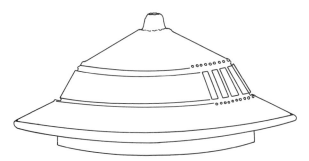

Diagram 27 Fix a core of composition into position

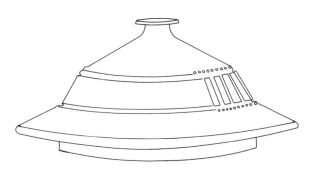

Diagram 28 Build up the final shape when the core has hardened

built up round the foundation. Work over the whole area continually. It is difficult to keep the shape correct if small sections are completed in isolation. Compare shapes and measure frequently to ensure correct modelling. When the composition is hard, corrections can be made by filing, but it is quicker to get the shape exactly right at the modelling stage. When the shape is satisfactory, leave to dry before attempting the final rubbing down.

Working on figure groups

It is important to make every effort to replace any missing item with its correct counterpart. If after research, and in agreement with the owner, a compromise has to be made, make sure that the addition will be in character. A flower wreathed garden hat, however well modelled and interesting to make, is inappropriate on a Grecian figure. Reference books with good illustrations of costume detail and accessories, musical instruments and weapons for the correct period are invaluable.

Replacing drapery
Areas of drapery will need similar treatment to missing chips. First, a support is fashioned to hold a foundation layer of composition while it hardens. Knead a ball of plastic modelling clay well and press into a suitable size and shape. It should be both wide and long enough to extend beyond the edges of the replacement. Fit it into position on the figure. This can be awkward where there is much ornamentation. Any curves or shaping can be modelled free hand in the plastic modelling clay to accommodate the foundation. Place a foundation layer of composition on the support and allow it to become hard. The final shape is built up on this hardened layer and any modelling of folds or other details added before the composition sets. Once the composition is hard the final abrading can be done.

Renewing ribbons
All ribbons should be made from composition which has been left to stiffen for at least an hour. Flatten it on either silicon parchment or a card dusted with dry clay making it the same thickness as the original china ribbons. The ribbons can be

Diagram 29 Pellets of plastic modelling clay are needed to support ribbon loops or bows

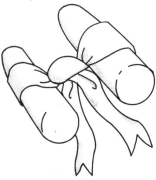

Fig. 57 Opening up a cone of composition to start a flower shape

cut to the right width with a sharp scalpel or scissors. Spread adhesive on the stubs to which the composition is to be joined and attach the new ribbon firmly in place. Smooth down the union well. If the ribbon is ruffled or looped it will need tiny wedges or pellets of plastic modelling clay for support. Make the ribbons as smooth as possible at this stage as rubbing down will be difficult on such fragile strips of composition. Bows should be formed by folding soft but firm ribbons and placing the loops in position with adhesive immediately they are made. They will then harden in a natural formation and not look stiff as they would do if left to dry before being attached.

Repairing basketwork
Woven edges and handles can be simulated by twisting two or plaiting three rolls of composition together. If this appears too sharply modelled roll the twist or plait gently on a piece of silicon parchment to consolidate it a little.

Modelling flowers and bocage
Replacement of flowers or foliage on figures and vases is a constant requirement. They must match the original exactly in size, petal thickness, quantity of petals per flower and plant type. One daisy among a group of roses will be easier and quicker to make but won't look convincing.

Most directly modelled flowers start as a pellet of composition which is pressed into a variety of shapes. Allow the composition to stiffen for an hour before using to make it easier to hold the thin

shapes required for petals. Flowers and leaves must always be bonded to the china with adhesive. They will not remain in place without it. Apply a thin coat of adhesive to the china and press the flower into position. Make any adjustments in shape to the edge of the petals or leaves to give a natural appearance while the composition is still malleable.

Making the different types of flowers
For a simple convolvulus type flower, roll a suitable quantity of firm composition into a ball, insert a round pointed modelling tool into the centre and flare out the edges into a cornet shape by revolving and pressing the tool outwards. It is then ready to place in position, which should be done immediately. It will then lie close to the china and not stick out at a stiff angle as would happen if it was dried first. Petalled flowers like forget-me-nots can be developed from this simple shape by cutting the appropriate number of nicks in the edge of the cornet form. Use either small sharp scissors or a scalpel, and cut the same number of petals as any remaining flowers possess. The edges of the petals can be rounded or indented with a modelling tool to match the surviving flowers.

Daisy type flowers can be made in two ways. Either form a cornet, increasing the number and length of cuts into the edge or flatten a length of composition into a strip, snip it into a fringe along one edge and roll up carefully. Separate and arrange the petals into a flower head.

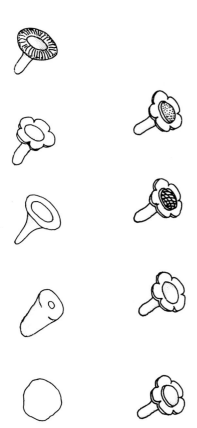

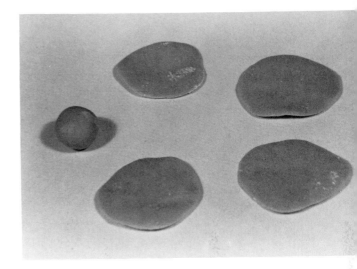

Diagram 30 Stages in modelling petalled flowers

Diagram 31 Flower centres. Top to bottom: indented, criss-crossed, concave, convex

The centre of open flowers can be finished in several ways. Sometimes a small dimple made with a pointed modelling tool is all that is needed. A raised centre is made with a small pellet pressed into position and either left as a dome, criss-crossed with a scalpel or indented many times with a pointed modelling tool. Whichever method is used the result must match any existing examples.

Roses are formed by flattening a number of small balls of composition into separate petals. It may be necessary to experiment to find the right quantity of composition needed to make the petals the exact scale to match existing flowers.

Fig. 58 Making a rose. Pellets of composition are flattened to make petals

Fig. 59 The first petal shape is coiled tightly to form the centre. The remaining shapes are arranged to overlap around it

Fig. 60 The completed rose. The number and size of petals must coincide with any original flowers

The first petal shape is coiled onto itself to form the heart of the rose. Further petals are assembled around this centre, each petal overlapping the previous one. Bend back the outer edges of the petals slightly with the modelling tool. The roses are more likely to be an open cabbage shape rather than the tight pointed modern form. Frequently the fingerprints of the original modeller can be seen impressed in petals and leaves indicating very clearly that the flowers were modelled by hand. Buds can be modelled from a pellet of composition and either left spherical, slightly elongated or well pointed. Sepals can be indicated by marks made with the modelling tool or pressed from strips of composition and added around the bud.

Leaves are made by pressing flat an oval pellet of composition and the shape accentuated with a modelling tool. The tip can be pointed and the edges indented if this is required. Veins on a leaf, if they are impressed and not painted on, can be marked into the soft composition with a modelling tool or, if sharply defined, by using a scalpel. Foliage, such as vine leaves or oak leaves, is easier to make by cutting the shape from a sheet of flattened composition. Press the composition to a thin even sheet on silicon parchment or a card dusted with clay and cut it to shape with small scissors or a scalpel. Refine the edges and add further detail with a modelling tool. Most leaves bend a little so arrange them in a natural curve over a pad of plastic modelling clay. The bocage on old Staffordshire figures, usually very stiff sprays of lobed leaves, was made in two thin layers joined back to back over a branch of clay. The join is clearly visible in any remaining examples of foliage and this method should be copied for the replacement.

Stems and tendrils are prepared from fine rolls of composition matching the diameter of the broken edges exactly and fitted carefully to the break. As it is extremely difficult to abrade fine stems down to size they must be fitted and smoothed carefully so the join is inconspicuous. Originally, fine stems were made by dipping thread in slip and arranging it in position while still wet. When the china was fired the thread burned away leaving only the vitrified clay.

Replacing parts of petals or leaves
If only a portion of a petal is needed apply adhesive to the broken edge and the back of the broken china petal. Prepare a whole new petal

Diagram 32 Modelling leaves

Diagram 33 Cutting oak leaf shapes

Diagram 34 Cutting ivy leaf shapes

Diagram 35 Cutting vine leaf shapes

Diagram 36 Composition rolled flat and fringed to make grass type bocage

Fig. 61 Leaves need a support of plastic modelling clay so they will curve in a natural way

Fig. 62 Cutting composition to simulate the grass-like bocage on flat backs

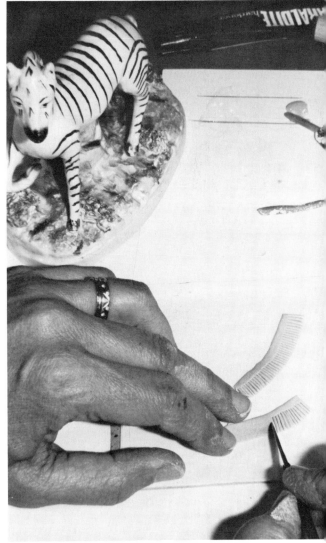

and press into position from the back of the broken piece, leaving enough exposed to complete the petal. Smooth the front of the petal into the original china to give a continuous surface. Trim excess composition from the back but leave a slight overlap as the seating is so small and this will give additional strength. When remaking large petals or leaves a plastic modelling clay support may be necessary.

The grass-like tufts found on so many Staffordshire flat backs was made originally by pressing moist clay through a mesh. This method can be used with composition provided the correct size mesh is at hand. Alternatively, a strip of composition can be flattened and one edge fringed. Ensure that the fringe is cut to the correct length and thickness. Coil this strip and while still soft apply the uncut edge to the group. The fringed ends must be arranged with a modelling tool to imitate the original tufts, which are usually curled or flattened a little.

Fruits also start with a pellet of modelling composition, the ball shape being modified according to the type of fruit. Apples are spheres of composition with a small dimple at top and base made with a pointed modelling tool. Pears need a conical pellet with the depression at the thick end. Both oranges and lemons have a pitted surface made with a pointed tool. Lemons are more oval in shape than oranges, almost coming to a point at each end. Grapes are slightly oval with the tendrils made from fine rolls of com-

Fig. 63 Attaching and arranging the bocage

position carefully coiled into position. However, it is usually the distinctive colours which leave no doubt about the fruit. The modelling should not be over accentuated.

Although the flowers and fruit look complicated, they are probably the easiest free hand modelling to do. A little study of the flowers on the original will indicate how they were made. Unless dozens of identical leaves or simple flowers are required it is quicker to model the individual replacements freehand. The amount of time taken to make moulds or bend sheet metal into cutters for stamping out shapes is usually greater than for modelling. The result of individual modelling is also of a better quality.

Making accessories for figure groups
Sticks, guns, musical instruments and any other object used to embellish a figure may be modelled separately and joined to the figure when set, but it will generally look and fit better if modelled directly onto the figure. When it is necessary to replace the hand as well as the object being held, a natural position of the fingers will be easier to achieve by modelling both the hand and the

object directly onto the figure at the same time. Composition which is surplus when modelling can be rolled into an assortment of small diameter lengths and left to harden to provide foundations for sticks or similar accessories. The ready-made core is put into position with adhesive and a small pad of soft composition, and supported with plastic modelling clay. A core for the hand can be arranged to grasp the object and the composition left to set. If no suitable core is available it will be necessary to make one, leaving it to harden on silicon parchment before using it. The final modelling is then built around this firm foundation. When modelling a hand the core should be finished where the fingers join the palm. If a hardened core goes further than the first knuckles it will impede the modelling of delicate fingers. These can be added at the second modelling stage. Use composition which has stiffened for an hour before being rolled into separate fingers. Make sure that the separation between the fingers as well as the knuckles is well defined in the modelling. Three scratches with a file across a boxing glove of composition will not look like fingers. The modelling of hands is dealt with in more detail later in this chapter.

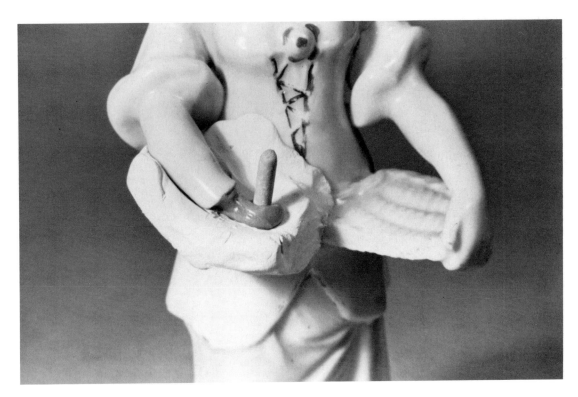

Anatomical replacements

Modelling limbs

When making replacement limbs the style and character of a figure group must always take priority over strict anatomical accuracy. The proportions of the limbs are often elongated to add grace and movement to a pose. The most frequent replacements are arms and legs or parts of these. This modelling, particularly the hands, is probably the most complicated and difficult the restorer has to cope with. A little knowledge of anatomy is essential if limbs are not to look like plaster casts. A simple guide to the structure of arms, hands, legs and feet is included after the basic method of procedure. Measurements must be accurately taken between joints with dividers and calipers whenever possible. However, when both limbs are missing the classic proportions of the human figure can be used as a guide, checking with any breakage scars for indications of size and position.

First a stable foundation for the modelling must be constructed. A core can be made and left to harden on a card and then attached to the figure. This is similar to the method for making a handle. Alternatively, a plastic modelling clay sling can

Fig. 64 The core or bone supported by a pad of plastic modelling clay. This figure holds a bunch of flowers which will be arranged around the core

be attached to the figure following the line of the missing limb. The core of pliable composition is positioned with adhesive on the china and left to harden in the sling. This method will work just as well for legs as arms if the figure is placed on its back or side. The support becomes more a splint than a sling and as before the composition is left to harden on the figure. The principle of constructing a foundation for limbs is probably better understood if in this case the core is thought of as a bone. This in turn is surrounded by composition which represents the building up of muscle and tissue. After the core has hardened check the measurements between joints and the angle of the limb. If they are not right, correct or replace them now, because if the proportions are incorrect at the start the limb will never be satisfactory. It is quicker to correct them at this stage than try to compensate by adding masses of composition which will need a lot of rubbing down in the end. Make sure the limb looks natural from all angles, not just from the front. Adding necklaces, bracelets or flowers to hide a bad mend is an admission of failure and inspires mistrust.

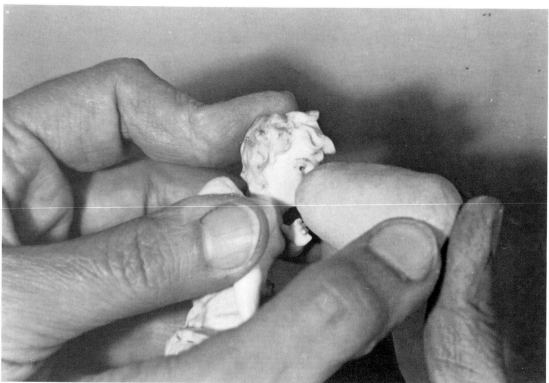

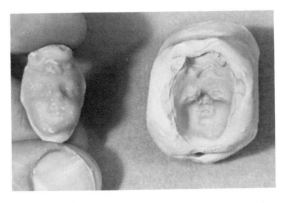

Fig. 65 A mask taken from a cherub used to replace a child's head

Fig. 66 Taking a plastic modelling clay mask

Fig. 67 The mask and the plastic modelling clay mould

Fig. 68 A collection of masks is useful when a pattern is needed for a replacement

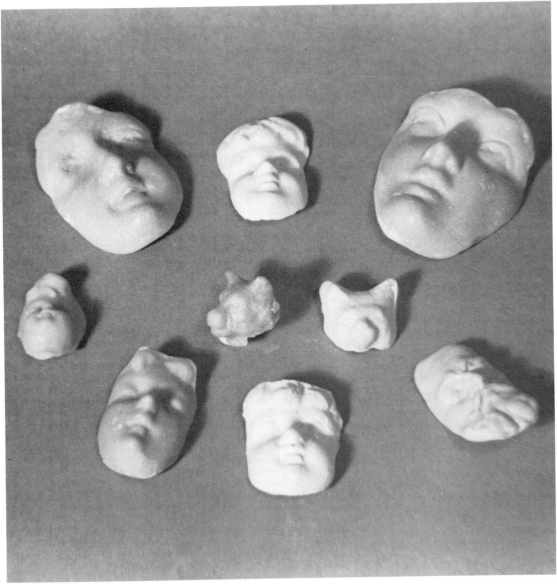

Modelling a head

A headless figure is not an everyday problem but the difficulty and time taken to model a head by hand makes it an expensive job. A practical alternative is to use a simple press mould of plastic modelling clay to take a mask from a suitable model. If an identical figure is available a mould can be made of the whole head. However, if the twin is not available a mask of the face only can be made from a similar model and all the other details added by direct modelling. The face to be used must be the right scale and have an appropriate depth of modelling. A Meissen figure will not double for a Staffordshire flat back. It must have the right style of features; plump cherubs will not turn into languishing shepherdesses but they do make excellent children. Many factories used the same mould to compose several different groups, merely changing the decoration and details. Staffordshire chimney ornaments will often double as either male or female, the difference being in the painting of heavier features and a change of hairstyle.

To take a press mould, form a ball of plastic modelling clay into a smooth cone and dip it into cold water to prevent it sticking to the china. Press the narrow end onto the most prominent part of the face, which is usually the nose and chin. Push gently but firmly until the face only is covered by the plastic modelling clay. Push as far as the hairline and under the chin to the neck. Remove the plastic modelling clay cleanly without twisting. Even a slight turn will splay the plastic modelling clay and change the shape of the mould. The result should be a clear impression of the features. Any minor irregularities can be corrected with a small modelling tool. If the impression is not clear try again, making sure that the face of the model is quite clean and the plastic modelling clay well dampened. Features are usually less pronounced in a mould than they appear to be on the original figure. This is because they are emphasized by the painting and are not necessarily less pronounced due to a poor moulding.

The mould is filled with a thin sheet of freshly made composition. Ease the soft composition into the mould with a small modelling tool, coaxing it gently but thoroughly into the nose and mouth cavities. Leave the mask to harden for 24 hours, then remove from the plastic modelling clay and clean thoroughly. The mask is now ready to be positioned on the broken neck, adjusting the angle to make the new head look in the right direction. If most of the original neck is intact the mask can be secured directly onto it with adhesive and a pad of filler. Use plastic modelling clay to prop the mask into place while it sets.

Should a neck also be required a core must be built up from the shoulders first, and when hardened the mask is fitted to this core. The neck core can be put in place when the mould for the mask is filled and both will then be ready at the same time. The face can be turned to look right or left, up or down. Place the mask with sufficient room for the chin to extend beyond the neck, bearing in mind that the core is thinner than the finished neck. Leave the mask to harden in position. The neck can now be built up, modelling smoothly into the chin and over the back and sides of the head, joining up with the mask. Ears, hair, hats or any other accessories can be added as modelling progresses. The features will need emphasizing slightly to compensate for the thickness of the base coats of paint, and glaze which will tend to flatten out the depressions. Finally, the head must be checked for flaws and brought to a fine surface for painting. Faces always need a super-fine finish as even the slightest blemish at such a small scale looks like a bad scar. It is convenient to build up a collection of masks from a variety of china figures so that when a replacement is required the model is readily available.

Although figures present some of the more difficult problems in modelling, once past this stage they are usually simple to paint because there are no large, plain areas to cover.

Anatomy as applied to china restoration

The time and skill needed to replace an entire figure would only warrant the expense in a very important group. In a piece of great quality such an extensive replacement would add little to its value or interest. It must be clearly understood that a replacement does not restore a piece to mint condition.

Although limbs are often covered by clothing or drapery the underlying structure and proportion of bones and muscles must be considered or the results will be stiff and distorted.

The mass of the shoulder projects like a ledge beyond the body, with the arm inserted into its under surface. The upper arm is thicker from

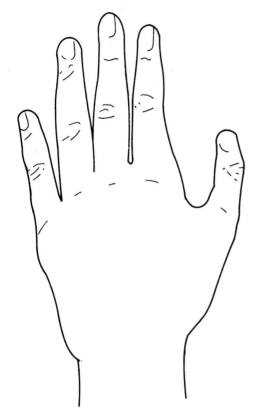

Diagram 37 The hand, showing relative positions of finger joints and thumb

Diagram 39 A fully modelled hand

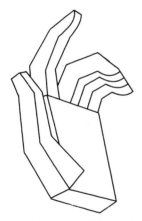

Diagram 38 Simplified shapes of the hand and fingers

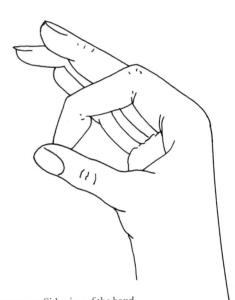

Diagram 40 Side view of the hand

front to back than from side to side and tapers slightly above the elbow. The point of the elbow is under the centre of the shaft of the upper arm when bent, not in line with the back of the arm. Immediately below the elbow the forearm is at its heaviest. The mass is convex at the back and concave in its front plane. It tapers to the wrist as the muscles descend into tendons. At the wrist the bones come close to the surface making it angular; it is nearly twice as broad as it is thick.

Hands are the most common replacement needed for figures. They contain so many parts and are so variable in action and character that they warrant special study. It is a worthwhile starting exercise to trace the outline of one's own hand with the fingers spread, marking in the position of wrist and knuckles. Note particularly how the thumb is placed in relation to them. At the back the hand is flat except when the fist is clenched. On the inside the palm is like a shallow bowl with squared sides. It is well cushioned on both sides near the wrist, the bulk of the muscles forming the base of the thumb, extending half-way across the palm. A further pad lies along the base of the fingers. The mass of the hand is greater on the side of the thumb than on the little finger side. It is broader at the finger joints than at the wrist but thicker at the wrist than near the fingers.

Fingers are composed of three bones, each of diminishing length towards the finger tips. The length of the first bone is equal to the remaining two. As the palm extends half-way along the first bone the distance between joints on the inside of the fingers appear to be the same. This is best seen when viewed from the side. Collectively the fingers taper. Each finger tapers in itself with a tendency to converge towards the middle finger. When the hand is in action the two middle fingers are inclined to go together. A side view of a finger shows the top to be flat with angular joints while the underside is rounded, particularly at the tip beneath a flat nail.

There are only two bones in the thumb. The whole length of the thumb is equal to that of the second finger measured on the outside. It reaches to approximately the middle joint of the first finger. When measured from wrist to finger tip the hand is equal to the length of the face from chin to natural hairline. At the knuckles the width of the hand is about half its length.

The lower limbs should not be considered as two straight sticks joining at the top. They are a reverse or S-curve in both the front and side views. The axis comes at the bony structure of the knee. This shape starts with the bone formation and is enhanced by the padding of the muscles. The mass of the thigh is well rounded and tapers down to the knee. Calf muscles envelop the sides and back of the bones below the knee, widening rapidly for about one third of the distance to the ankle before tapering to the foot. The shaft of the leg above the ankle is round, changing into more angular planes as the bones of the ankle become apparent. From the front view the leg does not set squarely above the foot but slightly to the outside of centre. In profile the leg enters the foot slightly forward, over the instep, throwing the weight on the arch, not the heel. The respective position of the two lower leg bones, which form well marked prominences, is an important characteristic of the ankle, the outer bone being lower than the inner one.

The main body of the foot is formed in the

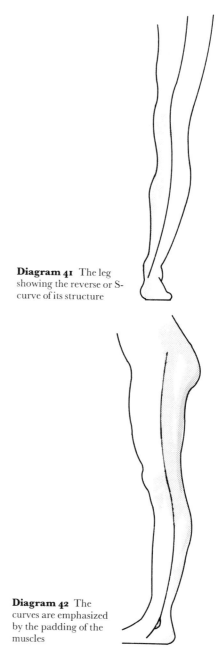

Diagram 41 The leg showing the reverse or S-curve of its structure

Diagram 42 The curves are emphasized by the padding of the muscles

shape of an arch which is greater on the inner edge. The heel and the ball of the toes form the supports. It is broadest at the ball tapering forward into the toes. From the ball backwards the width diminishes gradually into the rounded surface of the heel. There is a similarity in the principle between the skeleton of the foot and that of the hand, although the proportions of the bones are different.

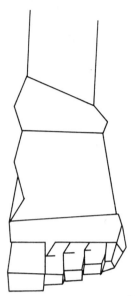

Diagram 43 Simplifying the main shapes of the ankle and foot

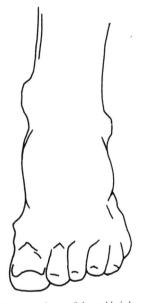

Diagram 44 The outer bone of the ankle is lower than the inner one

Every part of the figure has its shape, place and characteristic. The fullnesses and hollows which bear definite relations to each other should be observed. It is a mistake to finish any particular part of the limb too much in advance of the rest. It should be developed gradually and consistently over the whole area.

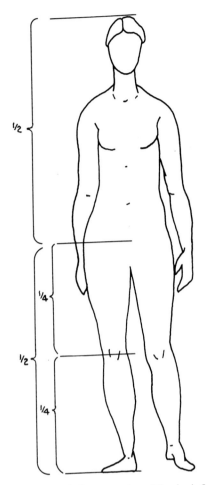

Diagram 45 The relative proportions of the classic figure

Rubbing down

Abrading is used to remove excess adhesive and composition, to do the final shaping when modelling and to prepare a perfect surface for painting. It is perhaps the most important single factor for successful results. It certainly occupies the major proportion of the restorer's time and is not a task to be skimped. Accurate modelling is the way to minimise labour, but even so a final rubbing down is always necessary to prepare the surface for the paint. Never attempt rubbing down composition until it is completely hard. If the abrading is started while the filler is even slightly rubbery it will be dragged from its seating. In addition the abrasive paper or file will clog so quickly that it will not cut through the composition.

Always use the abrasive papers cut into narrow strips and folded over into small pads; about 3 mm ($\frac{1}{8}$ in) turnover is sufficient. This way the chances of harming surrounding decoration and glaze are reduced to a minimum. Using a large sheet of abrasive paper allows no control over the size of area being scratched. Practise abrading to the limits of the filler only, putting no pressure on the adjoining china. As soon as the surface of the abrasive is clogged with filler fold the strip over onto a fresh area. Once the cutting edge has gone, any further rubbing is really polishing. Abrasives with a strong, flexible plastic backing are made but they are expensive and not freely marketed. They are springy and difficult to fold into pads for fine work but are useful in shaping free hand modelling. Where a large surface has to be abraded use a circular rubbing action to avoid long scratches. Abrasive paper can be folded into tiny triangles or wrapped round orange sticks to get into small difficult corners. A long bamboo stick with an abrasive strip wound round the end will reach inside deep vessels.

Various abrasives are embedded in rubber cones and wheels for use with flexible drive drills. These, unfortunately, have a limited use for the china restorer. The heat generated by the edge of an abrasive wheel, either of carborundum or rubber impregnated with aluminium oxide, will be in excess of 600°C (1100°F). This will burn the composition if the wheel is used dry, and when lubricated the resulting slurry obscures the work in progress. Its use is limited to small areas and short bursts to avoid overheating the filler. The expense of the equipment may not justify the time saved. Abrading with a drill which throws the dust out in a cloud should never be attempted without an adequate respirator and protection for the eyes.

Small, fine cut or fine grade needle files are useful for rubbing down, particularly when shaping free hand modelling. Good quality steel files will keep their edge and outlast several cheap ones. They are supplied in many shapes, but round and flat shapes with tapered ends are the most frequently useful. Files are brittle and misuse will snap them. Never use them to probe or chisel the composition. As soon as they become clogged with composition clean them by rubbing across a file card. Curved files or jewelers' rifflers are useful for concave surfaces although an abrasive strip over a finger serves the same purpose. Always store files in a dry place or they will rust.

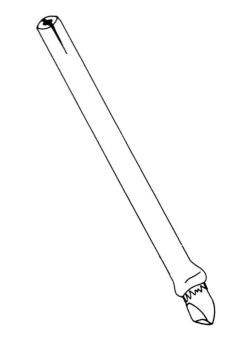

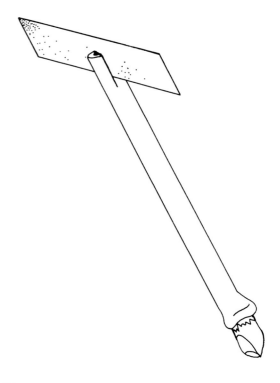

Diagram 46 Making a modelling tool to reach inside a deep vessel. Make a slit in the end of a piece of dowel or bamboo

Diagram 47 Insert a narrow strip of abrasive paper

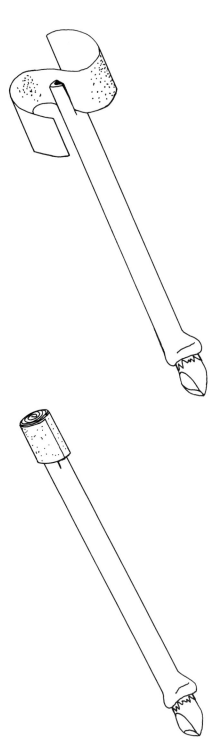

Diagram 48 Wind the abrasive paper around the stick

Diagram 49 As the abrasive surface becomes worn or clogged, cut away a section to provide a fresh cutting area

A stiff brush is necessary to sweep away any dust on the surface of the china. A brush with small bellows attached, as used by photographers, is most useful. Blowing by mouth will deposit moisture on the work.

Dust from rubbing down is very light and covers all nearby surfaces. Apart from taking the precautions of using barrier cream and wearing protective clothing, food should never be consumed while rubbing down and the hands should always be washed immediately work finishes.

Using the abrasives and files
When a large piece of composition which has been applied with more enthusiasm than care needs removing, a small coarse file with well spaced teeth and/or a coarse grade of abrasive paper can be used to begin with. Do not continue too far with a coarse file or abrasive because the resulting scratches will dig deep into the composition and need refilling. Once the unwanted bulk has been rubbed away the medium grade abrasive paper or a needle file is used. The final abrading, almost a polishing, is done with fine flour glasspaper. Pay particular attention to all depressions and grooves. If any dust remains it will become trapped beneath the paint and cause blistering when it is stoved.

Shaping flat areas
Follow the contours of the china, do not rub the filler flat on a rounded surface. Particular care must be given to the shaping of the edges or rims of plates or bowls etc. Some are rounded off, some are angular and some round on the faceside and angled on the reverse. The area where filler and china meet must be invisible except for the colour. Any hump must be rubbed down flush with the surrounding surface and any pin holes or crevices revealed must be refilled.

Once the shape is right the surface is brought to a satin smooth surface with flour glasspaper to give a perfect surface for painting. The surface needs to be checked under a magnifying glass for flaws. All trace of hardened composition on the surface of the china where it is not wanted must be removed carefully with abrasive or a sharp scalpel. Use extreme caution anywhere near gold decoration.

Shaping free hand modelling
Files are more useful when shaping free-standing modelling than they are on flat surfaces. They will

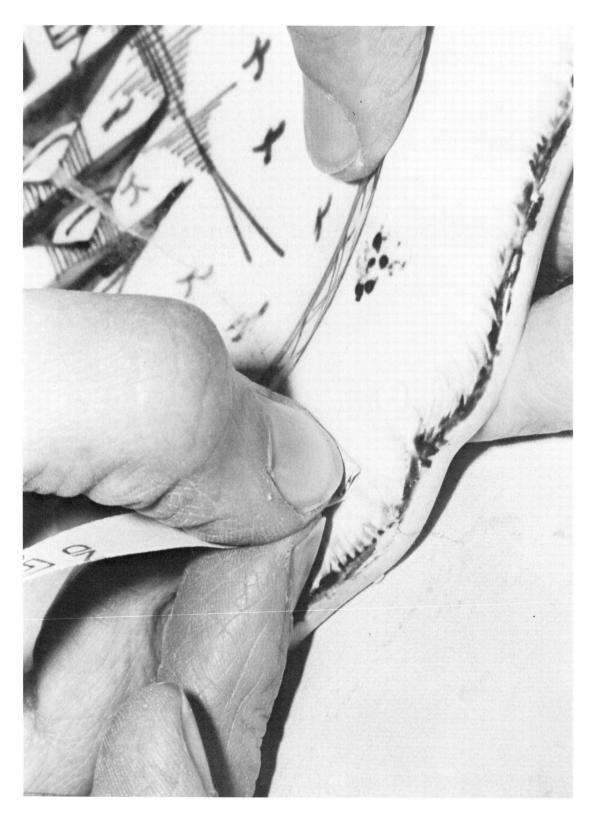

Diagram 50 Care must be taken to continue the original shape on the rims of bowls or plates

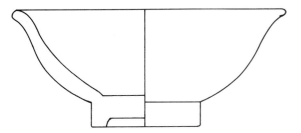

Diagram 51 Do not rub flat edges where the rims are rounded

bring pressure to bear on a part which cannot be reached with abrasive paper. Use them in long, lengthways strokes, not sideways. Flexible plastic abrasive sheet is very useful for rounding the backs or arms, handles and similar parts. Cut it into strips, hold either end in each hand and pull to and fro. Paper-backed abrasive can be used in the same way. If the strips tend to tear they can be mounted on self adhesive transparent tape for strength. Abrasive paper can be folded into a knife edge or rolled into a point to get into a small gap. Once the shape of the china is true a final abrading with flour glasspaper should make the surface smooth and china-like ready to receive the paint. Check that no hardened, unwanted composition remains on the surface.

Faults in filling and modelling

If the fillings in rivet holes rise when pressed home it is because there is either a pocket of air or inadequate adhesive at the base of the hole. The remedy is to remove and replace the filler, adding sufficient adhesive and packing it well in.

Cracks appearing at the edges of the filler after hardening and which may not be noticeable until after painting and stoving may be due to one or a combination of several causes:
the surface of the china may have been greasy, wet or dusty before filling;

Fig. 69 Rub down carefully where there is surface modelling, to continue the contours of the pattern

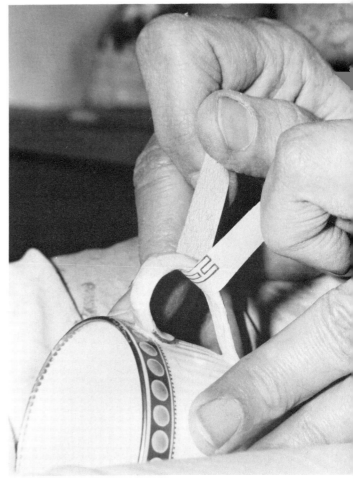

Fig. 70 Shaping the inside of a handle

perhaps too little adhesive or no adhesive at all was used along the join;
too great an amount of titanium oxide was used in the adhesive or composition;
the clay may have been damp when used. It would then shrink when drying. Always store it in an airtight container;
the layers of composition were too thick. Maximum thickness to be applied at one time is 0.5 cm ($\frac{1}{4}$ in);
the filler was stretched when being put into place;
an unsealed crack leading into a chip expanded when heated, forcing the filler out of its seating;
the filler was not pressed firmly enough onto the edges of the break;
the second layer of filler was applied before the foundation had hardened, disturbing the adhesive before it had fully set.

The solution, whatever the cause, is to remove the filling. If it remains intact it can be reseated with adhesive and left to harden. Otherwise, make new composition and refill. Seal any cracks before refilling.

Should the surface appear flakey or pitted when rubbing down, either the epoxy resin and clay was insufficiently mixed before use or there was too much clay on fingers, tools or the surface of composition when filling gaps. This loose clay becomes trapped in the filler. Correct by rubbing down to a sound surface and refill.

There are several reasons for the filling being too dark and difficult to obliterate with paint:
the epoxy resin was mixed in unequal quantities;
too much hardener was used resulting in a deep brown composition;
insufficient clay or titanium was used in the mixture;
too much methylated spirit was used to lubricate the modelling tools.

Fig. 71 The right lower arm, hand and handle of the hurdy-gurdy have been remodelled and are ready for painting

If an extra basecoat of paint will not obliterate this satisfactorily the only solution is to replace the filler with a correctly made one.

If the filling remains soft and rubbery then perhaps unequal quantities of epoxy resin were used. Too much adhesive in proportion to hardener will prevent the filler setting completely. Ensure that sufficient time has been allowed for hardening. The temperature may be too low for filler to harden. Never try to retard setting by storing made up composition in a refrigerator. Epoxy resin contaminated by grease, water or cleaning chemicals will not set properly. If further time in a warmer atmosphere does not harden the filler it must be removed and replaced with a fresh mix.

Time spent on rubbing down to obtain a fine finish is never wasted. Apart from finishing the shaping it provides a good key for the paint, which can never be any better than the surface it is applied to. As skill in modelling develops so the time spent in rubbing down diminishes.

5 · Making Moulds and Taking Castings

Making a mould must be regarded as an alternative to modelling only in suitable circumstances and not as a substitute for free hand modelling ability. Casting is a double operation, first the making of a negative in which secondly to cast the positive image which will be used as the replacement. To be worthwhile for the restorer to choose casting rather than free hand modelling to make a replacement there would have to be a need for several identical pieces or one with complicated surface modelling. The work and time involved may well exceed the time taken to model free hand.

To be able to cast a missing piece it is essential to have an identical pattern from which to obtain the mould. It must be the exact size as well as the right shape. Careful measurements must be taken to ensure that the newly cast piece really will fit into position. Even handles at either side of the same object may have warped unequally in manufacture so that the remaining handle will not serve as a pattern for the replacement. The area to be used as a pattern must be sound so that there is no risk of further breakage during mould making. There must also be sufficient space around the area from which the mould is to be taken to accommodate the casting material. Once made, the moulds are filled with the usual epoxy resin and china clay composition. For filling moulds it should always be used when freshly made and soft.

Moulds fall into two categories: rigid and flexible. Rigid moulds (e.g. plaster, dental impression compounds and waxes) cannot be used where there is any undercutting or indentation angled away from the surface. These will trap the moulding materials to the master, making removal impossible. When a rigid mould needs to completely encase the section to be copied, for instance in the case of a handle or knob, it has to be made in several removable sections or pieces and reassembled for filling. Flexible moulds (e.g. meltable rubber and liquid latex) are useful where there is deep undercutting – on a figure perhaps. The disadvantage of flexible moulds is that care has to be taken not to stretch or compress them when inserting the filling. Whichever material is used to make the mould the method of filling it and attaching the casting to the china remains the same.

Materials and tools

Dental plaster; for making moulds

Dental impression composition (Stents Composition); for press moulds

Dental modelling wax (de Treys Universal Wax); toughened wax in thin sheets for shallow press moulds

Moulding rubber; for making flexible moulds

Liquid latex (Copydex); for making flexible moulds

Wood sawdust; to strengthen moulds

Releasing agents (mineral oil, petroleum jelly, soft soap, thick liquid detergent); used between mould and pattern or casting to facilitate separation

Mixing vessels (plastic bowls or disposable food containers); for mixing plaster

Modelling tools scalpels etc.; as used previously

Many otherwise useful moulding materials are unsuitable for china restoration owing to the high temperature required in their application. 120°C (250°F) should be regarded as the maximum heat tolerance for valuable china, particularly when applied to one small area only.

Dental plaster

This is a fine grade of plaster of Paris giving very good definition. It is a powder which is mixed with water and used as a semi-liquid. This is then poured into a leak proof container surrounding the area to be used as the pattern. There must be enough space around this area to construct the container and allow at least 1 cm ($\frac{1}{2}$ in) of plaster around the edge and the same depth of plaster above the highest point to be moulded. Plaster less than 1 cm ($\frac{1}{2}$ in) does not have sufficient strength for handling. The container is most conveniently made by forming a box of plastic modelling clay. Once mixed with water, dental plaster sets quickly and dries slowly. Everything must be ready for use before mixing the plaster as it becomes too thick to pour within 5 to 8 minutes. This method would be very useful when replacing an area which is very boldly decorated.

Constructing a container
Choose a sound identical area of the article or its twin to provide the pattern. Knead sufficient plastic modelling clay to form the wall of the container at least 1 cm ($\frac{1}{2}$ in) above the highest modelling and long enough to go around the chosen area. Allow a margin of at least 1 cm ($\frac{1}{2}$ in) beyond the area which is to be filled. This is to enable the mould to be fixed into position later. Arrange the retaining wall on the decorated side of the area of china to be copied. Join the plastic modelling clay to the china, making sure the base of the wall is well secured to the china to form a water proof joint or else the wet plaster will flood out.

Coat the china lightly with the chosen releasing agent to prevent the plaster sticking to it. Do not allow the releasing agent to collect in the depressions or they will not be filled by the plaster, producing an indistinct impression. Any surplus ridges or spots of the agent on the china will come out as part of the surface in the plaster mould. It is essential that the releasing agent is applied thoroughly but sparingly and evenly.

The container for the plaster needs to remain in a horizontal, level position while the plaster is poured in and left to set. This will ensure that the plaster in the mould is an even depth. The article will probably need to be propped up with plastic modelling clay or held level in a carton cushioned with screwed up paper. Do not use the salt tray for this purpose; if there is a spillage while pouring the plaster the salt will dissolve. The plastic modelling clay container is now ready to receive the liquid plaster which becomes the mould.

If the piece which is missing was part of pierced

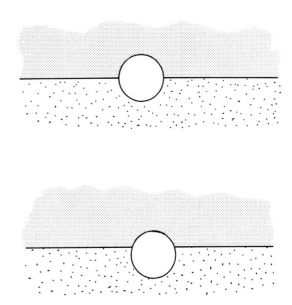

Diagram 52 Do not submerge china to more than half its thickness in plaster (top) or it will be trapped beneath the curve (bottom)

or openwork decoration, a base as well as walls will be needed. Knead a piece of plastic modelling clay until smooth and flatten it until it is large enough to block off the area to be moulded. A margin of at least 1 cm ($\frac{1}{2}$ in) is needed beyond the area for repair. Press this flattened base firmly onto the least decorated side of the china which is being used as the pattern. Push the plastic modelling clay halfway through the openwork. If the base is left below the central point the plaster will flow beneath the curve of the china and be trapped; it will then not be removable without destroying the mould. Place a plastic modelling clay wall around the perimeter of the area above the base on the decorative surface of the china. Make sure all the edges of the plastic modelling clay are firmly sealed to the china to prevent leakage. Apply releasing agent to the china. Make sure the container is horizontal and level. It is now ready to be filled with plaster.

When the area to be moulded is sited at the edge of the china the container must be extended outwards. Without a margin of plaster beyond the edge it would give a poor impression and be very weak. Flatten and shape the plastic modelling clay to give a base covering the area of the missing piece plus 1 cm ($\frac{1}{2}$ in) overlap each side and extending 1 cm ($\frac{1}{2}$ in) beyond the edge. Place this

79

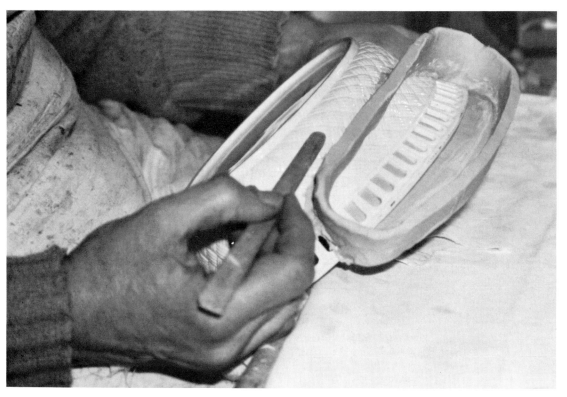

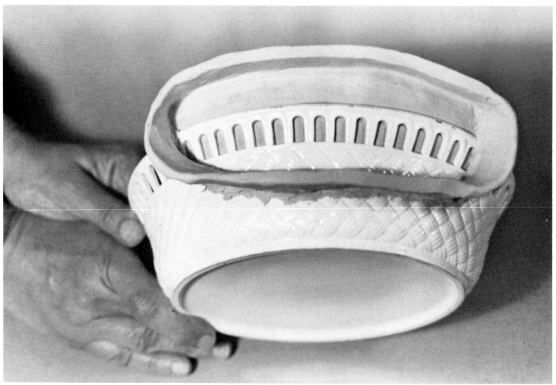

beneath the china pattern and press into position, making sure the base comes exactly halfway up the edge of the rim and halfway through any openwork to avoid trapping the plaster. Build a plastic modelling clay wall onto the china encircling the area to be moulded and around the outside edge of the plastic modelling clay base. Make sure it is a good leakproof fit. Apply releasing agent to the china. Level the container and fill with plaster.

Mixing and using the plaster

A wide flexible vessel in which to do the mixing is most convenient. Choose a vessel large enough to hold the water plus the plaster and allow room for stirring efficiently. Sufficient plaster must be mixed to complete the pouring in one operation. An estimate of the quantity required can be obtained by filling the plastic modelling clay container built to receive the plaster with water and using this amount of water for mixing.

Always add plaster to the water, not water to plaster. Pour sufficient cold water into the vessel and add plaster by sifting through the fingers to eliminate lumps. Stir gently with a thin stick to avoid introducing air bubbles. Continue adding plaster until the mixture is a smooth creamy consistency. It is then ready for immediate use. Pour into the prepared container in a steady stream. Do not delay, the plaster quickly becomes too thick to pour freely and is then unable to fill fine indentations. Deep depressions which tend to trap air can be filled first with a dab of plaster applied with a soft paint brush. This must be done swiftly or the plaster will be too thick. When the container is full vibrate gently by tapping to assist any air bubbles to rise to the surface. The plaster mould must be left to set and dry. It will be well set within an hour but not be dry or strong enough to remove for 24 hours. Allow it to dry and harden naturally.

Clearing up plaster

Neither plaster nor the rinsings from vessels and tools used in preparing the plaster must ever be poured down a sink or drain. Unless the drain is provided with a special trap the plaster will cause a blockage. Leave the plaster in the mixing vessel

Fig. 72 Seal the plastic modelling clay firmly to the china to ensure a leakproof join

Fig. 73 A plastic modelling clay container ready to receive the dental plaster

Fig. 74 Mixing dental plaster by sifting through the fingers

until set, when it can easily be turned out in one piece from a flexible bowl. Even better, the whole thing can be thrown away if a surplus food tub has been used. Tools should be scraped and washed with water in a bowl immediately after use. The cleaning water must be retained until the plaster has settled before disposing of it by draining off the water and collecting the residue for refuse disposal.

Preparing to use the mould

When the plaster is hard and dry remove the plastic modelling clay. Ease the plaster carefully away from the china taking particular care not to crumble the edges and any sharp modelling. Fit the mould around the broken area to make sure it matches the surrounding china, checking that any fluting, scallops or similar shaping follows along the pattern. The mould must now be fixed firmly in place. It has to remain rigid while the composition is inserted and allowed to harden. Gum paper strips or elastic bands with plastic modelling clay props will hold the mould in the correct position. If the mould is large it will be heavy so make sure the support is adequate.

Filling the mould

Applying releasing agent to the plaster surfaces which are to be filled with composition to facilitate later separation. Apply adhesive to the broken china edges and fill the mould with freshly made composition, coaxing and pressing into the contours. Make sure the union between china and composition is very firm, also that the mould is held in alignment with the china surface or there will be a step at the join. If the china is over 0.5 cm ($\frac{1}{4}$ in) thick it is advisable to fill the mould in two

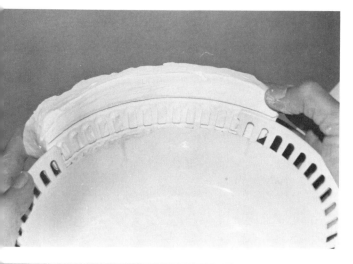

layers, just as when using a plastic modelling clay press mould. The composition must be left to harden for 24 hours before the plaster is removed carefully. Provided the releasing agent was applied correctly firm even pressure should remove the mould easily. In any difficulty run a scalpel between the edges of the composition and plaster. Once the mould is off, the composition can be cleaned and trimmed with a file if this is necessary. Fill any pin holes or flaws with composition before finishing with fine abrasives ready for painting.

Moulding in the round
When making a mould to completely encircle the pattern, for instance in a cup handle or a leg, a rigid mould has to be made in more than one piece to enable it to be removed. Once made the individual parts of the mould are filled with the usual composition and reassembled. Either the filled mould can be assembled on the article being repaired or the duplicate of the missing piece can be hardened in the mould before being removed and bonded to the china.

The first piece of the mould needs a plastic modelling clay container built round the pattern exactly as for the single piece mould. Build the base and push it precisely half-way up the object to be copied. Fix the wall securely around its perimeter to hold the plaster without leaking. The wall must be high enough to allow for at least 1 cm ($\frac{1}{2}$ in) of plaster above the highest point of the china. This will hold one half of the plaster mould. Coat the china surfaces which will come into contact with the plaster with the releasing agent to avoid sticking. Fill this first piece of the mould with plaster and leave to set.

After about two hours the first piece will be firm enough to continue with the mould making if handled with care. The plastic modelling clay should be removed without disturbing the mould and will reveal the object being copied half-submerged in plaster which now forms the base for the second part of the mould.

A plastic modelling clay wall is now added around and 2 cm (1 in) above the plaster, or at least 1 cm ($\frac{1}{2}$ in) above the highest part of the china. Two shallow depressions should be made

Fig. 75 Fitting a plaster mould into position

Fig. 76 A two piece mould. The location holes, foil and plastic modelling clay walls in place to receive the second pouring of plaster

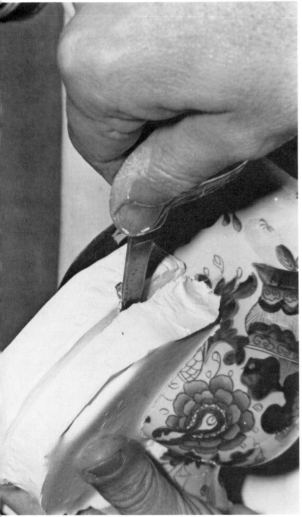

with a scalpel into the plaster base. These will be filled with plaster and form locating keys when reassembling the mould for filling with composition. Add two or three small pieces of aluminium foil or silicon parchment at intervals round the edges of the plaster. Make sure they reach the outside rim so they provide easy points of access for a knife blade to gently lever the mould apart. Apply releasing agent to all china and plaster surfaces within the plastic modelling clay container. Support the container keeping the top level. Ensure that the mould is well packed up underneath to take the weight of plastic modelling clay and wet plaster. The strain on a long thin piece of china, a handle for instance, is very considerable. Fill the container with freshly made plaster exactly as before and leave the completed mould to harden for 24 hours.

Releasing a multiple piece mould from the pattern
Remove all the plastic modelling clay from the plaster. Insert a thin bladed knife where the foil is showing between the layers of plaster and lever very gently. Go round each slot in turn, never using force or the levering may place too great a strain on the china. Provided the coating of releasing agent was applied thoroughly and the pieces were made as exact halves with no undercutting, the mould will part easily. If in spite of all efforts the mould remains firmly attached to the china the only solution is to crumble away the mould with pincers. This will destroy the mould and it will have to be remade, taking greater care in its preparation.

Using a multiple piece mould
Make sure the mould fits the china being repaired and is a good clear impression. Apply releasing agent to the areas of the mould to be filled to prevent the composition and plaster sticking together. Don't use an excessive quantity or it will collect in the hollows and not give a sharp casting. Make fresh composition and use it immediately to fill each piece of the mould. Press it into flat sheets of a suitable size and shape, easing it into the prepared mould with a small modelling tool. Fill every depression well or the casting will need building up later to correct the shape. A shallow

Fig. 77 The plaster must be poured swiftly and steadily into the container

Fig. 78 Parting the mould by leverage at each side, not the centre

83

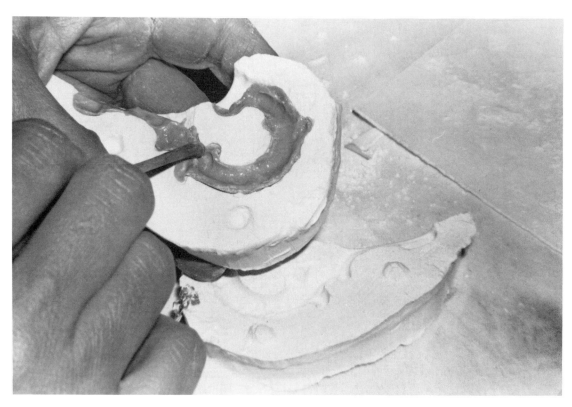

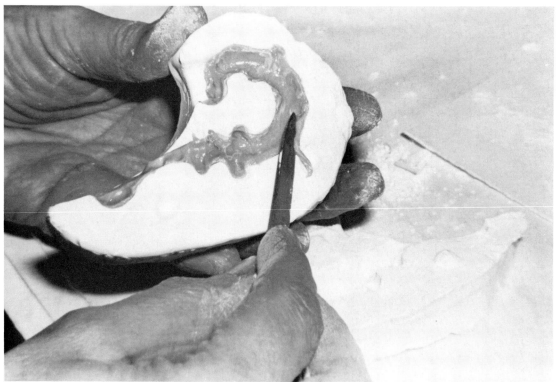

groove should be left along the centre of the composition to allow room for the filler to spread when the parts of the mould are squeezed together. Trim the edges of the filler exactly level with the rim of the mould. Do not overfill or the casting will be oversize because the pieces will not fit together closely when assembled. The replacement can either be cast with the mould in place on the china or made separately and bonded to the china when set. The advantage with the first method is that the join between china and filler will match perfectly; additionally, time will be saved with only one hardening stage.

When casting and bonding in the same operation, coat the broken china with adhesive, position the filled mould one half at a time, making a smooth union between composition and china. Secure the mould very firmly with gum strip bindings and provide adequate support for

Fig. 79 Fill each piece of the mould with composition, leaving a small depression along the centre

Fig. 80 Trim the edges of the filling composition flush with the surface of the mould

Fig. 81 Where a handle is partially intact fill the missing section only. There is no need to make a complete handle

the weight. Allow the mould to remain in position until the composition is hard. Remove the mould, which should part easily and leave the replacement in position. Clean away any plaster left from the mould. Check for pin holes or other defects in the surface which will need either filling or rubbing down. After a final abrading with fine glasspaper the new surface is ready for painting.

If the new piece is to be cast separately the parts of the mould are filled with composition, strapped together securely and the filler left to harden. Once the composition is cured the plaster mould is removed and the edges of the new piece filed to fit the broken edges exactly. Apply adhesive to all the areas to be bonded, press the replacement into position and leave well supported under pressure to harden. Remove the support and any remaining traces of plaster, check that the surface is perfect and prepare it for painting.

Moulding heads
If an exact duplicate is available for copying, a plaster mould can be made. This must be constructed in at least two, sometimes three pieces to allow for the undercutting beneath chin and hair. It is usually most convenient to take a mould

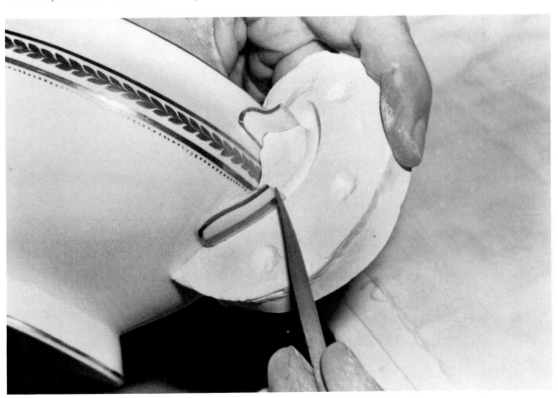

from the back of the head first. The figure must be placed face down and a gallery of plastic modelling clay built out around the back of the head to hold the plaster. Build out the container from along one side of the neck across the highest point of the ear, over the crown and along the other side, crossing the back of the shoulders to join up with the plastic modelling clay to form a continuous barrier for the wet plaster. The first section of the mould is filled with plaster. Everything is carried out exactly as for moulding a handle or limb. Allow 2 hours for drying before preparing a second section.

When the features are very flat it is possible to mould the face in one further section. Should the chin form a barrier to the removal of the plaster mould the face must be moulded in two separate sections. Make the division down the centre of the forehead, along the ridge of the nose to the point of the chin; continue under the chin and down the centre of the neck and then across to join onto the plaster. Use the same techniques as before, allowing a two hour interval for drying before removing the plastic modelling clay. The remaining area can now be filled with plaster to make the final section of the mould. The completed mould is left to dry and harden for 24 hours, after which it can be carefully dismantled and used to cast a complete new head in composition.

Moulding knobs

This can be tackled in exactly the same way as taking a mould from a head. The knob, and whatever it is attached to, must be supported lying on its side. The first piece of the mould is taken no more than half-way up. The mould is then completed in one or two pieces, depending on the degree of undercutting. If there is a great deal of undercutting it may be preferable to make the mould in three pieces.

For heads and very ornate knobs it is worth considering the use of moulding rubber or liquid latex as an alternative moulding material.

Dental impression compound

This is a rigid compound which becomes soft when heated and can be used for a simple press mould. The compound regains rigidity on cooling and makes a firmer press mould than plastic modelling clay. As it hardens rapidly it needs no container so it can be used in a confined space, but it cannot be used where there is any undercutting. It can be removed easily from both china and composition without the aid of any releasing agent. As the mould is rigid it can also be used to cast large areas.

Using dental impression compound

Precise instructions for using dental compounds are included in every package and may vary slightly with each manufacturer. They are applied as tablets which are dipped into near boiling water until softened right through. While hot they are kneaded in the fingers until smooth and of a suitable shape. Press immediately onto the surface to be copied. It helps to get a good sharp impression if the china is slightly warm. The compound hardens in a few seconds and can be lifted off easily when cool provided there is no overhang. It is ready to be strapped into position and filled as soon as required without further preparation.

Fig. 82 Dental impression composition

Fig. 83 Dental impression composition gives good definition of fine detail

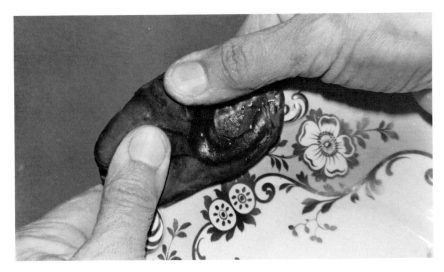

Fig. 84 Pressing the warmed dental impression composition on to the pattern

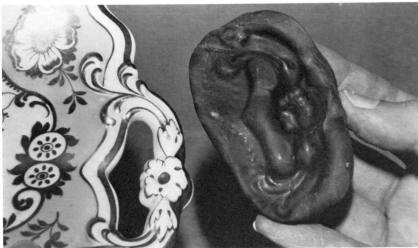

Fig. 85 A good clear impression. The modelling on the original is accentuated by the gilding

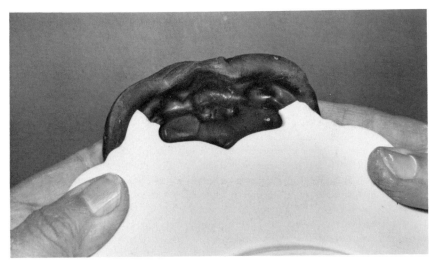

Fig. 86 Fit the mould onto the broken area and fix securely

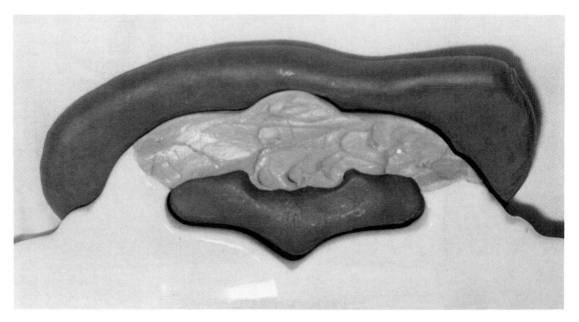

Fig. 87 Fill in the gap with modelling composition

Fig. 88 Dental universal moulding wax

Apply adhesive to the broken edges of the china and fill the mould with freshly made composition. Make sure the mould is not pushed out of position when pressing in the filler. Leave the casting to harden and, when the mould is removed, perfect the surface of the composition ready for painting. Dental compounds are reusable but become very brittle if overheated.

Dental universal wax

This is made as thin sheets of toughened wax which are useful for shallow press moulds. They are too thin and weak for use when moulding and casting large areas unless melted into a block. Dental impression compound serves this purpose more conveniently. Wax gives a very smooth surface but as it sets rigid it cannot be used where there is undercutting, nor is it suitable for deep modelling or fine sharp detail. The wax softens at a low temperature and hardens quickly.

Using dental universal wax
Cut sufficient wax to overlap the broken area by approximately 1 cm ($\frac{1}{2}$ in) all round. Warm the sheet of wax between the hands until bendable and press into place on the china. Do not heat the china or the wax will melt and run where it is not

wanted. No releasing agent is required. The wax can be lifted away after a few seconds.

Fit the moulded sheet very firmly into place behind the broken area of china matching up any relief moulding and the edges. The overlap left at the perimeter of the wax can be bent over the edge of the china to help hold it in place. As the sheets of wax are so thin they may need additional support with plastic modelling clay. Fill the wax mould with fresh composition; no releasing agent is necessary. Make sure the wax is close up to the surface of the china and is not pushed out of place when filling. Leave the composition to harden and finish the surface in the usual way. The wax can be reclaimed by warming gently and leaving to flatten on a sheet of glass. Only a small amount of heat is required to soften dental universal wax.

Moulding rubber

A reusable rubber medium which melts with varying degrees of heat and remains flexible when cool. It is easily removable from both china and composition without a releasing agent, but gold should be covered with mineral oil before applying moulding rubber over it. As the mould is flexible it will need careful handling when filling to avoid stretching or distorting. Some moulding rubber shrinks and some requires to be liquified at a temperature too high to be safely used with valuable china.

Using moulding rubber
Precise instructions regarding melting temperatures, which vary slightly with each product, are given with the packs. Temperatures above 120°C (250°F) should not be used with china. Always work in a well ventilated place as heating will release fumes. The rubber should be melted in a waterjacketed container for safety, but if great care is taken a strong pan can be used over a hot plate. Never use a naked flame. Place the granules in the pan over a very low heat until molten. The resulting syrup is ladled with a spatula onto the area to be copied. When sufficient thickness has been built up, at least 1 cm ($\frac{1}{2}$ in), a little more if space permits, the mould is left to cool completely on the master. Ease the rubber away from the china at the edges and remove carefully. If the mould is trapped behind china and cannot be stretched sufficiently to remove, a small slit can be made with a scalpel to ease away the rubber. When using such a mould care must be taken not to press the slit open with the filler. A piece of self adhesive tape can be used to hold its edges together if necessary.

The mould is ready for use immediately without further preparation and can be filled with epoxy resin composition in the normal way, either being filled with composition and hardened in its final seating or hardened separately and bonded to the china when hard. The filling of the mould and the final finishing is similar to a plaster mould, the main difference being the ease with which the mould is finally peeled away from the casting.

Moulding rubber is reusable. Any left unused in the pan is left to cool and then peeled away for use another time.

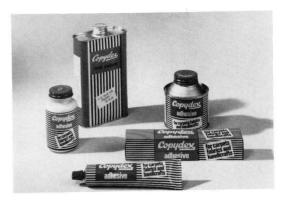

Fig. 89 Liquid latex for making flexible moulds

Liquid latex

Although not primarily intended as a moulding material it is easily obtainable and makes excellent flexible moulds. It is usually sold as an adhesive for fabrics. It is non-shrink and remains flexible when set, although the final coating will need reinforcing with fibre. No releasing agent is needed. It peels easily from both china and composition surfaces. Any gold leaf decoration should be protected with a light film of mineral oil.

Using liquid latex
A good flexible mould can be made by coating the area to be copied with a coat of liquid latex directly from the tube or jar. If applied too thickly the liquid will tend to run off the high areas. After a few minutes disperse any bubbles and lay extra latex on any thin patches to make a smooth, even coat. Leave for several hours to set. This first thin layer will have very little strength but will dry to a smooth transparent skin which gives good reproduction.

When firm and transparent a second application of latex mixed with wood sawdust is pressed over the skin. Use sawdust which is fibrous but not too coarse; pine wood cut with a hand rip saw makes the ideal texture. Sawdust which is too fine will not give sufficient strength. Mix the sawdust and liquid latex together very thoroughly on a sheet of silicon parchment with a spatula and press the mixture firmly over the first skin at least 1 cm ($\frac{1}{2}$ in) thick. Leave the mould to set for 24 hours. Peel the mould away at the edges carefully. If it is trapped behind china and cannot be stretched sufficiently to be released make a small slit and ease it away. Use this mould exactly as

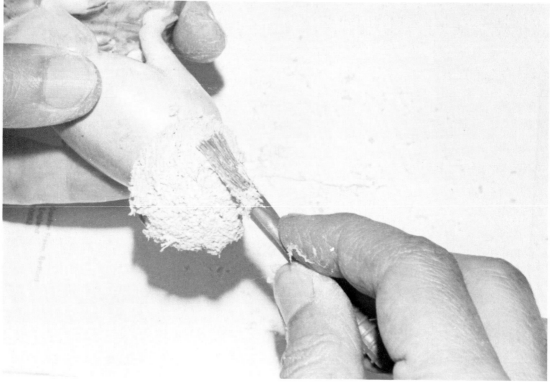

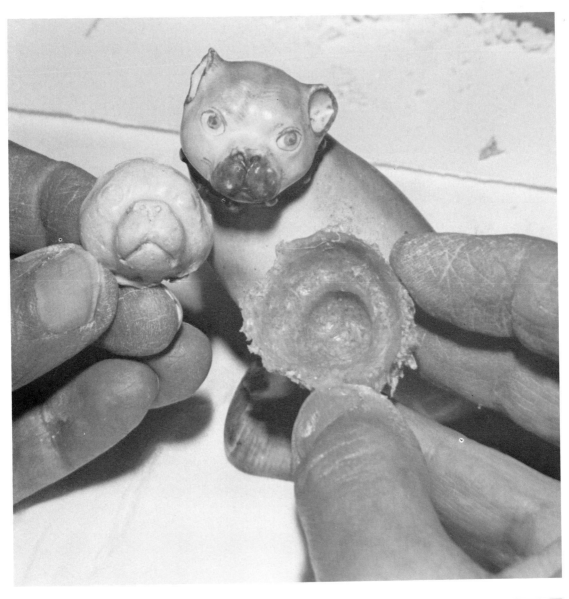

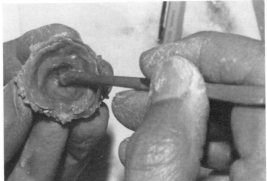

Fig. 90 Mixing liquid latex and sawdust. The initial coat of latex, only, is in place and set

Fig. 91 Applying the final coat of liquid latex which is reinforced with sawdust

Fig. 92 Mask, original pattern and the latex mould

Fig. 93 Filling a mould with composition

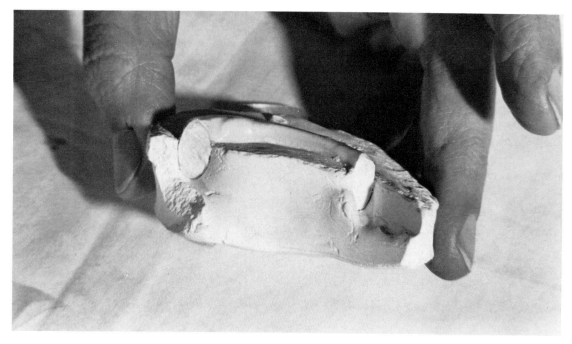

before. Fill the mould with epoxy resin composition as for previous castings. Liquid latex is not reusable. The moulds will keep for a while but eventually become hard and curl up. Flexible moulds can be distorted so they are not suitable for large flat areas, but they are ideal for chunky undercut shapes.

Plastic modelling clay

A non-hardening composition useful for simple shapes. It is very quick and easy to use for chips and small plain areas. It cannot be trapped by undercutting, but because it has no elasticity it will not regain its shape when withdrawn from a receding surface. Definition is not as sharp as other moulding materials. It sticks to china unless wetted but as it remains soft it can be removed by scraping away, which will of course destroy the mould. It is reusable many times but will eventually become too stiff to use easily.

Using plastic modelling clay
As the clay does not harden, the moulds should always be thick and chunky for strength. Plastic modelling clay is soft when warm so it will retain its moulded shape better if chilled before being filled. Simply knead a piece of plastic modelling clay until smooth and malleable. Dip it into cold water to prevent it sticking to the master and press

Fig. 94 The penalty of making one piece of the mould too deep. Efforts to remove the plaster mould broke the china

straight down onto the pattern area. Withdraw the mould immediately, lifting off cleanly. Do not twist or the impression will be distorted. This press mould is ready for immediate use but chill in a refrigerator if necessary. The new piece can be cast separately and bonded into position when set. Alternatively the mould can be firmly set in position by smoothing and spreading the edges over the surrounding china and the filling inserted directly into the mould. Remove the mould by peeling away and finally scraping clean with a scalpel.

Plastic modelling clay has many uses for the restorer. These are described on many occasions throughout the chapters on bonding and modelling.

Faults in moulding

Moulding faults which originate in the bonding and the preparation of composition are identical in cause and treatment to those encountered in free hand modelling.

If a plaster mould is crumbly and breaks easily either the plaster has become damp at some time before it was used and should be discarded, or insufficient plaster was mixed with the water.

When the surface of a plaster mould is covered in holes and crevices it indicates that the plaster was too thick when poured. This may have been due to it not being used quickly enough once it was made or to the use of too much dry plaster in the mix. In addition the mixture could have been stirred too violently and the bubbles not allowed to rise.

Should the plaster stick to either china or filling composition the releasing agent was applied too sparingly or unevenly, leaving patches uncoated. If running a thin blade around the edges and gentle pressure will not part the mould the only remedy is to destroy the mould rather than risk breaking the china. Crumble away the plaster with pincers and a file and then make a fresh mould.

If there is a step at the edge of the replaced piece the mould was not strapped closely enough to the china. It would take longer to abrade the whole area down to the right level than to recast the piece. Remove the new piece by filing through at the join. If the replacement can be salvaged it can be reseated; if not, make a fresh casting.

Rubber and latex will stretch, particularly if the mould is too thin and the filling is forced in place too hard. This will then give a casting which is indistinct or too large. Fill the mould gently and give extra firmness by embedding it in plastic modelling clay for the filling operation.

Moulds are most useful when a good pattern is procurable. Unfortunately a mould cannot be turned inside out to make a right hand from a left one, so the occasions for use are limited. Like all china restoration techniques it is not as simple as it first appears. To make a good mould takes practice and neatness.

6 · Applying Basecoats

The whole object of overpainting repairs is to make them less unsightly. The area of china covered by paint should be the minimum possible. A small hair crack, cleaned, bleached and sealed against further penetration of dirt may be more acceptable than a large area of overpainting. A large area of composition or a long dark break however, needs masking with paint to make the object more visually pleasing. There is no hope that overpainting, however well matched and applied, will hide a mistake or a badly prepared surface. It will be more likely to accentuate it, catching the light and showing up every flaw. On the other hand, if the colour doesn't match exactly and the edges of the paint do not fade invisibly into the surrounding china the appearance of an accurate, well finished repair will be ruined.

Overpainting joins and fillings requires skill and patient practice to acquire the knack of thinning out at the edges of the paint to make it merge with the surrounding china. On a large plain area or long crack this cannot be done by hand and an airbrush is needed to cover any extensive repair.

Matching colours depends on the eye. There are no recipes for mixing Worcester or Wedgwood white. Each piece of china is an individual item; indeed, the colour needed can change from one area to another on the same object. Colour must always be matched under the type of lighting in which the china will normally be displayed. Blues are particularly prone to changes under artificial illumination.

Materials, tools and equipment

Synthetic resin glaze (Chintex); used as a medium with pigments

Artists' oil colours (Winsor and Newton); pigments used to give colour and body to the glaze medium

Thinners (Chintex Thinners or Joy Thinners); solvent for synthetic glaze

Stoving equipment, oven or warming cabinet; for curing glaze

Brushes; for mixing and applying the paint

Stiff card or cartridge paper; used as a palette for laying out pigments

Dippers; containers for mixing paints

Tracing paper; used for tracing patterns

Pencil (H or HH); used for tracing patterns

Abrasive paper, flour glass paper; to rub down base coats

Glass fibre eraser; for very fine rubbing down

Airbrush (DeVilbiss, Paasche, Badger, EFBE); used for spraying on basecoats

Compressor; for supplying air to airbrush

Bench rest; bracket for holding airbrush

Masking tape, film and fluid; all used to screen areas from spray

Airbrush cleaning fluid; aerosol can of airbrush cleaner

Paint is a mixture of colour and medium prepared for the specific purpose for which it is to be used. In china restoring it must:

obliterate the repair;
have tenacity on the china as well as composition;
withstand cleaning and handling;
not fade or discolour with time;
not peel or crack;
have a china-like appearance.

A clear synthetic resin glaze specially prepared to fulfil all these needs is mixed with selected oil colours. This medium is water white and remains clear indefinitely. It will withstand boiling water, most detergents and mild domestic chemicals. It wears well unless attacked with very harsh abrasives. Most important, it will adhere to a slippery china surface. It requires stoving at a low temperature for maximum durability. Synthetic

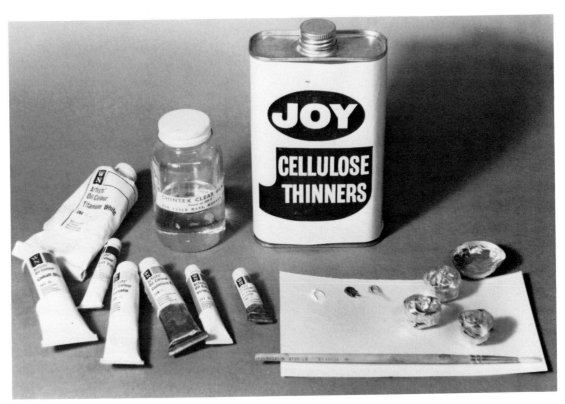

glaze medium has a shelf life of six months. As soon as it becomes slightly stringy or heavy to apply a fresh supply should be used.

Artists' quality oil colours must be used to colour the medium. Do not economise by using student or budget grades of paints as they are not sufficiently durable. Neither are they colour fast or so finely ground, and often their oil content is incompatible with the glaze medium used. Many pigments will change with stoving or age and a few are not inter-mixable, so unless tests for stability are made it is essential to keep to the tested colour list given below. Provided they are thoroughly mixed with glaze medium and given a finishing coat of glaze to protect them from wear and oxidisation they will retain their original colour. Artists' oil colours last indefinitely provided they are kept tightly closed in their tubes. Once laid out on a palette they remain usable for about 24 hours if covered to protect them from dust and fluff. These 18 colours will give a sufficient range to match any colour needed for china restoration.

Yellows: Aureolin, Chrome, Raw Sienna
Greens: Viridian, Sap
Blues: Cerulean, Cobalt, Prussian, Ultramarine

Fig 95 Materials for painting

Reds: Cadmium, Rose Madder
Browns: Burnt Sienna, Raw Umber, Burnt Umber
also: Lamp Black, Titanium White, Paynes Grey, Cobalt Violet

Between each coat of paint the resin medium has to be cured by stoving at 115°C (240°F). This can be done in an electric or solid fuel domestic oven if it is scrupulously clean and the temperature can be held constant. It should be kept solely for this purpose and used in a well ventilated place. Gas ovens can cause discoloration and fume streaks on the painting. The fumes produced by curing synthetic resin in an oven with a naked flame can be toxic. When curing synthetic resin on large objects an electric, thermostatically controlled warming cabinet will be required.

Pure sable brushes from the water colour range are the most suitable type. Usually, comparatively small areas are to be covered with paint, so a small brush seems the obvious choice, but thin brushes result in streaky basecoats. A full bristled brush with a good natural taper should be used; a size four chisel pointed brush is quite small

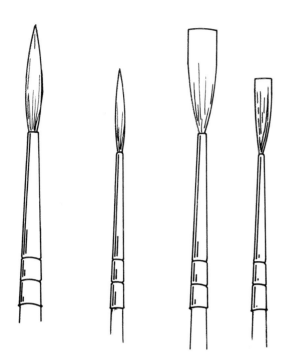

Diagram 54 Making disposable dippers. A disc of aluminium foil is pleated into a cup shape

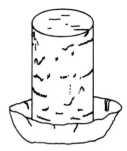

Diagram 55 A cork can be used to help in shaping a suitable dipper

Diagram 53 Pencil and chisel pointed sable brushes

enough. Best quality sable brushes known as liners and writers are particularly suitable. Brushes are a very personal choice. Before purchasing they should always be tested for:

strength and spring in the bristles, so that they will hold their shape and be controllable. A limp floppy brush will never work well;

sufficient volume to hold a reserve of paint, or it will dry too quickly;

a good tip which does not split or have odd whiskers. Test new brushes by dipping in water and shaking to determine the quality of the bristles.

In addition a stiff bristle brush is both a necessity and an ecomony for mixing. A soft brush will not distribute the pigment evenly throughout the medium and the hairs will be broken in the effort to do so. Synthetic bristle or nylon brushes tend to curl at the tip after a short time when used with restoration materials. Always store brushes clean and in a dust and moth proof box.

It is essential that the thinners used is compatible with the medium. Unsuitable thinners will become curdled and lumpy when mixed with the glaze. Thinners are highly volatile and flammable. Always work in a well ventilated place.

A palette is required for laying out the pigments. Stiff absorbent card is ideal. It has the

Diagram 56 Press the foil firmly around the cork

Diagram 57 The completed cup

advantage of absorbing some of the oil in the paint. Once again, old greeting cards can be used and discarded, saving time and cleaning materials.

It will also be necessary to have a deep narrow vessel for mixing glaze and pigments; a shallow saucer or tile allows the mixture to spread out and dry too quickly. A small metal dipper as used in oil painting is the right shape but it is difficult to completely clean a vessel which has contained synthetic resin. The glaze is very viscous and quick drying so a disposable vessel is a great help.

1 Remodelling handles

2 Bronze powders and pigments

3 Colour cards

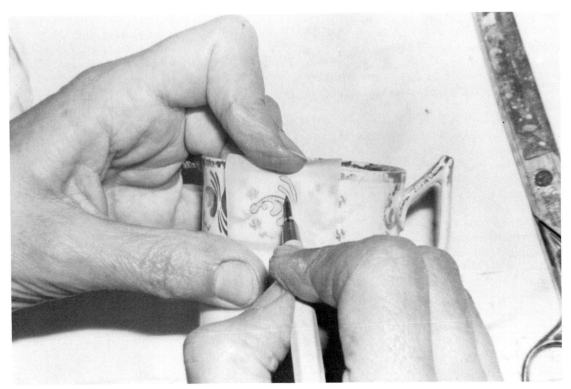

Fig 96 Tracings. Cover the design to be copied with tracing paper and draw over the pattern in pencil

A foil cup can be quickly made from either heavy duty or doubled aluminium foil. Smooth a small disc of foil around a cork to obtain a good shape; do not leave any wrinkles or they will trap pigment and hinder even mixing. If this proves to be too fragile, the aluminium foil can be used inside a dipper, thus making a disposable lining. Never mix in a plastic container; it will dissolve.

Before beginning the basecoats it is as well to take a tracing of any pattern which will be obscured by the over painting. Good quality tracing paper and a hard pencil, grade H or HH, is required.

The basecoats will need rubbing down between each application of paint. The abrasives used for this must be very fine so as to smooth, not scratch, the paint surface. Flour grade glass paper is suitable and for a final smoothing use a glass fibre eraser. This looks like a propelling pencil but has glass fibre bristles instead of a lead, which make a very fine but tough abrasive. Care must be taken not to get fragments under the skin. Only a very short length of the bristles should be exposed or they will snap.

For an invisible finish on large areas, especially on long breaks or cracks, an airbrush is indispensable. This is a precision instrument which deposits a fine, almost imperceptible layer of paint over the surface. When well handled it produces extremely fine lines and softly graded tones as well as areas of even colour. The paint is built up by successive coats on the damaged portion leaving the edge with an almost invisible veil of painting fading into the china without a step.

Not all makes or models of airbrushes are suitable for use with a synthetic glaze. They need to be:

suitable for use with thick mixtures;
unaffected by resins and cellulose thinners, with no parts made of plastics or rubber;
capable of delivering an extremely fine line of paint;
easy to clean, preferably with a gravity feed paint cup and no pipes or pots to clog and which would be difficult to clean.

As well as the airbrush a constant supply of clean dry air delivered at 2.5 bars or atmospheres (35 lb per sq. in) is required. This may be obtained from an electric powered compressor, a foot pump similar to those used for inflating tyres or an aerosol can. In choosing, consider the amount of work it will have to do as well as the price. The footpump is used to raise the pressure in a storage tank from which the air is taken to the airbrush. In use, the pressure remains correct for only a short while before it becomes necessary to pump again. This means breaking off from the work, and it is a laborious system if there is much painting to be done. The aerosol can is suitable for occasional use, but applying two coats of paint over a long crack across a plate and then cleaning the airbrush will almost exhaust it, and so it becomes an expensive source of air. It is however, a useful standby which, in the event of a failure of the main equipment, at least makes it possible to clean the airbrush before the paint sets in it. The most satisfactory, easiest, but initially most expensive, air supply is from an electric compressor. For the best results it should have an air reservoir and a control valve to deliver air constantly at the predetermined pressure, with a moisture and dust filter incorporated. In all cases the airbrush is connected to the air supply by a flexible tube.

A bench rest or similar device is needed to hold the airbrush when not being held in the hand, as it cannot be laid down on the bench when full of paint. These are supplied by the manufacturer and are sometimes included with the airbrush, but with other models they are an optional extra.

Masking tape is a crepe textured self adhesive strip specially manufactured for use when spraying.

Masking film is a transparent plastic sheet which is self adhesive, manufactured for use when spraying.

Masking fluid is a liquid latex applied by brush for masking small areas.

Airbrush cleaning fluid is supplied in aerosol cans to give a pressurised jet of cleaning fluid. Do not allow it to come into contact with the skin. This solvent will harm rubber and most plastics.

Warning: The fine spray produced by an airbrush is highly volatile and the workspace should be very well ventilated. Preferably an extractor fan vented to an exterior outlet should be installed. An efficient respirator should always be worn, not just a gauze dust mask.

Preliminaries
Taking a tracing
When it is necessary to take a tracing of any decoration which has to be touched in this must be done before the basecoats obscure the design. Lay a piece of tracing paper of suitable size and shape over the area to be copied, securing it if required with gum strip. With a sharp, hard pencil draw in as much of the decoration as will be needed onto the tracing paper. Detach carefully and coat the paper on the reverse side with graphite, scribbling evenly with an H or HH pencil. Do not use carbon copying paper for this purpose as it contains wax over which paint will not take. The tracing is carefully preserved for future use when the basecoats have been completed.

Sealing hair cracks
Any hair cracks that are to be painted over must be sealed before a basecoat is attempted. Heat the china in the oven to $65°C$ ($150°F$). While the china is still warm apply clear glaze to both sides of the crack with a soft brush. As the china cools the glaze will be sucked into the crack and will seal it. Allow the article to become quite cold before stoving it for 20 minutes at $115°C$ ($240°F$) to cure the glaze. When the china has cooled the glaze remaining on the surface is rubbed down to a smooth surface with flour paper. The crack can then be obliterated with the normal basecoats.

Techniques

A minimum of two coats will be required, exactly matching the ground colour of the china. The first coat must completely obliterate the required area but be liquid enough to flow on evenly and settle without ridges or grooves. If the proportion of pigment to glaze is too great the coat will be too soft and rub off easily, even after stoving. Subsequent coats need more glaze and less pigment, giving a complete match to the original surface both in texture and colour. As small an area as possible should be covered by the paint, overlapping first the repair and then each previous coat just enough to avoid building up a hard edge.

It is as well to master the techniques of mixing basecoats to the right consistency and applying them correctly before embarking on an actual restoration. Practice is needed to get the feel of the materials. The paint should be fluid and milky, not buttery. It should drip easily from the brush. The technique is more akin to laying water colour washes than oil painting.

First basecoat

Pour sufficient glaze into a dipper to give a depth of 3 mm ($\frac{1}{8}$ in); any less will become tacky before the colour is mixed. Add sufficient Titanium White oil colour to ensure that the filler will not show through. Stir well to incorporate the pigment. No streaks must be visible, but do it gently to avoid introducing bubbles. The mixture must still be thin enough to drip from the brush and remain shiny when applied, but it must be thick enough to mask the repair with one coat. When the balance between the glaze and Titanium White to give complete coverage has been established, small quantities of additional pigments can be added to match exactly the body of the china. Unless the first coat is an exact match it will show through the subsequent translucent one.

If a lot of adjustments have been made and the proportion of pigments to glaze is now too great, add a little more glaze to correct the consistency of the mixture. Add one or two drops of clean thinners to the mix to disperse any bubbles and compensate for the thickening of the glaze with pigments. Two small pots of thinners will be needed; one for washing brushes and a second, which is kept very clean, to add to the colour mixes. Do not put thinners into a plastic container as it will dissolve most plastics.

The mixture remains workable for 20 or 30 minutes at a room temperature of 20°C (70°F), proportionately less as the temperature rises. When working on a very warm day or in a hot climate the life of the paint mixture can be extended by standing it on ice. This can be achieved by placing a plate over a shallow dish filled with crushed ice and working with the dipper on this. If an old fashioned warming or invalid dish can be obtained and filled with the ice this is an ideal arrangement. This will ensure that the paint is not too tacky to use by the time the correct colour is mixed.

Make sure the area to be painted is dust and grease free. The surface can be wiped with a rag or cotton wool swab damped with methylated spirit. Rubbing down creates a great deal of dust which clings to the china. When working on the inside of a pot make sure that the whole of it is clean, not just the area to be painted, or the dust will settle on the wet paint with every movement.

Applying the basecoat by hand
The paint is laid on smoothly with sweeping strokes from the centre to the edge of the break. Retouch as little as possible. Use a full, long haired sable brush. A thin brush cannot hold enough paint for the mixture to remain fluid and float off smoothly before becoming stringy and tacky. The edges of the paint must be thinned down. This is done, primarily, with the sweeping action of the bristles across the surface using the bend and spring in the bristles to flick up at the end of each stroke. Do not apply the paint in a hard, bold band across the repair; work lightly across the china. Do not attempt to brush the paint out or go over the surface a second time. Finally, use a very little clear glaze on the tip of a clean brush to disturb and smooth away the edge before it dries into a hard step.

If this coat is not satisfactory, remove it immediately by wiping away with thinners and try another application until the right effect is achieved.

The technique for applying a coat of paint thickly enough to obliterate all trace of the repair and at the same time fading it out at the edges requires a lot of practice. It is not desirable to repaint more decoration than is absolutely essential; keeping as much of the original as possible is important. The undercoat which is not immediately over the repair but, because of the overlapping technique, is obscuring the pattern more than necessary, must be removed at this stage. With a fine stiff brush or a sharpened orange stick dampened with a little thinners, go over the decoration, carefully cleaning away the paint which overlaps the edges of the repaired area. Do not touch the thinned down edges of the background between the decoration; remove the basecoat only where it is concealing the pattern. The basecoat should be left directly over the repair or in time the epoxy resin will darken slightly and show beneath the transparent decorative painting. This clearing of paint must be done with each coat of paint before stoving. Should dust or fluff settle on the wet paint do not attempt to remove it while the surface is still tacky. Stove the object first; the dust will be removed when rubbing down once the china is cold.

Clean brushes thoroughly in thinners, removing all pigment completely before a final rinse in clean thinners. Do not allow the paint to harden in the brushes before cleaning. Make sure all flakes of pigment are cleaned away, particularly at the base of the bristles. Thinners dissolves the glaze quickly, but particles of pigment can be left behind to contaminate the next coat of paint. Do not leave brushes to soak in thinners or else the bristles will curl at the tip.

Stoving

The primary coat must now be stoved at a temperature of 115°C (240°F) for a minimum of 20 minutes. Unless the china remains at a constant temperature for a full 20 minutes, curing will not be complete. When dealing with a large, heavy object allow time for the oven and china to come up to temperature before calculating the 20 minutes stoving time. Articles should be placed on a baking tray, particularly if they are small or liable to overbalance. The other advantage is that the handling can be confined to the tray, not the painted edge of the china. It does not matter if the china is stoved immediately after painting or is left until a batch has accumulated. The setting of the paint will not be harmed either way, but the longer it is left the more dust is likely to settle on the work.

Abrading the first basecoat

Once the work is stoved it is left to cool completely before being gently rubbed down until smooth. The rubbing down must be done very lightly, barely using the weight of the finger and taking care not to rub the edge of the paint into a hard line. Use narrow strips of finest grade (flour) glass paper and rub only on the paint, avoiding the decoration and gilding. To get a really fine surface a glass fibre eraser should be used last of all. Only a short tip of fibre should be exposed and rubbed gently on the surface. Although the glass fibre bristles are very fine their abrasive power is great and damage can be done with over-enthusiastic use. The abrading will make the basecoat look a shade or two lighter but it will revert to the original colour with the subsequent coat of paint. The rubbing down, besides proving a fine smooth surface, gives a good key to the next coat of paint.

Second basecoat

In this mix a higher proportion of glaze is used. Less pigment will be required as this coat does not need to obliterate the repair, but must copy the texture of the china. Pour an adequate quantity of glaze into a dipper as before but mix in less Titanium White; sufficient to give the look of the china glaze rather than the china body. This coat must imitate the surface of the china. The pigments used for matching will be the same as used in the initial, obliterating coat, but this time it must have a translucent quality just as the original china has. This is achieved by increasing the quantity of glaze used in the mix. Again, an exact match must be obtained or the painted area will be obvious. Remove all dust and fluff from the surface and make sure the brush to be used for painting is clean and dust free. Use the same sweeping action of the brush across the area to be painted, from the centre towards the edges. Use the brush lightly, barely contacting the china with the bristles. Fade the edges of the paint into the china with a little clear glaze, taking the edge fractionally over the preceding one to prevent a build up of paint into a hard line where the restoration ends.

To remove this second coat if it is not up to standard, do not wipe it off with thinners as this would disturb the primary coat as well. It should be stoved in the normal way and rubbed down to the preceding coat with abrasives. Make sure the surface is not dusty and apply a fresh coat of paint.

When a satisfactory surface is achieved this coat also must be stoved at 115°C (240°F) for 20 minutes. When it is cold rub it down, first with flour glass paper and finally with the glass fibre eraser, working gently at the edges so that they are not rubbed into a hard line. This coat of paint, because of the higher proportion of synthetic glaze, will be much harder than the first. Two basecoats are the minimum required and should also be the maximum aimed at. Frequently results do not come up to expectations and extra coats must be applied. Every one must be stoved and rubbed down. As each coat will increase the thickness of paint and the area covered, try to apply only the minimum needed to give a perfect surface. It also saves time and temper!

To paint a pure white coat over the repair first of all serves little purpose as this coat will be too light and bright, and will then need obliterating. Added to which the white will probably break through when rubbing down and give a patchy appearance to the undercoats. Basecoats must match the body of the china exactly, even though the final glaze on the original may be a deep rich

Fig. 97 Painting a basecoat. Covering a chip by hand

Fig. 98 Use a brush dampened with thinners to remove unwanted basecoat on the decoration

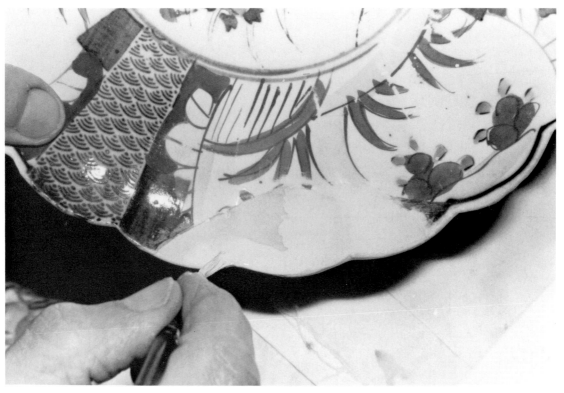

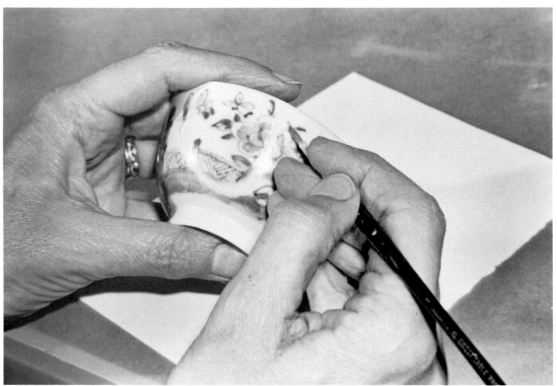

blue or green. The body colour needs to glow through the deep colour to give translucence to the final coat, just as it does in the original enamel.

Black or dark brown china, where the clay from which the object is made is dark, are the exceptions. Here both basecoats need to be dark enough to match the body exactly but with sufficient opaque pigment included to obliterate the filler.

Because of the sharp contours on handles and knobs the basecoats on these are easier to apply than on flatware. Again, no more china than necessary must be covered with paint. Do not paint the complete handle or knob in an effort to disguise a small join. It is the china which is of interest and value, not the paint. The line where paint and china meet must be faded away imperceptibly, first with the action of the brush and finally with a little clear glaze. A hard band of paint covering the break is as unsightly as a dark join line.

The overpainting must continue over any decoration which the repair crosses. It must be as narrow as practicable, leaving as much of the original pattern as possible clear of paint. However, unless the repair is obscured by the undercoats the touched in decoration – which will probably need transparent colours – will be marred by the shadow of the filler which will get darker with age. Figure groups, bocage, plates, bowls and all china that has a glazed finish needs this preliminary preparation.

Colour matching
Experience in colour mixing is invaluable, without it a lot of experimental practice will be required. Most students find colour matching difficult and frustrating, usually because time is not spared for practice and learning. Hundreds of suggestions for blends could be given but the restorer needs a formula for arriving at the correct combination and proportion of pigments. Undoubtedly the ability to analyse colours into their constituent pigments increases with practice. The only way to learn the properties of the contents of the paint box is to mix the pigments together and see the results. Keep records of the experiments which can be referred to until, eventually, matching any colour becomes instinctive. Pigments have various qualities of transparency and the ability to absorb or reflect light as well as having their own particular colour. These properties must be explored and exploited

to fully match and imitate the subtle differences in china. It is useful to paint a set of cards with each pigment on its own card to test against the china for colour comparison. If they are shaded down from concentrated pigment, diluted gradually, to a very light wash, a complete range of tone is available.

Matching white porcelain is the most frequent need. Most white china is grey when compared to white paint from the tube. It must be decided whether this greyness tends to blue, brown or cream in tone. Once this is established it is necessary to compare the available pigments within that colour range and choose the nearest. Never mix black or Paynes Grey in a basecoat. Neither of these pigments reflects light, and grey made from them appears as a dirty patch. If the grey has a blue overtone the choice is between:

Cerulean: a cold pale blue;
Cobalt: warmer and denser with a rather flat effect;
Ultramarine: which has a definite purple tinge, and
Prussian: a strong colour with a green tinge.

Once the nearest blue is selected a very small quantity can be added to the initial mix of glaze and Titanium White. Mix in the pigment gradually by brushing a little of the paint out on the palette and then transferring a little to the dipper, rather than by picking up a random blob on the brush. Mix it thoroughly until no streaks are visible and test a small dab against the surface to be matched. Compare the colour of the paint with the colour of the china. Consider:

is the paint too light? If so add more pigment gradually. It can soon be overdone;
is the paint too dark? Add a little more white;
is the paint too blue? If it is, does the china appear brown or cream against it?

If the china looks brown by comparison with the dab of paint consider if it is a cold grey brown, in which case Raw Umber is the brown to use. If it is a warm reddish brown add Burnt Umber, or Burnt Sienna, which is an even warmer brown. If the comparison makes the china look creamy add a little yellow, deciding which yellow is needed by the same method. Cold colours are the ones having a greater proportion of blue in their make-up. The warm colours contain the sunny colours yellow and red to a greater degree.

This methodical selection and comparison, if

used thoughtfully, is the basis of good, accurate colour matching.

A simple record of various mixtures and the pigments used is helpful at first. Time spent in experimenting with colours is not wasted, as it will save hours of random experiments later.

Finishing basecoats

Sometimes, although the colour match is good, the final appearance of the basecoat lacks an indefinable quality. The china glaze reflects the light and the paint looks dead in comparison. Close inspection and consideration is needed to ascertain just what is missing. Perhaps the colour changes near the edge, or the colour intensifies in bands where the action of the potter's fingers made shallow grooves in the wet clay. If the china is transparent the decoration may be casting a shadow through the paste, or the oxide used in the decoration may have run into the surrounding glaze. The original glaze possibly has hundreds of microscopic bubbles trapped in it which look like a fine white mist when viewed under a magnifying glass. All these qualities can be reproduced with a further application of glaze mixed with oil paint. The colour can be modified or darkened in the necessary places by a coat of glaze and pigment without the addition of white. The tiny bubbles can be simulated with synethetic glaze and a minute quantity of white.

All these effects should be tried out first on a practice plate, otherwise hours of work on preparing base coats can be wasted. A few old plates or tiles painted with colour trials will provide a valuable record.

When an item is heavily crazed, a thin film of glaze and colour will serve to disguise the repair better than trying to imitate the lines of cracking.

All these additional coats of paint must be floated on lightly, never brushed out, or the results will be streaky. Preferably an airbrush should be used for this. It can diminish or intensify the colour imperceptibly, which is a very difficult thing to do by hand.

For plain china without decoration or gilding the overpainting is now complete and only awaits the final protective coat of glaze.

Faults in hand painted basecoats

Many faults which originate in the preparation, bonding and modelling stages only show up when painted and stoved. The remedy is to remove the paint completely and correct them. Do not add ashesive or filler over a painted surface; it will stick to the paint only and peel off later. As the paint is to be entirely removed it can be flooded with thinners and wiped off.

Pock marks appearing along the break line indicate that air is trapped in a badly filled join and is escaping through the paint, leaving small craters. The paint must first be removed and the pin holes filled. Use epoxy resin adhesive alone if the holes are very small. If this proves insufficient, epoxy-resin mixed with china clay must be rolled into a thin thread and inserted over adhesive along the holes and pressed in firmly. The filling must be allowed 24 hours to harden, after which time it can be rubbed down and repainted.

Paint that pulls back from the china when applied, like a spot of oil on a wet surface, indicates that there is grease on the china. It was possibly left by plastic modelling clay, or an excess of barrier cream on the hands which was transferred to the surface of the china. The article must be thoroughly cleaned with methylated spirits until free from grease.

When the fault lies in the colour or consistency of the paint itself always remove the offending coat. Left in place it will need a second obliterating coat to cover it. This adds undesired bulk and serves no useful purpose. If it is the first basecoat it can be removed with thinners. Make sure it is completely removed. The second coat must not be removed with thinners or the solvent will attack the previously applied paint as well. Use flour glass paper to rub it down instead. If carefully done the initial coat can be retained, provided of course that the first coat was perfect before the second was applied.

When the paint rubs off easily because it is soft, even after stoving and cooling, remove it completely and repaint using a higher percentage of glaze medium in the mixture. Using the abrasive too vigorously, or too coarse an abrasive, will also remove more paint than necessary. Rubbing down paint must be done gently, it is not as tough as epoxy resin or filler.

When the coats of paint are dull and matt it indicates that either the pigment or thinners content in the mix was too high.

If the repair shows through the paint, insufficient white was used. Make sure the mix really obliterates before adding further colours for matching. Check also that the filler was not too dark to begin with, in which case it may be necessary to apply a second obliterating coat. Try to avoid this in future by using a little more titanium oxide in the filler. When several coats of dense paint are used the thickness of paint over the repair is too great and will form a bulge which will catch the light.

The cause of paint changing colour when stoved may be any one of several reasons. It is a good plan to check the tubes of paint with the colour list and make sure no unlisted colours have crept in unnoticed nor any of an inferior quality. Paints containing carbonate of lead will inevitably discolour through oxidisation. Never use Flake White, Cremnitz White, Foundation White or Flesh Tint as these all have lead in their composition. Student and economy colours contain cheaper ingredients which cannot be expected to withstand baking. Perhaps the oven was not quite clean or the oven cleaner was not rinsed off thoroughly and was releasing fumes when hot. The shelves and baking trays must be clean too. The china must be clean inside as well as out before restoration starts. Figures are often very dirty inside and this can seep through. The paint may have been contaminated during mixing, perhaps by a dirty dipper or brush. All containers and brushes should be used solely for china restoration. The correct thinners must be used. White spirit or methylated spirit are not compatible with the glaze medium. This is usually apparent immediately because the mixture curdles, but contamination through a paint rag or by using an old brush could occur. If all these possibilities can be ruled out the cause may be fatigue on the part of the restorer. The eye gets so weary of comparing colours it resorts to self-deception. A change of focus and a rest is all that is required. Yellow stains appearing on the surface of the china when heated are smears of epoxy resin, which discolour when heated. Remove them with a scalpel or glasspaper. Never smooth off unset joins or fillings with methylated spirit or water as it just spreads a film of diluted epoxy-resin over the china. It also impairs the strength of the epoxy resin. Make sure finger marks and smears are removed before painting.

Bubbles sometimes appear in a coat of paint after stoving; they are usually more noticeable in the second coat. The paint must be rubbed down to below the level of the bubbles before applying a fresh coat of paint. The trouble was probably caused by applying paint onto a dusty surface or by using a dusty brush, or bubbles may have been present in the mixture before painting, in which case stir the paint more gently and add one or two drops of thinners immediately prior to using. Make sure the surface to be painted is smoothed, not lacerated by the abrasive. Scratches will trap air under the paint, which then expands and erupts on heating.

All these things can happen; it does not follow that they will. They mostly occur when the rules are overlooked. Initial attempts at painting are usually depressing, and the dual problems of colour matching and fading away the edges seem insoluble. But both of these troubles can be overcome by practice, not just by trying once or twice but by careful, sustained training of hand and eye.

Attempting to overpaint long or large areas by hand, especially on plain china, is a wasted effort. They will show up as hard ribbons of paint when held in a good light. Success at the early stages depends on choosing the right type of repairs to experiment with beforehand. Repair shell chips, handles, knobs, simple drapery and bocage on figures to begin with. This way skill is developed in handling the materials. Spending a lot of time trying to do the impossible teaches very little.

Airbrushing
The airbrush
The first airbrush was patented in 1893 and although they have developed since then they contain the same principle parts. The paint is sprayed by the action of air rushing past the end of the paint nozzle, so creating a vacuum which draws the paint out and atomises it to produce a fine mist. The paint nozzle contains a needle, the position of which controls the paint flow. This is the way all airbrushes required for fine spraying of thick materials must function. If the action blows air through the paint the results will not be satisfactory with a synthetic glaze mixture. Such airbrushes are cheaper in manufacture but are intended for coarser application of much diluted paint.

Choosing an airbrush
When buying an airbrush choose a model that:

is easy to clean. Make sure there are no narrow

Fig. 99 DeVilbiss airbrush E63

Fig. 100 Efbe airbrush B1

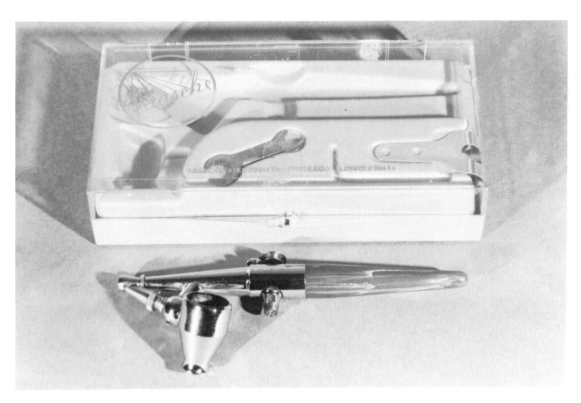

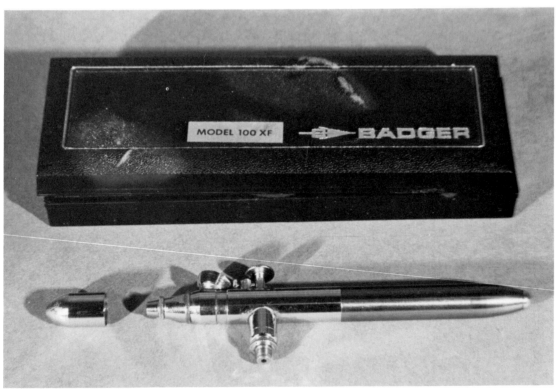

pipes or passages for the paint to clog;

has easy access to any washers that may need renewing frequently;

emits a fine spray. A 0.3 mm nozzle aperture is ideal;

is well balanced and comfortable to hold. If there is any strain from airline or control lever it with be tiring to use;

gives alternative right or left hand fixing if it has a side mounted colour cup;

has clear instructions for use and cleaning.

Choosing a compressor

There are many types of compressor available ranging from those with a piston pump to those with a diaphragm pump. The important thing is that the pressure of air delivered to the airbrush can be controlled. In some cases this is done by the use of a reservoir fitted with a gauge and regulator. If a diaphram pump is connected directly to the airbrush without a reservoir this produces an uneven, pulsating delivery. This can be partially controlled by using an extra long airline.

It is important, also, that the air is clean and dry. Moisture condenses in the reservoir, which has to be emptied periodically. When a reservoir is not used a filter and water trap must be included in the airline.

Choose a model which is compatible with the airbrush and make sure that the threads on the connectors match. A noiseless compressor is a great advantage to the operator and any close neighbours, but increases the cost of the equipment.

Checking an airbrush

Warning: Good ventilation is essential; ideally a spray booth with an extractor fan should be used. Inhaling atomised vapour is highly dangerous so an efficient respirator must be worn. The filter should be changed immediately the slightest smell is noticed. Never smoke or have naked flames, pilot lights or convector heaters burning nearby. Wearers of contact lenses must always wear protective spectacles; the fine spray can cause intense irritation to the eyes and damage the lenses.

All makes and models of airbrushes should have

Fig. 101 Paasche airbrush H

Fig. 102 A prototype gravity feed Badger airbrush GXF. The production model has minor modifications

Fig. 103 A Simair automatic control, double outlet, noiseless compressor

Fig. 104 A Simair foot controlled, single outlet, noiseless compressor

clear instructions for operating and cleaning the equipment. These must be completely understood before spraying commences. Study the diagrams and instructions together with the airbrush. Make sure the removal of any parts for cleaning or replacement can be done with confidence. Get to know your airbrush inside as well as out. Checking that both air and paint flow are working efficiently before loading the airbrush

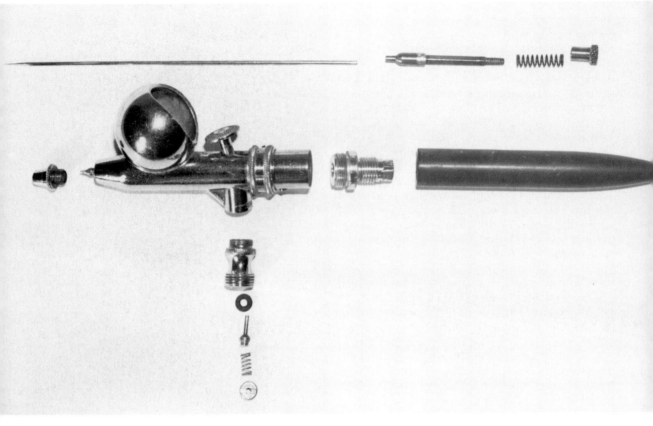

Fig. 105 The parts of an airbrush

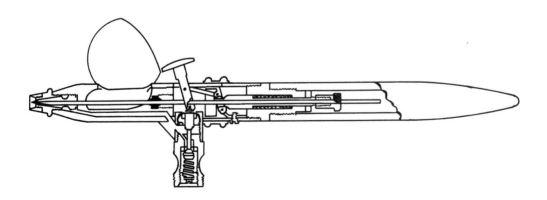

Diagram 58 Diagram of assembled airbrush. Although the construction may vary slightly between models, the basic principles are the same

with paint will save time in the long run. Switch on the compressor and blow a little air through the airline without the airbrush attached. This will get rid of any dust or moisture which may have collected in the airline. If no air blows through at this stage check the pressure gauge to make sure the air pressure is correct, the control to the airline is open and all fittings are airtight. See that the supply is unobstructed; by a chairleg or a foot on the airline for instance.

Attach the airbrush and operate the air lever button to blow out any dust. This will also prove that the air is flowing freely all the way through. If no air is emitted the air passage through the airbrush must be checked. Check washers to make sure they are properly in place and are not swollen, perished or split. Ensure that plungers are moving freely and are operating the valves as they should. If all these moving parts are functioning correctly it is most likely that the air passage is blocked either with dust or spilled paint. To clear it the aerosol solvent should be tried first. The pressurised jet will dislodge any particles of fluff or hairs and minor paint blockages. This should be all that is necessary in the air passageways. However, if the cause is a build up of stale paint left from careless cleaning it will be very stubborn to move. It may be necessary to soak the airbrush in thinners until the combination of pigment and glaze medium is broken down sufficiently to dissolve. The complete airbrush should never be left to soak in thinners unless all washers, seals and non-metal parts are removed first. Thinners will adversely affect all rubber and most plastic components, handles etc.

Having checked that the air supply is working properly the next step is to check the paint flow. All airbrushes differ a little in design and the individual instructions must be followed. Most have a single finger button which when depressed releases air and when drawn back controls the paint supply. On some models the finger button controls the air supply only and the paint flow has a separate and independent control.

Pour a little clean thinners into the colour cup and blow this through to make sure the paint passage and nozzle are clean and unblocked. If, although the air is coming through, there is not a jet of thinners when the paint control is fully opened, there is a blockage between paint chamber and nozzle. Check that the needle is moving to let the paint through. Make sure it is

not pushed into the nozzle so tightly that the lever cannot operate it. If the needle is quite free in the nozzle but does not move when the paint control lever is operated, adjust the securing nut which holds the needle in position. Check that the washer in the nozzle is not displaced, split, swollen or perished and replace it if it is. If the nozzle is blocked by a build-up of hardened pigment it must be soaked in thinners and cleaned with a stiff brush. Before removing the nozzle retract the needle to prevent damage. Remove any washer before immersing the nozzle in solvent where it may need to soak for some time. Reassemble carefully according to makers' instructions.

If the contents of the colour cup are bubbling it indicates that the nozzle is at least partially blocked or not properly seated. The air is forcing its way back through the paint chamber and not ejecting the liquid. Make sure the washer is in place and all screw fittings fully tightened.

Apart from the very exceptional failure of a part, the usual cause of trouble is dirty equipment. Following through these routine checks will prevent faults or remedy them before they need the services of an airbrush mechanic.

Using an airbrush

Glaze medium and pigment must first be thoroughly mixed in a dipper and a small quantity of the mixture poured into the bottom of the colour cup. Do not overfill or the paint will spill into the control lever mechanism and block it. Add several drops of clean thinners to make the paint sufficiently fluid to spray through easily. Up to 25% of thinners by volume may be added without harming the mixture.

Hold the airbrush at an angle of approximately 45° to the surface to be sprayed and about 1 cm ($\frac{1}{2}$ in) away. Changing the angle and the distance slightly will produce a range of effects; these should all be explored during practice. The greater the distance between airbrush and the work the wider the band of spray. Holding the airbrush at too low an angle will make the spray drift too far across the work. Always work with the minimum of air and paint flow so there is as little overspray as possible. The extent of this overspray is better understood if, as an experiment, light paint is sprayed onto a dark tile, or vice versa. Keep the airbrush moving all the time or a pool of paint will form at every pause. A lot of trial and error will be needed to get the technique right so

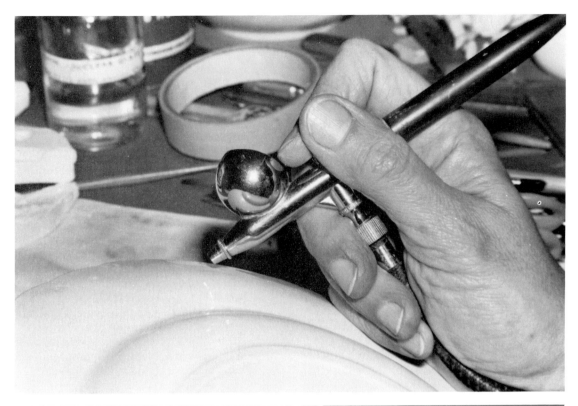

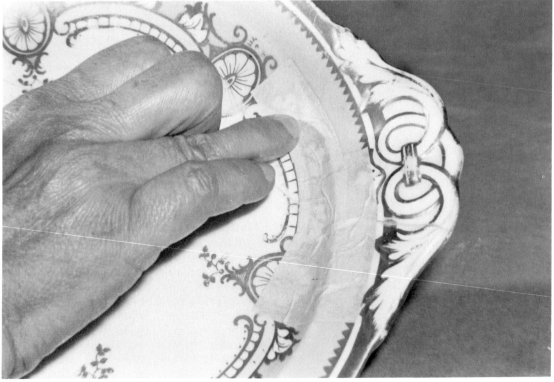

try on an old plate first to get the feel of the tool.

The control button is operated with the index finger, pressing down to control the air supply and pulling back to release the paint flow. Practise keeping the finger relaxed and with even pressure on the control button. Begin each stroke by operating the air pressure before allowing the paint to flow and end the stroke by cutting off the paint flow first and stopping the air pressure last. The sequence is:

press down – air on;
pull back – paint on;
push forward – paint off;
release upwards – air off.

If not done in this order a blob of paint will remain on the needle tip to be blown off at the beginning of the next stroke.

Fine lines are made by keeping the airbrush close to the work and with only light pressure on the control button for both air and paint.

To cover an area evenly with paint, spray a series of parallel strokes, each overlapping the previous one. Repeat the process until the paint is of the required intensity.

Shading can be done by gradually opening the paint control. To do this evenly requires practice and steady finger pressure. A sudden increase of pressure will produce a blotch of colour.

A spatter effect can be made by using a special spatter cap or the adjustment of a separate control according to the type of airbrush. A similar effect can be obtained by lowering the air pressure in the air reservoir to about 1 bar (14 psi). This can be useful for some mottled effects but its use is limited as it will also give a broken, sandy textured finish. It is difficult to obtain the correct size and shape of speckle to imitate the original one.

Masking

When it is desired to protect an area from the spray it is necessary to fix a mask over the surface to be shielded. The edge of the mask will create a hard edge to the paint so this is only of use when a definite line is required. A self adhesive strip with a crepe or crinkled texture which can be stretched to form curves is available and is most useful when painting bands of colour. Cut a sufficient length of the tape and press into place, easing it to continue

Fig. 106 Holding the airbrush at the correct distance and angle for spraying

Fig. 107 Using masking tape to shield an area from spray

the required line. Do not allow it to form angles around the curves. Make sure the edges are well pressed down and making good contact with the surface so that paint cannot be blown underneath them. The paint is then sprayed onto the china and over the edge of the mask.

The tape is removed when the paint is dry and before stoving. It will peel quite easily if it is not left on more than an hour or two. Heat will make it difficult to remove. When using transparent masking film the shape required is cut from the sheet. This stencil must be cut very accurately as any small angle or jagged edge will show up when sprayed. The paper backing is peeled away carefully and as the film is transparent it is easy to see precisely where to fix it. Press firmly into place without stretching or wrinkling. Paint will creep under the edges unless they are securely stuck down. Spray where required and leave the film in place until the paint is dry. Before stoving use a scalpel to lift one edge and peel off carefully without damaging the paint.

These self adhesive masking materials are made with a special, lightly tacky coating which will not damage the surfaces they are applied to and will peel away easily. Do not use freezer tape or the transparent self adhesive tapes used for parcel sealing. The adhesive on these will pull off paint and gold.

Masking fluid is a latex based solution which is useful for masking small areas. The solution is applied with a brush which should be kept solely for this purpose. Leave the latex to dry before airbrushing or the force of air will disturb the surface of the mask. Spray the article and remove the latex by gathering it up with a pointed india rubber eraser once the paint is hard. Do not leave the latex in position while stoving. The brush can be washed in warm soapy water and dried before storing.

Applying basecoats with an airbrush

The requirements are identical to painting basecoats by hand on small areas. Two coats will still be needed, the first to give cover and the second to imitate texture. The mixture of glaze medium and pigment will need thinning to make it a suitable consistency to go through the airbrush easily. Make sure the consistency is right for the appropriate basecoat before thinning. Do not substitute thinners for glaze medium; keep the ratio of the glaze medium to pigment correct for the respective coats.

Fig. 108 Masking film, masking liquid, airbrush cleaning fluid and masking tape

Using an airbrush for base coats solves the difficulty of fading away the edges but in doing so it deposits such a fine haze of paint that it appears as a matt halo surrounding the paint. This needs to be kept as narrow as possible by using only the minimum of air and keeping the nozzle close to the work. This halo can be further reduced in area by abrading with the glass fibre eraser once the item has been stoved. Remove as much of the spray halo between coats as possible otherwise, when overlapping subsequently, the area covered would be vast. An article with several breaks would have little original china showing. There is a great deal of prejudice against the use of spray painting, which is quite justified when it has been used indiscriminately.

Such a close even coat of paint is laid down that every pin hole and minute fault underneath shows up to an alarming extent. Use can be made of this by spraying a fine coat of paint over the repair in order to reveal any blemishes before starting the basecoats. The paint can be wiped away at once with thinners and the faults remedied before proceeding. Otherwise, after mixing a good colour match, the airbrush could reveal that the standard of preparation was not high enough.

Before stoving each coat in the usual way, decoration which has been coated by the overspray, leaving a cloudy appearance, must be cleaned. This is done by the method used for cleaning the decoration when painting by hand. Do not remove the basecoat immediately covering the repair, only the fine mist over the decoration at the perimeter.

Because the airbrush applies the paint in tiny droplets, the surface usually has a slight orange peel texture. This is remedied after stoving by light abrading. The centre of the work can be rubbed down gently with fine (flour) glass paper and then finished with a glass fibre eraser. The thin edges of the paint must be preserved but the matt border can be reduced in size by careful use of the glass fibre eraser.

To cover a crack or join

The crack must be sealed before attempting to obliterate it, otherwise the air trapped in the crack will blow through the paint and cause minute craters. For sealing cracks see the section on bonding.

Spray along the line of the break keeping the airbrush moving steadily and just swiftly enough to prevent the paint forming pools. Keep the nozzle close to the work or the band of paint will spread too far. The volume of paint and air must be kept to the minimum to prevent the paint being blown into ripples. This operation can be repeated, allowing a few seconds between runs for the paint to dry off a little, until the crack has been faded out. The usual two types of basecoat will be necessary, rubbing down the overspray each time after stoving.

Spraying large areas

Not only must the edges be tapered away to nothing but the paint must be applied evenly to the main area of the repair. It can either be sprayed as a series of parallel strokes or in a circular motion, each line of spray being slightly overlapped by the next one. If the spray is laid first in one direction and then diagonally across it the effect will be chequered and patchy. A to and fro action will result in a heavy deposit of paint when turning which will leave a patchy edge. Keep air and paint flowing steadily; some airbrushes have an adjustment which will preset the paint flow and hold it constant. This can be helpful for a really large area, but it is more useful for the restorer to be able to increase or decrease the quantity of paint delivered at will. When dealing with edges, heavily embossed areas, or small angles such as foot rims and beside handles, the paint must be applied very sparingly or the hollows will fill with paint and be lost. An excess of air will blow the paint into ridges.

Basecoats for handles and knobs

These are the jobs which are more successful when tackled by hand painting. The small area involved often means that far more of the article is sprayed than is intended. Most of the spray passes the handle of a cup for instance and smothers the bowl of the cup with a fine mist of paint. Masking in these circumstances usually leaves a hard edge around the painting. Figures too, usually fall into this category and are best done by hand. Quite often dark china or deeply coloured enamel areas must be hand painted. With dark colours the overspray is not only matt but looks grey; if this shadow is removed the hard edge problem returns, as the light catches this step even more on a dark surface than on a light one.

Finishing basecoats using an airbrush

The airbrush provides the ideal way of applying a finishing coat when, although a good match colour-wise, the two basecoats do not quite imitate the original texture. Use glaze medium and a small quantity of pigment to add pools or patches of colour, not at random, but to intensify the colour where the original glaze would have collected. The addition of a small quantity of white to glaze medium, sprayed lightly over the surface will recreate the effect of small bubbles so often found in the glaze of oriental porcelain.

The spatter cap can sometimes be useful. Trials must be made to establish that the spatter will match up with the original mottling. Nothing will be more obvious than even, round speckles alongside irregular ones. The colour also must match. Often several light applications will be needed either varying the intensity of the colour or changing it completely.

All these techniques must be practised so that the airbrush operator will know what effects are available. A record can be kept using white plates or tiles. Plates are better because they give practice in controlling paint on curved and sloping contours. Trials on card or paper which is absorbent do not give an accurate indication of the properties of airbrushing on china.

Cleaning after use

The air and paint passages are small and clog very easily, so the airbrush must always be cleaned immediately after use or if the work is interrupted, even for a short time – within one or two minutes rather than ten minutes.

Surplus paint should be tipped out and the paint chamber cleaned out with a little thinners and a stiff brush. This, also, is poured away. Spray through with clean thinners until a clear jet of thinners emerges. The tip of the paint nozzle and the needle must be cleared of paint with a paint brush, being very careful not to damage the point of the needle in any way, or leave a bristle behind. This is quite sufficient cleaning for the airbrush between colour changes. If the airbrush is not to

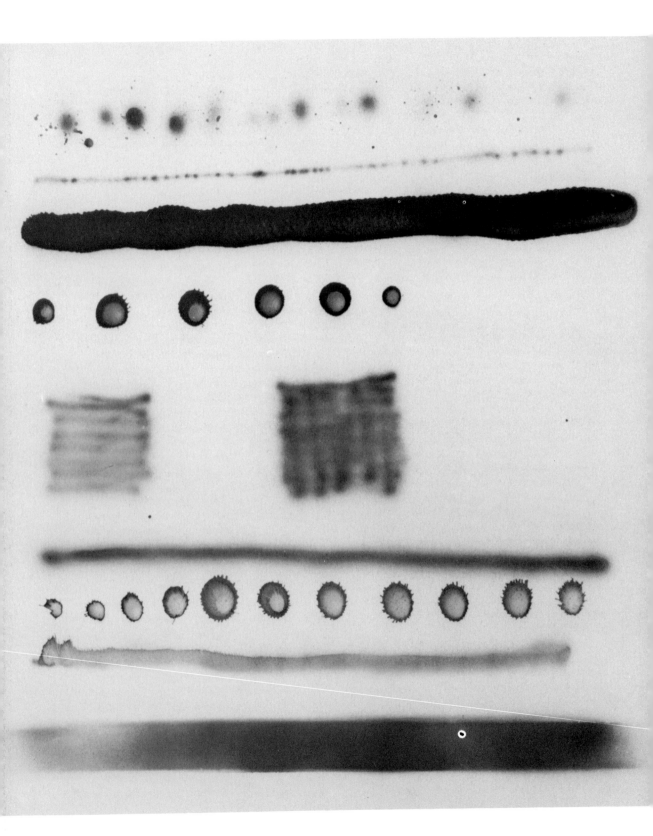

be re-used immediately, a little clean thinners should be left in the paint chamber until work restarts.

When the airbrush is not going to be used for sometime, more thorough cleaning will be necessary or the needle will be stuck firmly in the airbrush and pigment will also build up in the nozzle. Thinners and a stiff brush should be used to remove every trace of pigment and glaze medium before the airbrush is dried and stored away from dust. Follow the makers' diagrams and instructions for withdrawing the needle and other recommended maintenance cleaning.

After spraying through the airbrush with thinners for cleaning purposes, rinsing any rubber washers in soapy water and then drying carefully will help to prolong their life.

Faults in airbrush basecoats

When the sprayed surface has a granulated or sandy texture the paint was either too thick or the air pressure was too low. In the first case, provided that the proportion of glaze medium to pigment was correct, add more thinners. Thinners evaporates rapidly and it may be necessary to add a few extra drops as spraying proceeds, especially

Fig. 109 Airbrushing faults (*top to bottom*):
Spatters caused by allowing air lever to snap back into position
Uneven line caused by hestitant or shaky movement of the hand
Excessive air and paint flow
Excessive air and paint flow
Insufficient overlapping; Chequered effect caused by overspraying at right angles
Patch at each end caused by pausing at beginning and end of stroke
Paint runs caused by the paint being too thin
Hard edge produced by masking

in a hot atmosphere. The glaze medium only remains workable for 20 to 30 minutes so the mixing and spraying must be completed within this time. If the second is more likely, check that there are no air leaks at any connections and the pump is maintaining 2.5 bars (35 psi) while the airbrush is being used.

If the paint runs or forms dribbles on the surface the paint has been thinned too much. Add a small amount of unthinned paint mixture or wait a short while until the thinners has evaporated a little.

Blobs of paint spitting constantly onto the surface indicate that the needle tip is bent or that the nozzle is split. Needles can be straightened if not too badly hooked by rotating the tip against a hard smooth surface. A split nozzle needs replacing, but unless the needle has been forced into position or the airbrush dropped a split is unlikely to happen. If the blobs and spitting only occur at the start of a stroke, the air and paint control is being operated incorrectly at the end of the previous stroke. Curtail first the paint and then the air.

Faults in the preparation stage or due to the consistency of the paint are identical to those described and dealt with in the hand painting section.

With careful use and regular cleaning an airbrush gives years of service, but it is wise to keep a few spares in stock. Washers are very tiny and are easily lost during cleaning. Most manufacturers will service and repair airbrushes but a spare needle, nozzle and several washers can save a lot of delay and are not complicated to replace.

Controlling an airbrush takes time to learn, and it may seem as if one set of problems has been replaced by another. Practice and above all understanding of how an airbrush works will solve the problems.

7 · Decorating

Many students anticipate that the decorating will be the most interesting and exciting part of the job. All the work so far has been strictly disciplined and the smallest detail has needed close attention. Now, surely is the opportunity to apply swags of colour with zest. But not all decoration is that simple.

Unless the restorer is a confident draughtsman it is wise to tackle only the plainest decorations at first; simple bands, dots and sprig patterns are the ones to start on. This will provide excellent training and build up knowledge of the materials. It will take time to gain skill, but it will be developed with perseverance. Practice steadies the hand and enables the brush, which is an extension of the hand, to follow a prescribed line. It is most gratifying to discover that even a simple band of colour deflects the eye from the damaged area. As always with restoring antiques the temptation to put back worn decoration must be resisted.

Materials and tools

Synethetic resin glaze (Chintex)
Artists' oil colours (Winsor and Newton)
Thinners (Chintex thinners, Joy thinners)
Artists' dry ground colours (Winsor and Newton); used mainly with figure groups
Stoving equipment
Brushes
Stiff card
Dippers
Pencils (H or HH)
Orange sticks
Flour glass paper
Glass fibre erasers
Airbrush equipment

Most of the materials listed for decoration have been explained in Chapter 5 when dealing with the application of basecoats. The pigments listed there are adequate for the colours needed in decorating. Never make additions to the range of pigments before testing them thoroughly for compatibility and durability. The pigments must still be mixed into sufficient glaze medium to bind them to the china. It often seems wasteful to mix up a quantity of colour when only a small stroke is to be applied but it is most essential that the pigment is saturated by the glaze medium. A quick flick of pigment and glaze on a card will result in the decoration rubbing off, even after stoving.

The artist's dry ground colours are used for a few special effects, mainly in the painting of figure groups. The same pigments are required as in the oil bound colours list. It is important to obtain artists' quality pigments as they must be finely ground and permanent. They are supplied in 25 gram packets.

The brushes used for applying basecoats are suitable for decorating. The addition of a smaller brush of the same type and quality is useful when painting small patterns. A brush which is too fine will not hold a sufficient quantity of paint to complete a stroke before it dries out. Provided the brush is a good quality and is treated properly it will retain a fine point even though it is a large size.

The decoration must be stoved to cure the glaze medium. The usual temperature of 115°C (240°F) maintained for a minimum of 20 minutes is required for each stoving.

Marking out the design for painting

This is done with the aid of a tracing or by freehand drawing. For either method use a hard lead pencil, either H or HH, as a soft lead will make smudges of graphite in the paint.

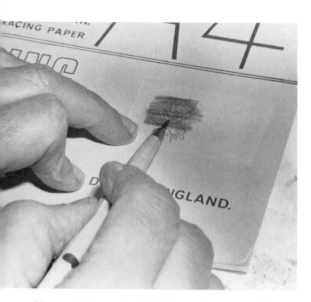

Fig. 110 Using tracings. Scribble over the reverse of the tracing with a hard pencil

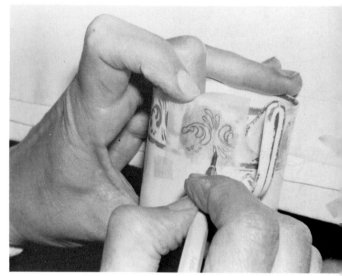

Fig. 111 Position the tracing, scribbled side down, and draw in the outline of the pattern

Using a tracing

Now is the time to transfer the pattern which was carefully traced before the basecoats were applied. Rub the pencil over the back of the tracing to give an even coating of graphite. Place the tracing in position with the graphite side in contact with the china, matching up the edges of the pattern with the original design. With a very sharp pencil trace over the main lines of the pattern. This will leave a clean, sharp outline of the design over the basecoats ready to be painted in.

Drawing free hand

At least a few measurements and guide lines should be made indicating the position and main components of the decoration, otherwise it is possible to end up with insufficient space in which to complete the last pattern. The amount of guide lines required depends on the restorer. A freer rhythm of brush work can be achieved if only an indication of direction and spacing is marked out. The detail is then put in directly with brush and paint. When the decoration is a simple edge band the guide line can be drawn using the fingers as a gauge. Hold the pencil in thumb and first two fingers and slide the third finger around the rim of the china. This maintains the pencil at an even distance from the edge. The sharp point of the pencil should just touch the china and be just

within the edge of the band. This strategem can also be used for gauging the distance of spots or sprigs placed around the edge of an article. To measure the distance between parts of a pattern a pair of dividers is needed. If the pattern is simple all that is necessary is a pencilled dot to indicate placing or a change in direction of a line. The dots can be joined up in pencil if more guide lines are needed. The pencilling must be done lightly so that lines will not show through the paint.

Much of the flower and landscape decoration on china was originally done by very fine artists. When the need arises to restore a break in these circumstances the re-painting must equal that of the original artist. If the student has no experience of drawing this is yet another skill to learn. For a restorer the ability to copy precisely is needed, there is no scope for originality in replacing decoration. Drawing skill is not only needed in marking out designs but throughout the painting of the decoration. The ability to draw is the coordination between eye, mind and hand, which is greatly improved by constant use. Practice with pen and paper to achieve coordination and a steady hand, and use a brush and paint to get the feel of the materials. Don't just doodle but build up definite patterns, starting and finishing each stroke exactly where planned. Copy the diaper patterns used on oriental porcelain and the repeat designs on old English table ware. Spode or Wedgwood are splendid for learning from.

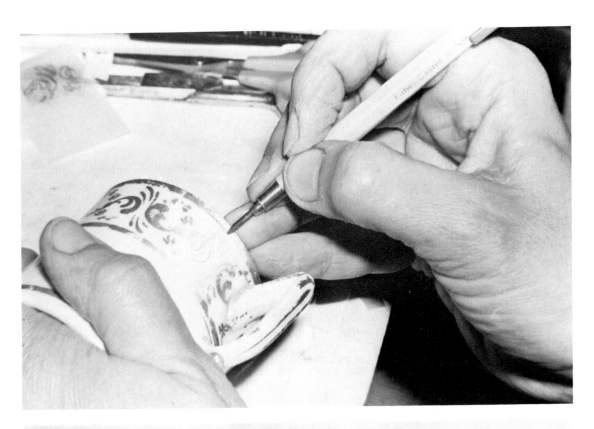

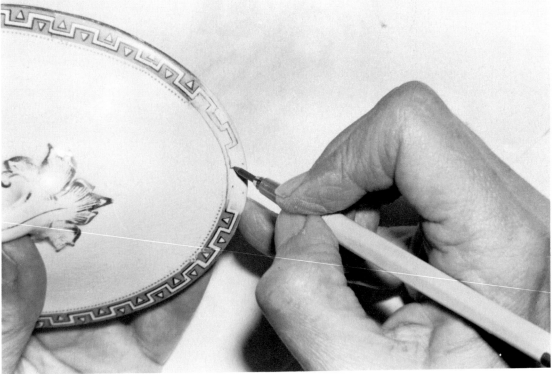

Fig. 112 Use a finger as a gauge to keep the band parallel to the edge

Fig. 113 Pencilling in a geometrical design which was first measured out with dividers

Fig. 114 English enamelling. The enamel is thinly applied and the strokes of the brush are clearly seen

Fig. 115 Chinese border pattern. A useful example for drawing practice

Diagram 59 Repeat patterns. Border or background pattern built up from a swastika motif

Diagram 60 It will frequently be necessary to copy this type of design

Diagram 61 Practise keeping the size and spacing of each motif even

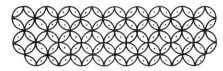

Diagram 62 Practice in drawing these patterns will improve co-ordination between hand and eye

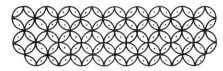

Diagram 63 Drawing should be practised with both pen and brush

Colour matching for decorating

Matching colours must be taken a step further at this stage. In the base coats the many variations of white from greys to creams was the chief concern. Now the rest of the spectrum has to be discovered. Matching the colour alone is not sufficient, its density, transparency, brilliance and intensity have also to be imitated if the decoration is to blend into the original. Recipes for mixtures are very little help as so much depends on the proportions of the pigments used. A few hours spent on methodical experiments, with the results recorded on a simple chart, will provide an excellent guide for future matching. It will also train the eye in the appreciation of the subtle differences between the pigments. Some of these are transparent and others completely opaque. As

soon as an opaque pigment is added to a transparent one the mixture loses transparency. It becomes more and more dense as further pigment is added as well as changing colour.

Try this experiment using Rose Madder with Cerulean Blue and Cobalt Blue in turn. The difference is subtle but useful. Experiment with mixing two colours, gradually increasing the quantity of one of them, e.g. Cadmium Red and Prussian Blue. Record each addition of colour. This will show how red decreases into purple and then the colour intensifies through to blue as saturation point is reached. It will also provide a good matching chart when the deep blues on oriental china are to be matched. If this experiment is repeated with the other colours, a very comprehensive colour chart will have been built up. This can all be done on heavy card. However, a much better idea of the effect will be obtained if china or tile is used, although unfortunately this will make a rather cumbersome reference file.

The addition of both Titanium White or Lamp Black in varying proportions also alters the character of the paint, and often this is all that is needed to bring a near match into a perfect one. Trials must constantly be made, and the restorer will never stop learning about the fascinating possibilities of colour.

Mixing paint

Mix glaze and pigment in a dipper so that the pigment is completely saturated by glaze. Even if only a small quantity of paint is required the pigment must be amalgamated with sufficient glaze medium or the paint will not adhere to the china. This may seem difficult when a dark, intense colour is required. To make the mixture workable one or two drops of thinners may be added, but more than this will weaken the holding ability of the glaze medium. The paint and glaze mixture for decorating does not have to obliterate the base coats, and it is therefore only necessary to add white if this makes the desired match. For many objects the basecoat glowing through a transparent colour gives the necessary luminosity for enamels. The paint will remain usable for 20 to 30 minutes at room temperature, after which period it will become progressively more tacky and stringy. Do not attempt to add thinners once this happens as it will destroy the properties of the glaze and evaporate too quickly to be of any use.

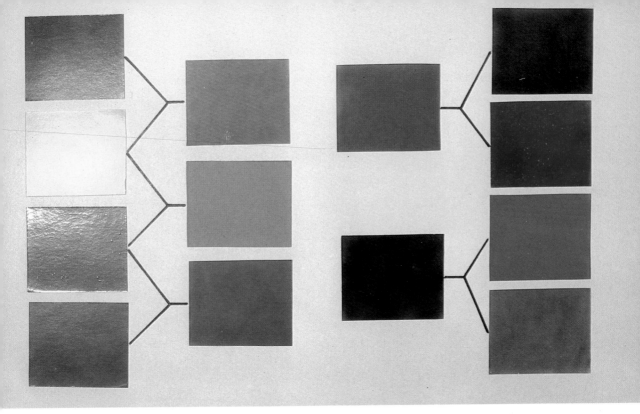

4 Primary, Secondary and Tertiary colours

5 Colour mixing; red through purple to blue

6 Gilding

Fig. 116 Wedgewood transfer printing which has a flat surface, level with the glaze

Fig. 117 Chinese hand painted enamel. The enamel is heavily applied, lying in pools and ridges on the surface

Applying the paint

The following methods of imitating decorations are suggested ways of achieving the right effect. They should be tried out in advance and recorded. Then, when the occasion for their use arises the starting point for final trials will have been established without wasting time on fruitless searches. It must also be remembered that methods which are successful with one colour will fail with another because the pigments differ in texture. Some techniques are tricky to manage and will need a little practice before using them on a piece of work. It is annoying to spoil a perfect undercoat by using an untried method of decoration unsuccessfully, and it is expensive in time too.

Consideration must be given to the type of decoration. Transfer printing and the European style of enamel painting are flat and lie close to or beneath the surface of the glaze. Thick pools of bright enamels are found on the surface of much oriental porcelain side by side with smooth painted inserts. Chinese blue and white decorations appear to be buried beneath a layer of glaze. Close observation of the original will be needed to suggest the means of imitation.

The paint is applied with a well loaded sable brush. If insufficient paint is used it will coagulate before the stroke is completed. A little experience will determine how much paint is needed on the brush to complete the stroke. When a very thin line is needed, lay the paint on as narrowly as possible. Then with a cleaned brush and a very little glaze medium wipe away the paint from each side of the line. Keep the brush clean by rinsing in thinners and wiping dry before dipping into a little more glaze medium to fine down still further. This method can be used for long lines or when doing small patterns. It will also trim up the edges of bands. It must be done swiftly and neatly as too much working over the surface will result in smears.

Until confidence has been acquired it is safest to stove after the completion of each colour. This way there is less chance of smudging the previous colour and, also, it will be easier to make a correction. If the stroke is misjudged do not attempt to wipe away with thinners, as this will dissolve the underpainting. Stove the china and when cold the error can be effaced safely with the glass fibre eraser.

Reproducing transfer printing

Originally transfer printing was done from engraved plates which used either lines or dots to form the pattern. This must be painted correctly if the replacement is not to look clumsy. Later techniques allowed solid blocks of colour to be applied. The lines or blocks of colour must be applied smoothly and thinly. Too great a thickness of paint will stand above the surface and catch the light, showing up badly. Lines can be thinned down if necessary but if they are lying close together this is not easy. A light touch and a brush which has a good point are usually enough. Where the shading is built up as a multitude of minute dots these must be replaced in the same fashion. Colour brushed on and left as a solid patch will not look right. Where the shading is sparse the tip of a brush can be used to dot the area. On larger areas a finger tip dipped into the paint, blotted on a rag or piece of paper and then pressed lightly onto the china gives a very good reproduction of stippling. A trial is necessary in order to convey just enough colour onto the china. Not everyone leaves the right kind of finger print; some are much coarser than others and a substitute is needed. A piece of abrasive paper or a coarse bristle brush may serve. Unfortunately cloth, which would give a good texture, also coats the paint with fluff.

For a large area of stippled background the most effective method of reproduction is to cover the whole area with paint and allow it to become tacky. Some of the paint is then removed leaving behind a speckled surface.

The removing is done with either a clean finger (if the finger prints are the right size) a stiff brush or the end grain of a piece of wood. In fact, anything clean and non-greasy which will produce the right size and degree of stippling. Judging the right moment to remove the paint is critical; the paint must come away cleanly leaving a definite impression. If it flows back into place it is too wet. Once it pulls up in strings it is too set. A small patch of paint should be applied to a spare piece of china as a testing ground, then the actual repair can be left undisturbed until the paint is at the right consistency. The paint will dry very quickly, so only small areas at a time should be prepared.

This method can be used for many different patterns. Sometimes designs are really a white silhouette on a stippled background, and the easiest way to copy this is to paint in the whole of

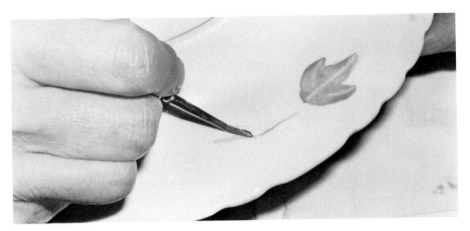

Fig. 118 Fining down a line with a brush and a small amount of glaze medium

Fig. 119 Reproducing stipple printing by applying the paint with a finger tip (*lower patch at right*). A flat coat of paint does not produce the right effect (*top patch*)

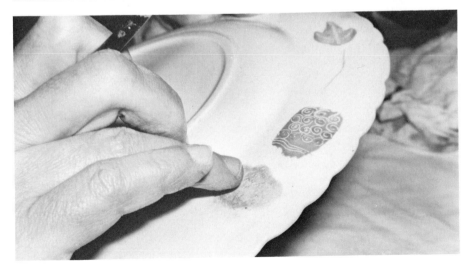

Fig. 120 Stippling paint onto the surface with a finger tip

123

Fig. 121 Leaf veins and lighter areas are imitated by removing paint from these areas while it is still wet

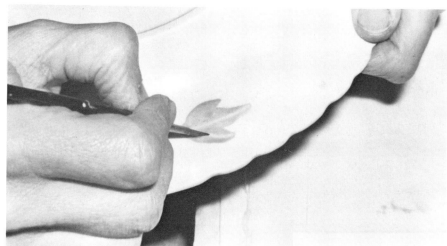

Fig. 122 Removing lighter areas of colour before the paint dries

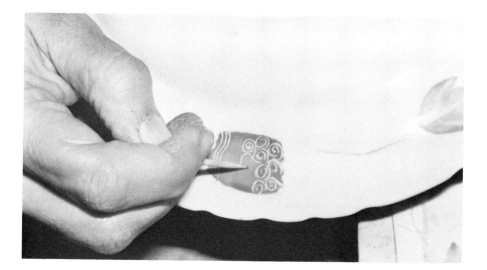

Fig. 123 Incising a pattern into tacky paint with a sharpened stick

the background and speckle it with the finger tip. Then remove the speckles covering the area which is to be white with a clean brush and glaze medium before the paint hardens. Work carefully, stroking and lifting the paint away; do not scrub at it. The pattern is usually completed with a thin outline of a darker shade which should be applied last.

Fine white lines and scrolls on a dark or strippled ground should be done by applying the ground first. When it has become tacky remove the lines with a sharpened orange stick. This is easier than painting the lines or trying to fill in the background around them. The same method can be used for spots or other small patterns. Never use thinner to remove portions of paint as it will remove too much.

In some early blue and white printing the cobalt oxide tended to run during firing. To simulate this marginal haze around the pattern a wash of pigment and glaze can be used. This can be applied smoothly either before or after the pattern is painted; the latter gives a mistier effect. In either case the paint must be stoved between the two applications. It should be paler than the decoration and if it appears rather bright it will need toning down with a little brown pigment. This coat of paint should be taken just beyond the edge of the pattern, but remember not to allow it to gather into a hard ridge at the edges. Stove the paint before completing the decoration.

Often the base coat under the decoration looks too light, although elsewhere the match is perfect. A wash of glaze medium mixed with the colours used in the base coats, omitting the white, should be applied over the decoration. This should be a very weak mix, barely coloured. Apply this wash lightly and smoothly; do not brush it out or the results will be streaky. Confine the area covered to the decoration; it should not show at the edges.

On early ironstone wares a transfer print was used to outline the pattern. This was applied first and oxide or enamel colours were then painted more or less within these borders by unskilled labour. To simulate this type of decoration the process must be reversed. Paint the colours first. The outline, which is mostly in brown, is applied round the edge once the colours have been stoved. When decorating in several colours complete one at a time. Work across the repair, completing each detail in order, as it is exasperating to complete the last colour only to find one small detail missing from the first colour.

Enamel painting, e.g. flowers and landscapes
The method of reproducing this naturalistic style of painting on china is nearer to applying water colours than to oil painting. A magnifying glass will be needed to show just how the enamel colours were applied originally. The paint must lie flat on the surface and sometimes the brush strokes will show. Paint must not build up in pools on the surface. A drop or two of thinners will be needed in the paint mixture to make working with it easier. When shading is to be done it is simplest to make the paint mixture to match the darkest area and add a little clear glaze for the lighter tints. Very often the shading can be done by applying the paint and removing it from the lighter areas with a clean brush and a very little glaze. Alternatively the area can be coated in clear glaze. The colour mixed with glaze is then introduced and allowed to flow where it is needed. It must be stressed that the pigment must be completely incorporated in the glaze medium. A very good imitation of china painting can be achieved with oil paint alone but without the glaze as a binder it cannot hold to the china.

Study will reveal a very limited range of colours on any one piece of china. Variation relied on shading a colour from light to dark and superimposing one colour upon another to make a third. It is a mistake to introduce too many colours in an attempt to match.

Raised enamel colours
When transparent, glass-like colours are called for they should be mixed without white so that the undercoat will glow through them. Apply the pigment and glaze medium in a pool, not enough to run out of place but so that it remains above the level of the surface. If greater height is needed, stove the paint and apply a second coat immediately over it. For Worcester-type jewel decoration this system can be used, but the paint must be built up layer by layer, stoving in between. Do not allow it to spread out.

Oriental enamel decoration, particularly Canton porcelain, frequently requires a small quantity of white in the mixture. Apply the paint liberally, so that it remains as beads on the surface. A drop of darker paint is frequently necessary at the highest point of the enamel. It is better to apply the paint in two coats if the enamel is very thick. Too much applied at one time will spread beyond its allotted space. Always examine the original work carefully to see just how it was

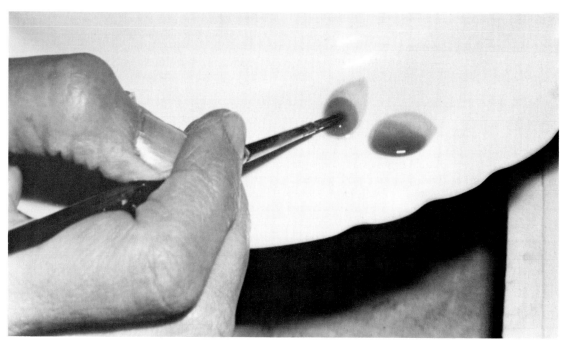

Fig. 124 Successive layers of paint can be built up to reproduce oriental-type decoration

done. A little experiment and practice before beginning can save a lot of time in the long run.

Thick coloured glazes
The glaze decoration found on stone ware, particularly the type used on studio pottery of the late nineteenth century, needs several mixes of paint. It is not enough to take a brush full of pigment and mix it on the china. Several mixes of different colours and glaze medium must be made separately and then laid on the surface, floating them into one another. This must be done in an orderly way, maintaining the continuity of the colour patterns in the surrounding glaze. The glaze must not be allowed to fill in the depressions or the shape will be lost. There is no need to apply and stove each colour individually in this instance.

Using an airbrush for decorating

An airbrush has limited use for decorating because its main value is in the application of areas of paint with no visible edge. It can be used to advantage when a broad area of colour is needed, e.g. for a background on transfer printed ware and for objects with a deep band of colour. A

mask will be needed to confine the spray to the limits of the decoration. It is also a great advantage to use an airbrush for spraying a fine haze of colour.

Spraying background colours for transfer prints
The area to be sprayed must be surrounded by a mask sufficiently wide to take all the overspray. Masking fluid is the most convenient method of screening when dealing with decoration. It is applied evenly with a well-pointed brush to surround the area being sprayed. If the design has any unpainted areas within these limits, these too can be masked. This will save removing the paint with glaze medium after the background is applied. The rubbery nature of masking fluid makes it difficult to apply in fine lines, but it is very useful for small dots and similar patterns. Allow the masking fluid to dry completely before spraying or the force of the air will blow it out of position. The matching paint is sprayed in a series of parallel strokes, each one slightly overlapping the previous one. If the colour needs deepening, go over the area again in the same direction. Strokes sprayed at right angles will give a chequered finish. Care must be taken when spraying that the paint does not build up in a ridge against the edge of the mask. To avoid this happening decrease the air flow as the mask is approached. Paint which is sprayed on dries

much quicker than it does when hand painted, therefore any removal of paint, whether by fingertip or with a brush and glaze, must be done quickly. For fine lines remove the nearly dry paint with a sharpened orange stick. Remove the mask when the paint has dried but before stoving.

Banding

The airbrush can be used to put on bands of most enamel colours. It is necessary to test first that the join between paint and enamel can be made invisible. The spray is very fine at the edges, which slightly alters the depth of colour. This is particularly noticeable on dark colours, where it appears as a grey film. Rubbing down or polishing the film merely makes it into a hard edge.

Graduated colour

The airbrush is indispensable for applying a shaded background, particularly if it gradually changes colour as well as density. This distinctive effect is almost impossible to imitate by hand.

The graduated background should be made with a series of parallel strokes. Starting with the lightest area the pressure on the control lever is increased at each stroke, which releases more paint and darkens the colour with each pass of the airbrush. It requires practice to control the air/paint flow lever precisely. If the finger pressure on the control is uneven the result will be stripey. For a very small area it may be easier to start where the colour is most intense and add a little glaze medium to the colour cup at the commencement of each stroke, although this does not give such an even graduation of colour, nor is it possible to go over the area again once the colour is diluted with glaze. Both the techniques need to be repeated many times before the right finger pressure is found instinctively.

If the shading is from one colour to another a separate mixture of both colours will be needed. The colours can be superimposed one layer over the other, or the colour can be changed in the colour cup as the spraying progresses. Each method will give a slightly different finish.

Spatter effect

This can be put on with an airbrush. The method of achieving this differs with the make of airbrush; either a special cap is attached or a simple adjustment interrupts the airflow and causes the paint to spatter.

Lowering the air pressure supplied by the compressor also induces spluttering and produces uneven droplets of paint. Although this is useful for some effects a random splashing of paint is of little use normally. The size and shape of the original spattering must be matched exactly. The paint flow must be regulated manually to match the volume of air and control the emission of the appropriate size of droplets, and this is not particularly easy.

Using artists' dry ground colours

A very delicate degree of shading can be obtained with artists' dry ground colours. These colours are finely powdered, pure pigments without the addition of oil or other fixatives. They are used over the usual two base coats which are colour matched to the body of the china. The surface for shading must be carefully prepared and rubbed down to a satin smooth finish because the fine particles of colour will cling to any roughness or scratches and make a very blotchy surface.

The pigments tend to settle in store and need grinding until smooth before use. Place a small quantity of pigment on a card and grind until smooth with a palette knife. Two or more colours can be ground together to obtain a perfect match. As the colours are ground they are spread out over the surface of the card, which enables minute quantities to be taken up.

For shading, the area is painted with a thin, even film of clear glaze medium. This is allowed to become almost dry. Judging the right moment is critical; the length of time required will depend on the temperature of the work room. When touched the glaze must just pull the skin. Use a knuckle to do the testing; it is more sensitive than a finger tip. It is advisable to apply a separate patch of glaze on which to do the testing so there will be no need to touch the actual work prematurely. Once the glaze is sufficiently set, the ground pigment is taken up on a clean, dry finger tip which is then dabbed lightly onto the glaze. This dabbing is repeated as often as necessary, applying extra pigment where the shading is heaviest. The powdered colour is left as a fine film embedded in the surface of the glaze. When the glaze is too dry to hold more colour it is stoved. The process can be repeated if necessary over part or all of the area until the right degree of intensity and shading is reached. The glaze soon becomes too dry to use in this way so all colours must be ground in advance and used swiftly.

Fig. 125 Grinding artists' dry ground colours with a palette knife

This is an excellent way of colouring flowers and leaves on figure groups, the small areas to be shaded lending themselves well to this method. Two colours may be used side by side; for example, a blue-green and a yellow-green on leaves. The blending of the colours in this way is softer than when applied as a wash.

Decorating figure groups

When imitating the skin tones on a figure the usual two base coats must be applied first. This will give a reflective backing for a transparent wash. Applied in this way the flesh tones will have depth and warmth which is lacking if the base coats are flesh coloured. A mixture of red and white alone gives a pink shade which is more suitable as a colouring for confectionery than figures. Experiments can start with Burnt Sienna, making small additions of yellow or red until a

perfect match is obtained. Male figures are usually a little deeper in skin tone than their female companions, and sometimes the addition of a little brown is needed for them. Many figures, both male and female, have a warmer accent, sometimes barely discernible, on the shoulders, elbows, wrists, knuckles and on the legs at knees, ankles and toes. Close inspection with a magnifying lens will show that the colour is in minute specks. An even wash of colours appears hard and unnatural, and fading it away at the edges is very difficult. Shading with dry ground colours solves the problem easily. Apply glaze medium thinly wherever the blush is needed, usually at the base of the neck and on the boney areas of the limbs. Allow the glaze almost to dry and then apply the well ground pigment. (See the preceding section on using artists' dry ground colours.) Use the pigments sparingly; it is easier to add more colour than to take any off. When sufficient blushing has been added stove the china in the usual way.

When a head is being replaced it is indispensable to have a clear illustration or model to study. Faces are very difficult to paint without giving them a made-up or cosmetic look. The eyes particularly must be closely observed. Various ways of indicating eyelids, with lines and small corner dots, have been used in the past. It is necessary to apply the paint in the same style. Eyebrows can be painted either as a single brush stroke or several short, fine lines. Noses must not be over-emphasised and lips should not be too bright; the red is usually toned down a little with brown or yellow, not white. Cheeks can be made to blush by applying dry ground colours. The surface of the face must be particularly carefully prepared and the glaze must be very evenly applied, otherwise the blush will turn into an unfortunate rash. Do not obscure the modelling by allowing the paint to fill in the depressions. Keep the colouring of features light or the effect will be too theatrical. Use Paynes Grey instead of black and always modify red before using it on cheeks and lips.

Note how the hair was painted. This can be done in one of several ways. The whole of the hair area can be coloured and while the paint is still wet fine lines can be drawn through it with a sharpened orange stick. This removes the colour in very fine lines, revealing the base coat. It must be done when the paint has set sufficiently to hold the lines but before it is so tacky that it pulls away in strings. Another method frequently encountered can be copied by painting fine dark lines over a lighter coat of paint. Where hair is more than one shade several mixtures are made and mingled on the head. Usually the lighter colours are used as highlights on curls and the darker shades placed in the hollows. Sometimes it is enough to use one shade of paint, applying it a little more thinly over the highlights and allowing the base coat to shine through.

Clothing and drapery must have the correct basecoats applied first. Any colour can then be added as a transparent coat over this foundation. The original enamels generally drained into the depressions and left the projections with less paint, forming a natural shading. As pigment and glaze also tend to do this the effect can be exploited, provided it is not done to excess so that it submerges the modelling. Stove and cool the figures before adding any decorative sprigs or details. The little motifs must be confined to their proper spacing and not used to conceal a fault.

If it is not desirable to use dry ground colours for shading petals and leaves; they can be painted with a wash of pigment and glaze. Veins should be added after the leaves have been stoved, then they can be fined down safely with glaze.

Baskets of fruit, guns, sticks and musical instruments are painted with pigment and glaze in the normal way. Never be tempted to take a touch of pigment and a dip of glaze on a brush and apply them. Always mix pigment thoroughly with sufficient glaze, even for just one grape.

Faults in decorating

If the paint runs on the surface it is likely that the mixture contains too much thinners. Only one or two drops should be added to a mix, just sufficient to thin the paint and make it workable. Wait a short while until the thinners evaporates a little and try again.

When the decoration will not stick to the undercoat the surface must be greasy. Clean it gently with methylated spirit. Make sure the brush is clean and has not been used for other materials. Never use more barrier cream than the skin can absorb or it will be transferred to the china and act as a barrier to the paint.

If fining down lines results in the whole thing being washed away check that glaze, not thinners, is being used.

When the decoration looks too well defined and too new, a coat of glaze mixed with a small quantity of the colours used in the basecoats can be applied over the top. If this is insufficient the decoration must be redone using a darker tone of paint.

Should the decoration appear bumpy and the line shakey, the cause could be an uneven painting surface. The solution is to rub down to make a perfectly smooth, flat surface. The decoration will have to be redone.

If a lot of close packed bubbles appear in grooves and depressions they are most likely to be caused by dust. Always brush or blow away the particles of paint after rubbing down basecoats.

If dry ground colours cling where they are not intended to be, the surface is either greasy or sticky. Stove the china and when it is cold wipe gently with methylated spirit. If this does not remove the unwanted smears they must be rubbed away with the glass fibre eraser.

No rubbing down is necessary after applying the decoration and the article is now ready for the next stage.

8 · Gilding

An elderly gilder, on being approached to take an apprentice, replied that he had insufficient time left to undertake the training as it took 25 years. This means that the china restorer has yet another exacting craft to learn. Another gilders' maxim is that the gilding is only as good as the surface it is applied to. This is certainly very true. Unless the restored surface is perfect the gold will show up every defect. Unfortunately the join between the old gilding and the new is very difficult to disguise. As compensation the addition of the gold decoration does give the final finish to china and seems to unite the whole of the decoration. Nothing revives china quite as well as a band of shining gold, but the temptation to rejuvenate antique china in this way must be resisted. Never put back worn gold, replace it only on the area of the repair. Even then, do not be lavish with it.

Materials and tools

Extra fine burnishing bronze; this is a very finely ground imitation gold powder

Copper powder; for repainting copper decoration

Aluminium powder; for repainting silver decoration

Transfer gold leaf; genuine gold supplied in thin sheets on tissue paper backing

Platinum leaf; tissue backed sheets of platinum

Synthetic glaze medium (Chintex); for binding bronze powder and leaf to china

Thinners (Chintex or Joy); for cleaning brushes

Brushes; sable brushes for applying vronze powder

Transparent plastic film (Librafilm) or thick polythene; used when burnishing

Agate burnisher or hockey-stick-shaped modelling tool

Scalpel, scissors; for cutting gold leaf

Cotton wool; used for swabs

Stoving equipment; for curing the synthetic glaze

Extra fine burnishing bronze is a gold coloured powder made from a mixture of metals. It is made in a selection of shades from pale lemon gold to deep red gold which can be intermixed to give a complete range of shades. It will tarnish if exposed to the air over a long period and should be stored in a well sealed container. The metal powders are used with glaze medium as a binder. The gilding is always protected with a coat of glaze medium which will prevent it tarnishing on the repair. Copper and aluminium powder is also available for simulating these metallic colours. Unfortunately the aluminium has a rather dull, almost galvanised, look. It is essential to get a superfine or extra fine grade of powder from a specialist supplier. The normal gold powder obtainable from art and do-it-yourself shops is too coarse and will never imitate the gilding on china satisfactorily. The ready made gilding preparations which are a mixture of bronze powder with wax and rosin are not compatible with glaze medium. They will tarnish quickly when left unprotected.

Pure gold is also available as a powder and can be used in the same way as bronze powder. It is only available in one shade, which limits the occasions when it can be used. It is expensive and is sold by half-pennyweight. Silver powder tarnishes too quickly to be practical.

Gold leaf is put up in various ways for different trades. Some is supplied on a transparent backing tape which is intended for application by hot irons, some as loose sheets which can be crumpled by a breath and need a great deal of skill in their application. The gold for transfer gold leaf is beaten into extremely fine leaves 0.0001 cm (0.000005 in) thick and mounted on sheets of tissue paper, which makes handling easier. It is supplied in books of 25 leaves. Gold leaf comes in six shades but it is not sold in a book of mixed shades. The six shades cannot be intermixed in any way, so the nearest match has to be used. Platinum leaf is used in place of silver as the latter tarnishes.

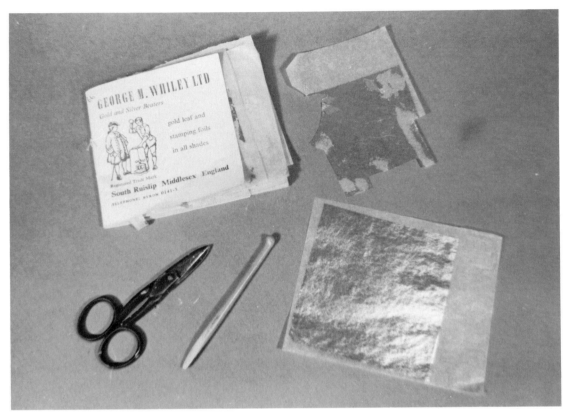

Fig. 126 Gold leaf

Synthetic glaze medium is needed to hold both bronze powders and gold leaf in place; without it the gold would not bind to the china. Thinners is necessary to make the glaze mixture workable when powder and glaze are used together and for cleaning brushes.

A separate set of brushes is needed for applying bronze powders. The fine grains of metal are difficult to remove with certainty from the base of the bristles. Some usually remain even after careful cleaning and are released when the brush is next used; if the brushes are kept only for gilding this is not detrimental, but it would be if the brush was subsequently used for a coat of white paint. The usual sable liners and writers are most useful. The liners are used for thin lines and small patterns, and the chisel ended writers are used for broad strokes and banding. A larger brush with soft hair will also be needed for applying gold powder by Method Two, described later. This can be made of ox hair or a mixture of ox and sable and should be about 1 cm ($\frac{1}{2}$ in) wide.

Transparent film is used to protect gold leaf when burnishing it. Provided it remains clean and unscratched it is reusable. Non-adhesive film used to protect books is excellent, or heavy duty polythene can be used. As the latter is more flexible it is particularly useful on an uneven or curved surface.

For burnishing, either a small agate burnisher made especially for gilding or a very smooth hockey-stick-shaped modelling tool can be used. If a modelling tool is used it must be kept solely for this purpose. It must be smooth and polished.

Scalpels and scissors must be very sharp or the fragile gold leaf will be torn and damaged.

Cotton wool will be needed for swabs.

There are no special hazards in using gilding materials. The precautions that were taken when painting apply here also.

Using bronze powder and gold leaf

The first essential, which is equally applicable to all methods of gilding, is to have a perfect surface to work on. The larger the area to be gilded the better it must be. The gilding is also going to be the least robust of all the decorations and must be treated carefully until the final protective coat of glaze has been cured. It may be difficult to decide whether bronze powder or gold leaf should be used. The china must be carefully examined to determine which method should be used. Where the decoration has obviously been brushed on around the base of rococo figures, in titles on Staffordshire figures or in tiny trails or sprigs of gold, then the choice should be to paint on bronze powder. For rich borders around good quality plates, or for bands on the plinths of vases or urns, the decision must be for gold leaf. The owner of the china should also be consulted. Apart from the cost of materials the extra time taken to apply gold leaf will add to the final cost.

Techniques

Marking out the pattern

Any guidelines or tracings for the patterns and banding should be put in with an H or HH pencil in the same way as for colour decorating. The bronze powder or gold leaf is quite opaque and there is no risk of the lines showing through, but they must be kept within the pattern area.

Using bronze powder

There is a choice of two methods for applying bronze powder. The first, which is the easier, is suitable for all types of decoration. Fine lines, small patterns or broad bands can all be done equally well.

The second method gives a superior finish on larger areas. Its successful application depends entirely on the perfection of the surface to which it is applied. One scratch or pinhole in the adjoining area will trap the powder where it is not wanted. It is not suitable for use on small patterns.

There is no reason why the two methods should not be combined if the decoration contains both small patterns and broad bands. The china must be stoved in between each application to set the glaze medium.

Method One. In this method the powder and glaze is mixed and used as a paint. The bronze powder relies for its brilliance on light being reflected back from its surface. Each grain is a minute disc or plate, not a sphere. If only a little powder is used in the mixture it is very dull, in fact it may even look dirty yellow and not metallic. For a rich gold, use only one or two drops of glaze,

adding as much bronze powder as it will hold and make the mixture workable with several drops of thinners. If a large amount of glaze were to be used it would require a great deal of powder, probably many spoonfuls to get a golden effect. As the proportion of powder to glaze medium is high the bonding properties of the gold paint will not be strong. Therefore care must be taken not to damage the gilding until a final glaze protects it. The bronze grains are heavy and tend to sink to the bottom of the mixture, so it must be stirred constantly while working to ensure even distribution.

The mixture will dry out quickly but it is possible to add another drop of thinners. This will keep it usable for a short time. It must be borne in mind that every addition of thinners will weaken the bonding strength of the mixture. The nearest shade of bronze should be selected to start the mix and additions of the appropriate brighter or darker powder made until a match is obtained. Stir each addition thoroughly or the result will be streaky. When the match is exact add the thinners. Do not add it at the beginning or it will evaporate by the time the mixture is needed.

The bronze paint can now be brushed on where-ever required. A loaded brush must be used or the paint will be too dry to take to the surface of the repair. The tip of the brush is used to draw fine lines, barely touching the surface of the china. It is not possible to thin the lines down with glaze medium when using metallic powders; brushing away with glaze causes a grey, smeary edge. Broader strokes with a flat, chisel tipped brush are used to fill in bands. The point where the old and new gilt meet must be disguised as much as possible either using the spring of the bristles to feather away the end of each stroke or by using a little clear glaze medium to soften away the edge into the adjoining gold. If the original gilding is worn the bronze is put on sparingly and toned down with a little glaze medium. If this proves insufficient it can be rubbed down after stoving using the glass fibre eraser. Always observe where the gilding is worn away. It will have disappeared on the high spots of fluting or rims and still be left in the hollows. On cups it will be worn where the fingers grasp the handle and where the mouth touches the rim. Do not just add dabs of gold without due consideration; they must be applied in the logical positions. When the gilt decoration is completed the china is stoved as usual.

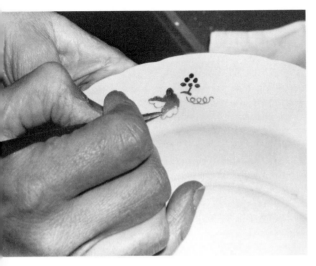

Method Two. This method gives a very good representation of good quality gilding, for example, on the handles and interiors of Royal Worcester porcelain. The glaze medium is applied to the repair wherever gold decoration is required and the dry bronze is powdered over the tacky glaze. Any surplus powder is then removed. This seems very straightforward but if there is the slightest roughness, scratch, grease or glaze in the wrong place the powder will cling to it. It is impossible to remove the powder, which looks like grey smears, without damaging the rest of the work. The powder has to be applied immediately the glaze is in the right state, so the bronze must be prepared and matched beforehand. The powder is mixed dry in a dipper to an exact match. Take up the bronze powders with a clean palette knife and mix with a dry brush. Once the correct shade is found the glaze can be applied to the china.

In order to see where the glaze medium is being laid a little oil colour should be added to it. It is best to use a little Raw Umber to colour the glaze as this will be unobtrusive in any worn areas where it may be necessary to rub down the gilt a little. The colour should not be deep, just enough pigment to show up the brush strokes against the background. Apply the glaze medium fairly thinly and very evenly. If it is too thick it will stand too high on the surface and show up as a lump. Any ridges or grooves will catch the light and show up alarmingly. If any glaze is put on the wrong place the china must be stoved to set the glaze medium. The glaze cannot be wiped away and left unstoved as it will leave a sticky smear which will hold the bronze powder. The pattern can then be put on correctly and the glaze left to become almost dry. To reiterate, when the drying glaze is tested with a knuckle it should be just tacky enough to pull at the skin, not stick to it. Do not carry out this test on the area being repaired as it is vital that the surface to be gilded is not marred by a skin print. Apply a little glaze elsewhere to use to test the state of tackiness.

Charge the large ox hair brush with plenty of bronze powder and dust it very lightly over the

Fig. 127 Using bronze powder mixed with glaze medium. Practice is needed in all the gilding methods before using them on restorations

Fig. 128 Dusting bronze powder over the surface of tacky glaze

Fig. 129 Washing away the superfluous bronze powder

surface once the glaze has reached the right condition, completely covering the glaze with a layer of powder. Allow it to settle. The glaze dries very quickly trapping the grains of bronze in the surface. Gently blow the surplus powder onto a sheet of paper for re-use. At this stage the work will look completely ruined, with gold obscuring everything. Gently swab away the excess powder with cotton wool and cold water. This can be done under a gently running tap or into a bowl with plenty of water. Allow the water to flush away the powder, do not rub it with the cotton wool. The loose grains of bronze will float off in the water leaving behind a perfect coat of gold embedded in the glaze. The swabbing must be done until all the loose powder has been removed. If this is well done on a perfect surface it is an exciting and spectacular operation. If the coverage is insufficient, stove the china and repeat the process. Should the gold need wearing away a little, this can be done with the glass fibre eraser.

Using gold leaf

There is very little to choose between the methods of applying gold leaf either in ease of application or in finished appearance. The restorer is advised to try out both methods. Then, in the light of experience, the most suitable method for the job in hand can be adopted. Both methods rely on the principle of using synthetic glaze medium to hold the gold leaf in place. Gold leaf is always handled by the tissue border. The surface of the gold should not be touched because the finger prints will hinder its adhesion to the china.

Method One. The gold leaf is prepared first. The outlines of the gold shapes wanted are traced onto the tissue backing of the gold leaf. This must be done very lightly or the gold on the reverse will be damaged. A well sharpened soft B pencil can be used for the tracing. The graphite will not come into contact with the glaze medium so there is no risk of smudging. Cut the gold leaf into the exact shapes of the gold decoration required; this must be done very exactly. It will require a razor, sharp scalpel or fine, sharp scissors so that a good clean edge to the gold is obtained. Put the prepared shapes under a small sheet of glass or between two pieces of card. They are so light that they will blow away with the slightest breath. Before the glaze is applied mark the positions that the gold shapes are to occupy on the repair. They should be marked in very lightly with a hard pencil.

Ideally use a faint dot just to indicate the position.

Apply clear glaze thinly and evenly over the surface to be gilded. It need not be confined to the exact areas of the patterns, at the same time there is no point in being too liberal. Wait until the glaze has become almost dry, at the same stage of setting as when applying both dry pigments and bronze powder by Method Two. Place the prepared gold leaf cutouts in their appropriate positions. If they are small it may be necessary to lift and place them with forceps. There is no second chance, because once the gold leaf touches the tacky glaze it will stick. If the placing is incorrect the remedy is to stove the china and remove the gold leaf with a glass fibre eraser. With the tissue backing still in place, use the burnisher to lightly stroke and smooth the gold onto the glaze. Carefully remove the tissue backing, lifting one edge with the scalpel and gently peeling away. It will almost fall off once the gold is attached to the repair. If the gold has only partially taken to the glaze medium and patches of gold remain on the tissue replace the tissue carefully, repeating the smoothing with the burnisher. Unless the glaze is too dry to act as an adhesive the gold will be firmly attached to the china. Should the pattern still be insufficiently covered in gold leaf, stove the china and repeat the whole process. When the gold coating is satisfactory, stove the china as usual to set the glaze. When cold the gold can be burnished. This will settle the gold smoothly in place. Cover the gold with a small piece of transparent film and rub evenly and lightly over its surface with a burnisher. Do not press too hard or the gold will be marked; the action should be one of flattening and polishing.

Method Two. Any guidelines or outlining of the pattern that is required must be put on the china first using a hard pencil. The gold leaf must be cut into suitable size strips in readiness for placing on the tacky glaze. They can be cut without detail and a little larger than needed to cover the final shapes required. Keep them carefully, as previously, while the surface is prepared. Glaze medium is now applied strictly within the boundaries of the design. A little artists' oil colour is added to the glaze medium – just enough to tint

Fig. 130 Preparing to lay gold leaf. Applying a glaze medium foundation

Fig. 131 A strip of gold leaf is laid on the tacky surface

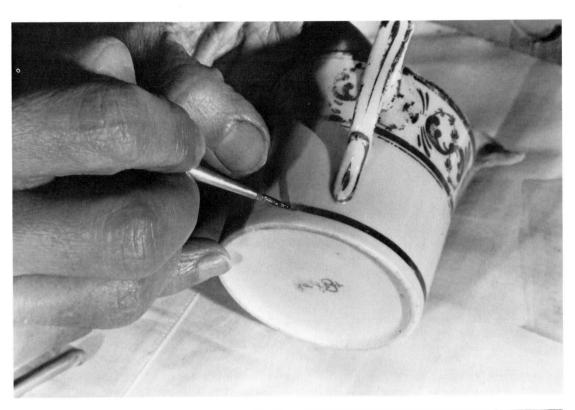

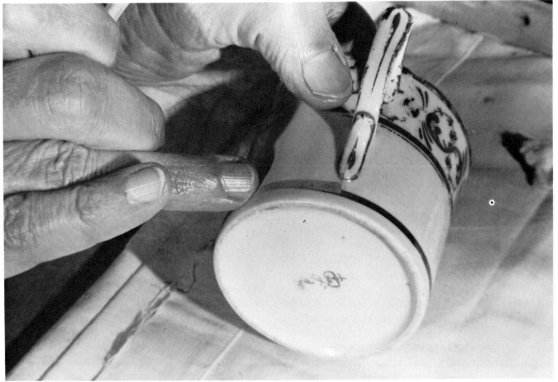

Fig. 132 Peeling away the tissue backing from gold leaf

Fig. 133 Burnishing gold leaf. Use a transparent film under the burnishing tool

it sufficiently to show up against the background – otherwise it is difficult to see where the glaze has been applied. Apply the mixture thinly and evenly. If the glaze is applied anywhere in error the china must first be stoved to harden the glaze, after which the mistake can be erased with flour glasspaper. A fresh coat of coloured glaze can then be correctly applied. Do not attempt to wipe away the error without stoving; wherever the surface is tacky the gold leaf will stick.

Allow the glaze to become tacky and press the strips over it, overlapping if the area is large. Press lightly but firmly with the finger, making sure all the gold leaf adheres to the prepared areas. Once the gold has stuck to the glaze the tissue backing will lift off freely. Stove the china at the usual temperature. When the china is cold, brush away any surplus gold leaf surrounding the shapes with a sable brush. If necessary the edges can be tidied up with the aid of an orange stick. Cut the orange stick to a chisel point and rub it until very smooth on flour glass paper. Use it to gently ease away any loose flakes of gold. Place transparent film over the gold and smooth with the burnishing tool. It must be done gently and will flatten and polish the metal. If the original gold is worn on the edges or raised areas the gold can be abraded a little with the glass fibre eraser.

With some very worn gilding, all that remains is the stain left by the flux used to apply the original gold. Do not attempt to replace any of the gold. Use Raw Umber mixed with glaze medium to touch in the missing areas.

Silver can be replaced with either aluminium powder used exactly as for bronze powder or platinum leaf applied in the same way as gold leaf. When only a little dull silver is needed Paynes Grey and glaze medium will serve very well without using any metal powder or leaf.

The gilding is now ready to be protected by a final coat of glaze.

Copper lustre

Very few attempts at restoring lustre ware are an unqualified success. The original china has a reflective mirror surface which is impossible to replace. On very small areas the second method of applying the bronze as a dry powder will give a mend which is not too noticeable. It may be better to concede that nothing gives a truly reflective copper or gold mirror finish and just make a very

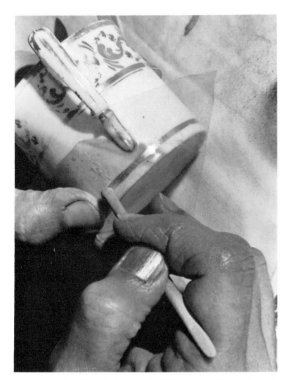

neat repair. The joins and fillings can be painted to match the colour as nearly as possible. Burnt Sienna or Raw Sienna modified to tone with the copper or gold and neatly applied will be less conspicuous than a patch of dull fuzzy gold.

Pink lustre

This can be repainted quite well. The main colouring, which is a mauve-pink, is added as a straightforward wash. Use glaze medium and the appropriate oil colours thoroughly mixed and apply to the surface, maintaining the continuity of the pattern. A little gold or copper powder, whichever is the closer match, is then added very sparingly. Use it either mixed with clear glaze medium as an additional coat of paint or dusted onto the pink coloured glaze medium while it is still slightly tacky. Very little metal powder is needed to reproduce the effect.

As isolated grains of powder tend to look like black specks, check it from all viewpoints to make sure the angle of the light does not alter the metallic effect. It is possible to obtain purple tinted metallic powders, but the colour soon fades to leave coarse grained, dirty gold specks.

Although an airbrush can spray an excellent coat of gold over a large area it is rarely useful in the small areas of repair on china. The overspray at the edge is very noticeable and when masking is used to prevent this the join is most pronounced. If the airbrush is used to apply a coat of glaze as a base for dry powder the texture effect of the atomised droplets will be apparent through the gold. The metallic grains will clog an airbrush very quickly. It would be wise to keep a second airbrush if one is required to be used frequently in this way. Cleaning is very difficult and small particles of bronze tend to appear in subsequent applications.

Faults in gilding

When bronze powder does not look smooth, either the wrong quality of powder has been used or insufficient thinners was added to the mixture.

If the bronze powder looks dull and leaden then too great a proportion of glaze to powder was used in the mixture.

If the bronze powder does not stick to the glaze it indicates that the glaze had become too dry before applying the powder. Do not attempt to patch up an area of bronze powder or the result will be lumpy. Stove the china first and then reapply the glaze; while it is slightly tacky brush on the powder.

If the gilt has a wrinkled appearance too much glaze was applied to the repair prior to dusting with bronze powder.

When dirty, indistinct marks appear on the surface after using the dry powder method of application, it indicates that the surface was either rough, greasy or sticky. To remedy this the china must be stoved, the surface cleaned with abrasives and a fresh start made. It may even be necessary to repaint the last base coat.

If the gold leaf does not remain on the china and will not come away cleanly from the tissue backing, the coat of glaze is too dry. Stove the china and re-apply both glaze and gold leaf.

When the surface of the gold leaf is irregular and lined, either the burnisher is not smooth enough or the transparent film is too thin or scarred. Alternatively, too much pressure is being used with the burnisher.

Because comparatively little glaze is in contact with the bronze powder or gold leaf it is not as tough as other decorations. Care must be taken not to rub or knock the gold before the final glaze is on and protecting it.

137

9 ⁖ Surface Finishes

There are wide differences in the surfaces of ceramic objects. They range from the shiniest glaze to a matt, almost gritty, texture. The degree of gloss frequently changes on the same item. Oxides used in colouring the original decoration affect the covering glaze, leaving dull patches or minute bubbles. The surface can be covered in fine cracks, sometimes deliberately induced, sometimes an unavoidable consequence of glaze reaction during firing. Foot rims are usually matt as the glaze was removed to prevent the object sticking to the kiln shelf during firing. Some glazes are applied thickly and have a deep, glass-like appearance, others crack or craze in the stress of firing. Stoneware frequently has no applied glaze, the clay itself firing to a vitreous, semi-shiny finish. Worcester animal and bird porcelains are frequently sculpted with a rough texture to give the illusion of fur or feathers. Wedgwood and their imitators manufactured jasper ware, which is a high fired stoneware with a matt surface available in several colours. Minton, Spode and their competitors imitated marble with Parian and Carrara wares. A matt white unglazed or bisque ware was manufactured for many years and reached its height of popularity in Victorian and Edwardian figure groups.

All these types of surface must be reproduced if the repair is not to look out of place. Occasionally it will be necessary to use a cold setting glaze medium if the ability of the china to withstand stoving is in doubt. Never glaze over the entire article to disguise the difference in texture between the original china and the replacement. The interest and value of the piece lies in the texture of the china, not the modern synthetic resin.

Materials and tools

Synthetic glaze (Chintex); for glazing and binding pigments to the china
Thinners (Chintex, Joy)
Broad sable brush; for applying glaze
Polymer drawing leads (Faber-Castell); used when reproducing crazing
Lead holder (Faber-Castell)
Steatite or magnesium silicate; matting agent
Cold setting glaze medium (Propol)
Dilutant for cold setting glaze medium
Artists' dry ground pigments, matting agents and colourants
Abrasive powder (Vim, pumice); used to tone down a glaze
Scalpels, cotton swabs etc.; as used previously

The repairs on a glazed object need a final coat of synthetic glaze both for the protection of the painting under it and to simulate the original surface. The usual resin glaze is used undiluted for this.

Thinners will be required for cleaning brushes.

A good quality, broad sable brush is required for applying the glaze. It must be kept for this purpose only. If it is used for painting there will be a risk of sullying the glaze with deposits left in the brush from pigments. The efficient application of a glossy coat of glaze is most important. It has to be smooth and shiny with no imperfections to mar the surface. The better the quality of the brush, the more easily good results will be achieved. Glaze should never be applied by airbrush. It will give a sandy or pebbled surfce, not at all like a smooth china glaze. A halo or dull rim will surround the sprayed area, making a most obvious change in texture. If this overspray is rubbed or polished away a hard edge will develop.

Drawing leads can be obtained in a range of colours to match the greys or browns in crazing. Leads in which the pigment is bonded in polymer, not wax, should be used, as it is possible to keep them needle sharp for drawing fine lines. They are

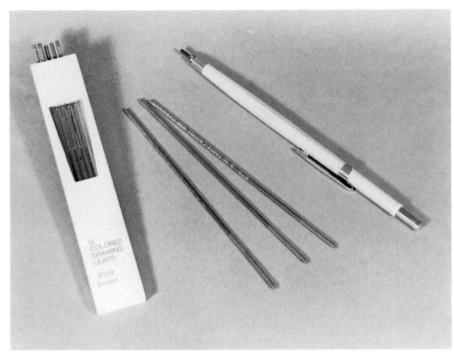

Fig. 134 Drawing leads and clutch holder

very strong and will not crumble or smear in use. The long, thin leads are used in a clutch pencil holder which has a special sharpener incorporated. Wax crayons should not be used; apart from the fact that they crumble and smear, glaze will not hold firmly on a wax surface.

Steatite or magnesium silicate, frequently listed as talc, is used as a matting agent for synthetic resin. (This should not be confused with bath dusting powder which is also known as talcum powder. It is a varying mixture of starch, boracic acid and zinc, and contains very little talc.)

A cold setting glaze must be used if there is a risk of stoving discolouring or harming china. This finish is neither as hard or durable as heat cured resins. China restored in this way must be washed with care and guarded against scratching. The cold setting resin is supplied as two separate liquids; a resin and a hardener. Once these are mixed setting takes place gradually over a period of 24 hours. It must be used with its particular dilutant and brush cleaner. Separate brushes should be kept for use with cold setting resin glaze medium.

Artists' dry ground pigments, in the same colours as required for decorating, are used when matching some matt surfaces. These give a different texture from steatite, so both methods should be tried and recorded for future reference.

Abrasive powder, either fine pumice or a dry domestic abrasive powder, can be used to subdue a glaze slightly. A paste or liquid metal polish should not be used as it will run into any cracks or crazing on the china; this leaves a residue which is particularly noticeable on dark china or over decoration. It will also harm any gold decoration with which it comes into contact, as it is slightly abrasive and will rub gold off instantly.

The usual selection of cutting tools, brushes, cotton wool, should be available.

Once again, it is necessary to practise the methods described to acquire ability in their application. Experiments will also provide a valuable record to indicate the best method to employ without making fresh trials each time.

Crazing

This is applied when all the decoration is completed immediately prior to the final coat of glaze. The cracks which form the crazing are in the glaze and will run across any decorative design, following a definite pattern which depends on the structure of the original glaze. The nature of the fractures, which are in the glaze only, must be studied when considering the method of reproducing them. They can be classified as:

a reticulation so close and stained that it shows
  more as patches of stain than separate cracks;
a coarse network of cracks which form either
  regular, brick-like patterns or irregular angular
  shapes;
long striations usually following the circumference of the china.

For reproducing very fine reticulation, painting
each hair line would be impractical and the
finished appearance would be clumsy. The
solution here is to apply a light coat of glaze
coloured to blend with the staining. Add a small
amount of the appropriate colour to the glaze
medium and mix thoroughly. For the best results
an airbrush should be used. Keep the colour weak
and spray on, graduating the intensity of the
colour to follow the original staining. Stove as
usual and when cold apply the final protective
coat of glaze by hand. This will look much better
than a cross hatching of lines.

A coarse network of crazing is reproduced using
a polymer bound drawing lead, sharpened and
maintained at a needle point. The crazing usually
appears grey or brown so the appropriate colour is
easily available. Abrade the paint sufficiently to
provide a key for the pencil lines. Concentrate on
drawing in the most pronounced lines, following
the original shapes and cracks across the repair.
Make sure the lines match up at the edges.
Discreetly done this is a satisfactory simulation. If
the drawing is overdone or the lines drawn in a
haphazard fashion the result is a meaningless
cobweb. Use an airbrush to spray a light coat of
clear glaze over the crazing. This will seal in the
crazing and ensure a neat, clean image. Stove,
and when cold the final coat of glaze is applied by
hand.

When the crazing is in the form of long
striations they are most suitably reproduced by
scoring them into a coat of glaze which is put on
evenly by hand, applying it in the same way as a
basecoat. Stove the china and allow it to become
quite cold. The lines are then cut into the glaze,
following carefully the route and pattern of the
original crazing. A scalpel which is very thin and
sharp must be used to do this, otherwise the result
will be a broad furrow accompanied by a ridge. A
very fine hair line cut in the glaze is required.

Take a small quantity of dry pigment which
matches the colour of the crazing and grind with a
palette knife on a card until smooth. It is applied
either with a soft brush or a clean, dry finger tip,
rubbing into the scores on the glaze. The fine
powder will be held in the cuts; any loose grains
can be blown and brushed away. The repair is
then given a final protective coat of glaze to seal in
the pigment and stoved as usual. This method
when skilfully done gives the best results, but is
impossible to carry out where the crazing is closely
netted. The effect achieved by scratching the
surface with a pin to represent crazing will not
bear close inspection.

For oriental ceramics with a thick glaze and
induced crazing, incising the glaze with a scalpel
is much the best method to use. Because of the
refraction of light through a thick, crackled glaze
the pattern of the crazing may change slightly
when viewed from different angles. The difficulties of matching such crazing must be
considered before undertaking repairs. A final
protective coat of clear glaze is necessary over the
crazing.

Glazing

Glazing must be done in a dust- and fluff-free
atmosphere. The wet surface of the glaze will trap
any particles that fall onto it and, as a glossy
surface is the aim, these cannot be removed by
abrading. Attempting to lift them off with a brush
will usually result in a disturbed, uneven surface.
Ideally, glazing should be done in a separate
workroom well away from any rubbing down.
The work bench at least must be cleaned down to
remove dust. Any dusty brushes, rag or similar
sources of contamination should be well out of the
way. The brush used for glazing should always be
stored in a box or case, not left out to catch the
dust. Never dip the brush into the bottle of glaze;
this will introduce all sorts of foreign bodies into
the supply.

Applying glaze

Make sure the surface for glazing is dust- and fluff-
free. Check that no dust from rubbing down is
held in grooves or depressions. Pour sufficient
glaze to complete the work into a clean dipper.
The brush to be used should be rinsed in clean
thinners and shaken free of moisture. This will
remove the air from between the bristles which
would cause bubbles to form in the glaze. The
thinners evaporates so quickly from the brush that
it will not dilute the glaze. Apply the glaze with a
well charged brush using a similar action to that
used in brushing on base coats. Start at the centre

Fig. 135 Applying glaze. Let the spring in the bristles sweep across the surface

of the repair and skim the brush across the surface, allowing the spring in the bristles to flick up at the end of each stroke. This will thin or 'feather' out the glaze at the perimeter. The glaze must diminish at the edges and fade into the original surface imperceptibly.

Attempting to wipe away a hard step will result in smears. Use sufficient glaze to cover well and flow into a flat even surface. Do not flood the surface or dribbles and ridges will form. The glaze must not be taken onto the china further than absolutely necessary. It must be confined to the area of the repair, only fractionally overlapping the underpainting.

This is not an easy exercise but the results will improve with each attempt. After the glaze is applied it must be stoved as usual to cure it. If the finished coat is not as good as anticipated it can be rubbed down after stoving and a second coat applied. Glaze is easier to apply and is less obvious on a convex area than a concave one, the edges being disguised in the curve of the surface. This means that particular attention must be given to the interiors of cups or bowls, making sure that no

hard step is left at the edges of the glaze. Glaze should not be allowed to fill up hollows in the modelling; the contours must be maintained. To get a deep glaze more than one coat can be applied, stoving between each application.

Glaze should be applied very lightly over any bronze powder decoration as this is always the least hardy part of the decoration and can easily be smudged by heavy handed treatment. When an airbrush is available a very light protective coat of glaze can be sprayed over the bronze and stoved. When cold the final coat of glaze is applied to the whole of the repair by hand.

Reducing a glaze

A glaze that is too glassy in comparison with the original china can be toned down a little with the aid of abrasive powder. Make sure that the glaze has been stoved and is completely cold and hard or the abrasive will be pressed into the soft glaze. Take up a little dry abrasive either on a small pad of cotton wool or a dry fingertip and work over the surface to be dimmed. Use a light, circular rubbing action, confining the abrading to the surface of the applied glaze only. Working with the fingertip will ensure that the pressure on the abrasive is light enough to avoid scoring the surface. Check progress constantly so that the glaze is not subdued more than intended. The gloss can be restored if the abrading goes too far with a further application of glaze. However, this is rather a waste of time and it is undesirable to subject the restoration to more stoving than necessary. Once the right effect is achieved the restoration is complete. Any excess abrasive is blown and brushed away.

Patches of glaze which are not uniformly glossy, owing to wear or because of the type of decoration, can be simulated by treatment with dry abrasive. Where the area to be abraded is small use a small piece of cotton wool wrapped around a thin stick instead of rubbing with the finger.

This method of matting a glaze will match in with semi-glossy surfaces but will not serve for jasper or similar ware.

Matt surfaces

There are two methods of applying a matt finish to jasper, Parian or bisque surfaces. Each will give a slightly different texture. It is advisable to try out both methods so that the most suitable one can be chosen as the occasion arises. The repairs proceed as usual until the painting stage is reached. Normal basecoats cannot be applied as they are shiny. Therefore the correct texture has to be applied immediately. It must be both dense enough to obliterate the repair and to imitate the texture.

The close grained matt surface of jasper ware is not an easy finish to reproduce. The paint for this surface is prepared with glaze medium and artists' oil colours with the addition of steatite as a matting agent. The greater the proportion of steatite the greater the degree of matting. A trial will be necessary to establish the exact quantity needed for the individual piece of china. The full degree of graining does not develop until the mixture is almost dry, but this only takes a few moments.

Pour a suitable quantity of glaze medium into a dipper and mix an exact colour match using artists' oil colours. Add a small quantity of steatite with the tip of a clean palette knife. Mix in thoroughly with a stiff brush and add a drop of thinners to compensate for the thickening properties of the steatite. Test on a piece of china for texture match. If necessary continue adding small quantities of steatite and thinners, mixing thoroughly each time until the resulting mixture matches the jasper ware.

This paint is applied in a similar way to a coat of glaze, laying it lightly over the repair and using the spring in the sable bristles to graduate the edges. The edges cannot be feathered away with clear glaze or a shiny rim will result. The glaze, paint and steatite mixture can be applied by airbrush if sufficient thinners is added for it to pass through the airbrush. This will somewhat weaken the durability of the repair and the coat should be applied by hand if possible. The thick mixture will swiftly clog the airbrush nozzle and cleaning must be constant and very thorough. This coat of paint is stoved as usual. It should not be rubbed down unless the results are unsatisfactory and make a further coat necessary. No final coat of glaze is possible.

For a rougher, more granular texture glaze medium can be mixed with artists' dry ground colours. This will give a more durable surface than the steatite mixture. Pour sufficient glaze medium into a dipper to complete the work. It is advisable to be generous with the quantity as matching up a second batch is difficult. Add the dry ground pigments until a dense, exactly matching colour and texture is produced. Use a palette knife to pick up the powdered pigments and mix in thoroughly with a stiff brush. Make sure there are no hard lumps or pockets of powder left in the mixture. Before using add a drop or two of thinners to bring the paint to a workable consistency. This mixture is applied to the surface to obliterate the repair and allowed to become slightly tacky.

Using a stiff bristled brush stipple the tacky surface. Continue stippling until the paint is dry enough to hold the granulation and no further effect is visible. Stipple evenly over the surface; do not thin out the paint in patches. The edges of the paint are stippled out to blend in with the china. The overlapping must be kept to a minimum, just enough to conceal the join. Fine down the edges with the action of the brush only; brushing out the edge with clear glaze would leave a glossy rim. This coat of paint is stoved as usual but should not be rubbed down. One coat should be sufficient as further applications will build up too much bulk. No final protective coat of glaze can be given.

Foot rims

It is unusual to find glaze on the foot rim of a piece of china. On earthenware items the clay shows through, not only as a change in texture but of colour as well. Frequently on chinese porcelain both the edge of a plate or bowl and its foot rim are a dull rusty brown. Any of the methods for giving a matt texture can be used around the rim. Where only the texture differs from the main glaze the simplest way is to rub down the gloss with dry abrasive after glazing and stoving. If a change of colour as well as texture is necessary, glaze mixed with oil colours and steatite is best. A coat of synthetic glaze should not be applied afterwards.

Using a cold setting glaze

The cold setting resin is used in exactly the same way as the heat cured medium for putting on basecoats, decoration, gilding with either bronze powder or gold leaf and for the final glaze. No significant difference is noticeable in the working properties of the two types of glaze. Equal quantities of resin and hardener are mixed in a dipper. The cold glaze mixes readily with both oil colour, dry ground pigments and steatite. A drop or two of dilutant can be added to adjust the consistency of the mixture when dry pigments or steatite are added. Each coat of paint or application of decoration must be allowed to dry naturally for 24 hours before either rubbing down or adding any further glaze. The china should be stored in a dust- and fluff-free place while drying. Brushes or the airbrush must be cleaned with the appropriate dilutant; thinners should not be used. The repair will need a final protective coat of cold setting resin glaze, unless a very matt finish using either dry pigments or steatite is required.

Faults in surface finishes

Bubbles which form in the glaze before stoving must be eased out to the edge immediately and dispersed. They must not be left or they will burst and form craters when stoved. They usually form when pouring the glaze or because the bristles of the brush are full of air. Never shake a bottle of glaze. Always rinse a dry glaze brush in thinners or dilutant before using it. If the bubbles do not rise to the surface of a dipper of glaze check that the glaze medium is not outdated and getting too thick for proper application.

When the bubbles do not appear until after stoving, several causes should be suspected. Check that there are no pin holes in previous coats of paint or decoration. The surface must be smooth; dust and scratches left from rubbing down leave pockets of air which are trapped under the glaze. The bubbles must be rubbed down until none remain to trap more air. A further coat of glaze must then be applied and stoved.

An uneven, streaky coat of glaze can be the result of outdated glaze. The supply of glaze should automatically be renewed at the end of six months. It tends to thicken very gradually, which goes unnoticed until the difficulty in application becomes extreme. Applying insufficient glaze or brushing it out too much will also give a poor finish.

A hard line around the area of the glaze must never be allowed to remain. Always feather off the edge with the brush. Work from the centre outwards, even for a crack. Never apply the glaze as a straight band.

Fig. 136 Propol cold setting glaze

143

A repair that looks too new and shiny should be rubbed very gently with dry abrasive, not hard enough to cause any scratching, but just enough to tone in with the original surface.

If the matt finish rubs off easily too great a proportion of either steatite, dry ground pigments or thinners was used in the mixture. All the soft paint must be removed before a fresh, correct, mixture is applied otherwise subsequent coats will peel off.

With the exception of faults which originate with the application of heat, difficulties encountered when using cold setting glaze medium can be overcome by applying the remedies for identical problems encountered with heat cured resin.

If the china is to be stored or packed for delivery it should be wrapped first in either acid free tissue paper or plastic bags. Newspaper, although excellent as padding for short periods, should not come into contact with the restoration or the china. Apart from the ink leaving dirty marks, the chemicals present in it, particularly if allowed to become damp, can cause deterioration and discoloration in some old glazes. As the environment and treatment of the china cannot be controlled once it has left the hands of the restorer no precise duration of repairs can be guaranteed. In a normal home atmosphere, with regular sympathetic cleaning, they will last many years. When china can be kept in an airtight cabinet it will remain cleaner and be less likely to sustain damage. Modern restoration materials should be expected to withstand reasonable handling and cleaning if china is to be studied, enjoyed and fully appreciated.

Fig. 137 The lower arm, hand and handle of the hurdy-gurdy have been modelled painted and glazed

144

10 Setting Up the Workshop

As well as the technical skills so far considered the restorer needs:

somewhere to do the work;
to know how to make and maintain tools;
to understand the need for safety precautions;
an understanding of the suitability of the job for the individual;
to know how to estimate the costs and overheads involved;
information on suppliers of equipments and materials; and
facilities for research (at least a library and advice on where to seek information).

The workspace

The needs of the workspace have to be balanced between what is desirable and what is possible. The choice will be influenced by economy, available space and the ultimate aim of the restorer. If the student wishes to do no more than small repairs by hand, a small space will suffice. Even then, the requirements for this should not be underestimated. Perhaps a statement of the minimum requirements will be helpful.

The workspace must have sufficient room to contain a stout bench which will not wobble or be harmed by spills. It needs to be large enough to give adequate space for working and to place the equipment within easy reach. A chair of suitable height will of course be necessary as well. A place is needed to clean and prepare china as well as an oven or heating cabinet for curing resins. Safe storage space must be found for both materials and china. The cleaning and storage facilities do not have to be within the workroom although it does save time and help to prevent accidents if china does not have to be carried backwards and forwards during restoration.

Choice of accommodation
Whatever accommodation is allocated it must be borne in mind that a great deal of dust will be created while working. As many of the solvents, adhesives and paints give off toxic fumes or are flammable, they must be stored and used in a suitable place. For the health of any other occupants of the premises the workspace should be confined to a separate area; a kitchen or any living area is most unsuitable.

The fine dust produced when rubbing down modelling composition or paint will float about and coat every available surface. This is harmful and must not be inhaled or ingested. It must be confined to the working area and never be allowed to come into contact with food, or equipment used in its preparation. Fumes from solvents and paints can cause health hazards so the appropriate precautions must never be neglected. (Cautions and precautions are given when these materials are listed throughout the book.) Good ventilation is vital and an extractor fan with an exterior outlet should be installed.

If airbrushing equipment is to be used (and only minor work can be done without it) the noise factor must be considered. The frequent running of some compressor motors can constitute a nuisance to close neighbours. Deadening the sound of a noisy compressor must be limited to a thick pad placed underneath as a free circulation of air around the motor is essential.

Heating
This is an important item when considering overhead expenses. Not only must the system of heating be economical to install and run, but it must be safe to use in the vicinity of flammable materials. The flammable liquids are highly volatile and will produce a spreading vapour which can be ignited by a spark. No naked flames, open fires or pilot lights should be in the vicinity.

Convector heaters which will circulate the heated vapours are particularly unpleasant. Good ventilation must always be maintained.

Lighting

Strong natural light at the bench is vital. Although some work can be done under artificial light, colour matching needs daylight. On dull days a good movable spotlight on the bench is necessary for providing illumination. It can also be used to highlight the imperfections in bonding and modelling by angling the beam across the surface of the work, even when the natural light is good.

Bench

A sturdy bench that will not be harmed by spilt chemicals, adhesives or paints is a basic essential. Plastic work tops are easily cleaned but some solvents will damage them. A wooden bench top enables equipment to be screwed in position; for example, the airbrush is much safer if its holder is secured in this way. The bench should be large enough to enable the tools, materials and the current job to be easily accessible. Nothing is more irritating or time wasting than constantly moving equipment into position. A bench where everything is crowded will add to the risk of chipping the china. Small tools and materials not actually in use can be stored under or at the side of the bench, preferably in cupboards so that there will be less danger of accidents.

It is very convenient to have a pad made from several thicknesses of absorbent, non-fluffy cloth on the immediate working surface. It makes a handy tool and brush wiper as well as offering a soft protective surface for the china to rest on. It will also absorb any accidental spills. When working on fragile figures or flower-encrusted china a pad of foam between the bench and the object will help to guard against crushing the delicate china.

Warning: If a pad does become saturated by any flammable or toxic liquid it should be disposed of immediately.

Chair

It may seem unnecessary to emphasize the importance of seating but unless the worker is comfortably positioned concentration is difficult. The chair should be the right height to enable the work to be supported on the bench, not balanced in the lap. Apart from the risk of the china

slipping onto the floor, maximum pressure cannot be brought to bear for bonding and abrading unless the work is firmly supported. Twice as much energy is expended if the article is supported in one hand while abrading with the other. Back ache and eye strain will be minimised if the workbench and chair are the right height for each other and the worker.

Cleaning

The restoration of any article begins with cleaning. A sink, drainer, hot water and space to use solvents or leave articles to soak undisturbed will be needed. Once again, some solvents are toxic so the restorer must be satisfied that accidental contact by other workers, children or pets cannot occur.

Heating cabinet

An oven or heating cabinet will be required for the low curing of resins. It should be sited well away from any flammables either in use or stored. As resins produce fumes when heated it should not be in the workroom. The type of stove needed is dealt with in Chapter 6.

Storage

Solvents and chemicals should always be stored in a cool, dark dry place, preferably under lock and key. If any doubt exists about the conditions needed for storage, the manufacturers of the materials will supply instructions.

Making tools

Provided tools can be produced quickly, making them can be a worthwhile economy, but of course there is little point in spending a long time making something which is inexpensive to purchase ready made. The main advantage in making equipment is in having the exact tool for the job. Saving unnecessary labour is the greatest possible economy. Take advantage of anything that cuts down on cleaning time but make sure that it will not be at the expense of efficient cleaning.

Making modelling tools and spatulas

Small, hand-made boxwood tools are very expensive. However, they can be converted from large tools intended for pottery, which are machine made and reasonably priced. Choose the widest and simplest boxwood shapes, which can then be split or sawn lengthways to provide two or three blanks. The tips can then be refashioned, first with a chisel or file to rough out the shape and then smoothed with glass paper. A pointed tool can be shaped in a pencil sharpener before finishing with glass paper.

Bamboo tools are very smooth and pleasant to work with. They can be purchased from pottery suppliers but these too are usually many sizes too large. They can be scaled down to size by splitting and reshaping the tips. Bamboo canes intended for garden use can be had in many sizes; these are well seasoned and suitable for cutting down before being whittled into smooth, useful tools. Thin, pliable slivers are very good for applying and spreading adhesive. Green bamboo canes must be left in the dry to season before being used. Dead canes are useless as they are brittle and splintery.

After shaping, any modelling tool must be smoothed and finished with glass paper. A clumsy, rough tool will never produce good results. Time spent in making a good tool is time saved when modelling.

Making probes
Although probes or potters pins are not very costly, they quickly become too blunt to get into small rivet holes. A supply can easily be made from thick embroidery needles and 1 cm ($\frac{1}{2}$ in) diameter wooden dowelling or rod. Saw the dowelling into approximately 6 cm (3 in) lengths and drill a hole at least 1 cm ($\frac{1}{2}$ in) deep in one end. Push the eye end of the needle into the hole, using a pair of pliers to grip the needle if necessary; it should be a tight fit. If there is any movement a little adhesive can be used to secure it safely into position; it would be dangerous if the needle could spring out of position when prising out a difficult rivet.

Making a bench rest for the airbrush
Take or cut a strip of aluminium approximately 2 mm ($\frac{1}{32}$ in) (14 British standard wire gauge) thick by 21 cm ($8\frac{1}{2}$ in) long by 13 mm ($\frac{1}{2}$ in) wide. Cut off a short length 8 cm ($3\frac{1}{4}$ in) long. Lay the two pieces flat and side by side on the bench with one set of ends level. Let these be the top ends. Using a square, mark with a scriber or fine felt tip pen the places where the strips are to be bent to form the shape shown in the diagram. Aim to make the shaped top just large enough to accommodate the airbrush. The two portions may be bolted, riveted or stuck together. If they are to be bolted or riveted it is best to mark and drill the holes before

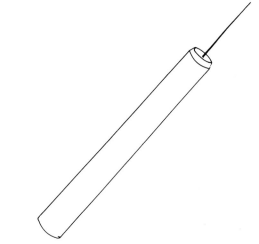

Diagram 64 Probe made from a needle inserted into dowelling

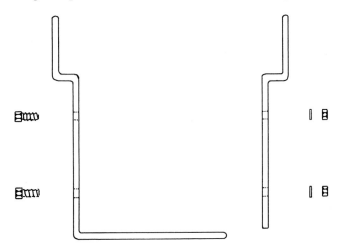

Diagram 65 Making a bench rest for the airbrush

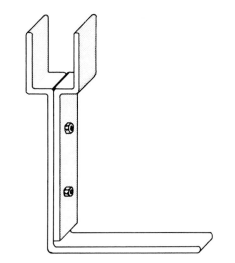

Diagram 66 This type of rest will hold securely all the makes of airbrush suitable for use in china restoration

147

the strips are bent. If laid one on top of the other the holes can be drilled through both pieces at once, thus ensuring perfect alignment.

The foot may be drilled if it is intended to screw the rest to the bench. It may be more convenient to use a G-cramp as this permits its easy removal. It does not matter which of the two bends in the short strip is made first, but it will be found easiest to make the foot bend first in the long strip and work along from that end. To bend the aluminium, clamp the strip into a metal jawed vice up to the mark made with the scriber or pen. No special tool should be necessary with this thickness of metal, not even a hammer; fingers should suffice. To obtain a small piece of metal such as this try a model engineering shop or a scrap metal dealer.

Making dippers and liners

Not only time but large quantities of expensive thinners can be saved by making either disposable dippers or liners which can be discarded after use. Discs of thick aluminium foil can be pleated or formed around a cork to produce an excellent paint container of just the right size. If these are found to be too fragile they can be used inside a metal dipper of the type manufactured for use with oil colours. Alternatively, a block of wood can be drilled with holes approximately 2 cm (1 in) diameter by 1 cm ($\frac{1}{2}$ in) deep to make a holder for the aluminium liners.

Disposable palettes

Palettes which can be disposed of after use are another economy, especially if they can be made from card which would otherwise be thrown away. Even if cartridge paper has to be bought specially it will work out cheaper than using thinners for cleaning. If only thin card is available, several layers can be stapled together for strength, the top sheet being peeled off after use. Non-stick parchment is also stronger used in this way. Waxed card must never be used as the coating will dissolve into the epoxy resin or paint mix. Throw-away dippers and palettes also save the fingers from contact with methylated spirit and thinners, so lessening the likelihood of skin irritation and dermatitis.

Caring for tools and brushes

Good quality specialist tools and brushes are expensive. They are not available from every art shop, so they are worth looking after. Make a point of cleaning them immediately after use and storing them carefully, and then they will last a long time. At least twice as much time is needed to remove resin or paint once it has hardened.

Modelling tools

Always clean tools used for modelling in methylated spirit before the resin has had time to set. Make sure that no small pieces remain; if they are left to harden they will scratch, not smooth the composition next time the tool is used. Hardened adhesive or composition will need removing with glass paper. There is already quite enough rubbing down to do on the restoration without wasting time on the tools. Do not hack at the resin with a knife or else the tool, not the resin, will be cut away.

Files

A file card should be used frequently while working, to keep files free from resin. Keep the file flat and rub it gently along the spikes embedded in the card. If the resin is allowed to build up on the teeth of the file abrading will become inefficient. When the file has been badly neglected and compressed resin has become hard, it can be removed by painting the file with paint stripper. Leave the stripper in place for 20 minutes and then flush off with water. Dry the file immediately and thoroughly. This treatment should only be used in extreme circumstances. A file card used properly should be quite sufficient. Files will wear out in time and should be replaced once the tooth has worn down.

Scalpels, knives and scissors

These must always be kept clean and sharp or they will drag and tear at the materials leaving jagged edges. Penknives and scalpels can be kept sharp on an oilstone, but scissors need professional grinding and setting from time to time to keep them in good order. Disposable scalpels can be used, provided they are disposed of immediately they loose their edge. They are quite cheap and should be renewed frequently. It would not be an economy to ruin a sheet of gold leaf with a blunt scalpel.

Fig. 138 A file card used for cleaning files and rifflers

Fig. 139 A recently introduced scalpel with a rectractable blade. Spare blade and two burnishing tools stored in the handle are included

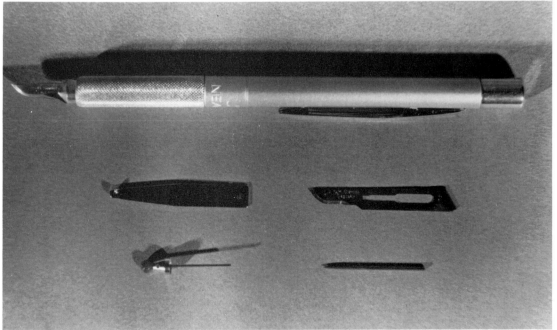

Brushes

A good quality sable brush, although initially very expensive, becomes a good friend. It is worth while breaking in a new brush before the favourite one is past its best. In that way a suitable brush is always available for a tricky piece of painting. Good drawing cannot be done with a limp, whiskery, inferior brush. Brushes should be chosen with care and looked after well, even cherished. Clean in thinners immediately after use, making sure no pigment is left to harden at the base. Once the paint is allowed to stiffen in the bristles they will be snapped off in the effort to remove it. Never leave a brush standing on its bristles either dry or in a cleaning fluid; this treatment will curl them beyond repair. Always store brushes in a dry, dust and mothproof place. Once brushes have been used with thinners they become unpalatable to moths, but new brushes should be stored with an insecticide.

Brushes used for parting or releasing agents when moulding, or with latex masking fluid for airbrushing, should be washed in warm soapy water, rinsed and thoroughly dried. It is a good plan to mark and keep separately the brushes used for different jobs to avoid any confusion.

Good brushes are made from complete hairs with each bristle tapering towards its point. Once the tip has been broken or worn away the brush cannot retain a fine point. The hairs are selected from different parts of the pelt according to the quality of the brush, the best coming from areas where the hair is longest, has the most spring and is least worn. Cheap brushes are made from long fibres cut to length. Any point is made by cutting the tip of the brush at an angle or by varying the length of the fibre so that if the point consists of one fibre only it could never be as fine as one natural hair.

Dippers and palettes

If it is impossible to use disposable dippers and palettes any tiles, saucers or pieces of glass used for this purpose must be particularly well cleaned as any residue will contaminate a subsequent mixture. Epoxy resin must be completely cleaned away with methylated spirit before it sets. Paint and synthetic glaze require thinners for removal. Synthetic glaze is particularly difficult to remove; even a smear of residue will contaminate a subsequent mix making it thick and sticky.

Neither of these two cleaning fluids should come into contact with the skin more than is absolutely necessary. They both have a degreasing action and if used frequently can cause the fingers to become sore and cracked in spite of regular use of a barrier cream.

Used thinners can be left to settle in a tightly closed jar and decanted for cleaning purposes when clear.

Cleaning airbrushes

Always follow the manufacturers' recommendations for cleaning an airbrush. Make sure that every trace of pigment and synthetic glaze has been removed with thinners before the job is considered finished. Any residue will block the instrument and a great deal of time will be wasted before work can recommence. Clear instructions and any special tools needed for routine cleaning should be included with the airbrush at the time of purchase. Precise instructions for cleaning cannot be detailed here as there are different makes and models on the market.

Compressors

The water trap on a diaphragm pump will need frequent emptying unless this is done automatically through the safety valve during operation. If the compressor has an air storage tank the condensed moisture will need draining off periodically. There will be a drainage plug beneath the reservoir for this purpose. Check regularly that the safety valve is working freely and not obstructed in any way. Also make sure hoses are in good condition and not perished. Unless the pump is a sealed unit check the oil level and top up if necessary.

Cleaning and keeping tools in good order seems irksome and unproductive when there is interesting china to work on, but unless it is done conscientiously and immediately simple routine cleaning will turn into major spring cleaning and lead to expensive replacements.

Safety precautions

Many dangerous practices have found their way into print, which immediately seems to give them authority. Others have been handed on and become common practice without due thought for possible hazards. Even everyday household chemicals must be used with proper care. Substances which seem inert and innocuous when used occasionally can be harmful when used frequently and intensively.

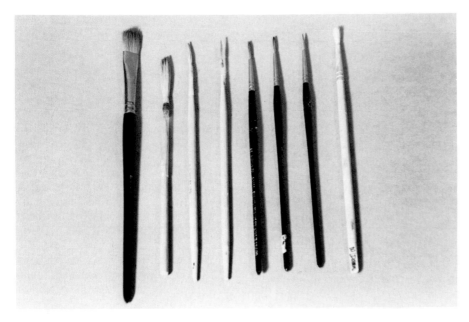

Fig. 140 Brushes suitable for glazing, painting and mixing. Make sure they are clean and that the points are reformed before storing

Diagram 67 Warning symbol for flammable substances

Diagram 68 Warning symbol for toxic substances. Danger from swallowing, inhaling vapours, fumes or dust and skin contact

Diagram 69 Warning symbol for corrosive substances

Diagram 70 Warning symbol for oxidising substances, producing great heat

Diagram 71 Warning symbol for harmful substances which can cause minor illness by swallowing, inhaling or skin contact

Safe storage

The hazards, shelf life and storage requirements of china restoring materials are detailed at the end of the chapter. All materials, whether obviously dangerous or not, should be clearly labelled so that no confusion can occur. The labels must be legible, indelible and permanent. Ready printed labels are available which comply with the latest safety regulations. It is a good idea to include on the label the remedy or antidote should the substance be misused. In an emergency the simplest instructions can be forgotten.

Flammables

These must all be stored in unbreakable containers in a dry, cool, dark place, preferably in an outhouse. Small quantities should be decanted into small closed containers for use in the workroom. Storage must be dry so that tins will not rust through and leak. Do not store incompatible materials near one another, so that if an accident does occur a further hazard will not be created. For instance, accidentally spilt acid (rust remover) should not be able to come into contact with the container of a flammable liquid (thinners, methylated spirit). It could damage the container and allow the contents to escape. All dangerous materials should be stored under lock and key. Never put solvents or chemicals into food containers. This may be an economical measure but in the workroom it can lead to confusion and accidents. Always make sure that materials are returned to their proper place in the store if removed for decanting.

Decanting

When decanting substances for bench use, pour gently to avoid splashing. Do not lean over the containers, and avoid inhaling the rising fumes. Always decant into clean containers; stopper and label each one immediately to avoid confusion over the contents.

Safe handling

There are three types of personal hazard to be considered while working. Chemicals or solvents can enter the body through the digestive system, the skin or the lungs. In the workroom it should be impossible to ingest any chemicals. Eating or drinking in the workroom or before washing the hands should never be permitted. Never use beverage bottles, domestic beakers or cups for storing or holding chemicals.

Contact with toxins either directly or from fumes or dust is less easily avoidable. The level of sensitivity will vary between individuals but apart from the short term effects from ingestion, inhalation and skin contact there is the admittedly small but serious chance of malignant diseases. Consequently it is wise to avoid contact with solvents and chemicals wherever possible. The use of respirators and gloves, and the use of tools not fingers, although feeling clumsy at first, soon becomes second nature. After all, the most delicate surgery is carried out by gloved hands manipulating tools. Surgeons are also compelled to wear a mask and frequently work using magnifying spectacles. It is a matter of habit.

Do not rely on barrier cream as a major safeguard. It should form part of the routine for the safe handling of materials. Filters in respirators must be renewed as soon as the slightest smell is detectable.

Never smoke in the workroom. Vapours inhaled through a cigarette are most harmful quite apart from the fire risk. Anyone suffering from asthma or other respiratory complaints will find that painting and particularly spraying will aggravate the condition.

Protective spectacles should be used when spraying, especially if contact lenses are worn. The vapour will irritate the eyes and may damage the contact lens.

Always seek advice for any rash, inflamation or cracking of the skin, whether on the fingers or any other part of the body. Allergies do not always show up immediately. An apparent immunity must not be taken as an indication that precautions can be ignored. Always:

avoid direct contact wherever possible;
wear protective clothing and equipment;
maintain good ventilation; and install an air extractor if possible.

Never mix chemicals or solvents unless they are known to be compatible. Always add acid to water, not water to acid, and wear gloves while doing it. Use tough plastic, not metal, receptacles for bleach and solvents when cleaning china because contact with metal may either neutralize or accelerate the action of the chemicals.

A first aid kit should be available. Cuts from broken china and burns from soldering irons should be covered immediately, before dirt or toxic dust have an opporutnity to enter the wound.

Fire precautions

The bulk of the supply of flammables, notably thinners and methylated spirit, should be stored apart, preferably in an outhouse. Indeed the storage of flammables except in very small quantities may invalidate the existing insurance on the premises if done without the agreement of the insurer. The danger does not only come from the flammable liquid but from the vapours given off. Special care must be taken when decanting, painting or spraying. Any swabs, paint rags or cellulose tissues impregnated with flammables must be completely dried off in a well ventilated place before being disposed of. For the restorer working alone using only small amounts of solvents and chemicals, safe disposal procedures may present a problem. Advice can be obtained through the Health and Safety Executive. A fire extinguisher and/or a fire smothering blanket should be easily accessible, not buried under boxes of china. Water should not be used to quench a fire where thinners, methylated spirit or electrical equipment is involved.

The bench magnifier is frequently overlooked as a source of danger. Left near a window where the sun's rays can focus through it, a plume of smoke will soon be produced which, if undetected, will spread. This may seem rather extreme but it has been the cause of panic in more than one workshop. Cover the magnifier or move it out of

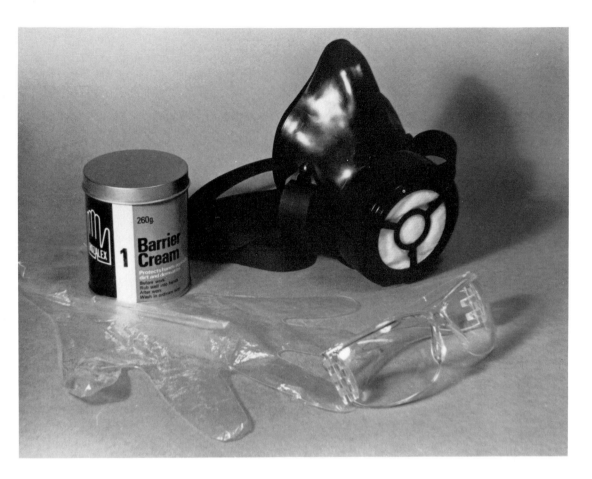

Fig. 141 Barrier cream, dust and vapour respirator, protective gloves and spectacles

harm's way; do not forget that the angle of the sun's rays will change while the worker is absent. Be careful to keep packing materials and boxes where they will not obstruct the circulation of air round compressor motors or heaters. Tidiness, forethought and sensible precautions will keep the risk of fire to the minimum.

Safety precautions for the china
The safety of the china as well as the restorer must always be in mind. Any new materials need thorough testing on china once it has been established that the materials are safe for the restorer to handle. They must first be tried out on an old worthless plate or something similar. Any product which does not have its active ingredients clearly listed or with which the restorer is unfamiliar should not be used until the technical procedures are fully understood. Any technique which would subject the china to a temperature at or above 120°C (250°F) should not be considered for use. Never use carborundum wheels, diamond

drills or anything which is designed to grind away the china, because it would then be damaged permanently. Strong glass etching acids such as fluoric acid should never be used to remove stains as the glaze, basically a glass, will be permanently damaged. Fluoric acid is the active constituent in some sanitary-ware bleaches.

Be very cautious about trying any unfamiliar material intended for industrial use. These so-called magic mixtures are sometimes brought along by the well intentioned for the restorer to try out. Many adhesives and chemicals are only permitted to be used under licence in strictly controlled conditions. These materials may be extremely hazardous for both china and restorer when used in normal workroom conditions.

Never do or use anything on a repair which will be irreversible.

A suitable occupation?

China restoration is an absorbing and compelling occupation for the right person. To others it is tedious and irritating. Beside artistic ability the restorer needs the patience and temperament to strive constantly for perfection. The work calls for someone who will not lose heart and temper on the occasions when the job is less than perfect and needs to be re-done. All the processes must be designed for the well being of the china, not the ease and speed of application regardless of results.

There are very few opportunities for employment with an organisation, so the china restorer is usually self employed. Without the stimulating influence of tutor and fellow students the intending restorer may find that the job is lonely and that enthusiasm wanes, especially when uncongenial work is waiting to be done. A self employed person must have the self discipline to work regardless of whether the job of the moment is boring, not to one's taste or the weather is wonderful outside the workroom window.

Unless situated within easy reach of a centre for the antique trade, the area may not provide sufficient work for a restorer. Although there is a great demand for skilled restoration, transporting work over long distances adds to the overall costs without adding to the value of the article concerned. Make sure of the market before building a workshop on a mountain top!

Because the restorer can be self employed, restoring china is often considered to be an ideal job for the retired, housebound or handicapped person. In many cases this is so. Anyone contemplating a career in restoring needs excellent eyesight, very good colour vision and great dexterity. A lot of china is quite heavy, so a good deal of strength and flexibility in the hands and wrists is required to handle valuable china safely. The job also entails sitting at a workbench for long periods, which can be tiring.

Before embarking on the procuring of fairly expensive equipment it is wise to consider all the conditions which will be encountered.

Cost

It is impossible to quote the prices for individual items as they are constantly changing. It would probably be helpful if the most expensive single item, namely the airbrush, is compared in cost to a good domestic sewing machine. The compressor is also in this price range. Paints vary greatly in cost according to the pigment used in their manufacture, and the availability of those pigments on the world market. Catalogues and price lists are usually available on application from manufacturers. Postage and packing must be taken into account and many firms impose a minimum charge for orders. Where it is possible to make local purchases, provided the tools and materials are of suitable quality, it is advisable to do so. Many large suppliers have overseas and provincial branches whose addresses can be found in the trade section of the area telephone directory. The addresses of manufacturers or main stockists of materials referred to in this book will be found collectively at the end of this chapter.

Costing

Only the finest quality materials can be trusted for durability, but the price of materials is insignificant in proportion to the labour involved when assessing the total cost of a job. It is simply not viable to restore low quality items unless they hold some great personal sentimental value. The value of the article can easily be below the price of the labour. It takes as much time to repair a break in an item costing a few pounds as one worth thousands. A rational and economic fee must be charged for the work or the restorer will be working to support, or at least subsidise, the client. The charges can be broken down simply into materials, labour and overheads.

Materials
It is difficult to put an exact price on a teaspoonful of clay or a squeeze of paint for each repair, so it is advisable to establish a standard sum to cover such items proportionate to the size of the job.

Labour
When considering labour costs the time spent in non-productive activities must be taken into account. Preparing and cleaning the workroom and its equipment, attending to clients, purchasing materials, keeping records and accounts, packing and delivering all take time. A proportion of this must be added to each job, otherwise the restorer finds he is paid for only a part of each working day. Keep a time sheet recording the total number of hours worked daily including general maintenance and routine tasks. Log precisely the amount of time spent directly on

each item from the initial cleaning to the final glazing. Over a period this will reveal the proportion of productive, direct, working hours to the time spent in hidden, unproductive activities.

For example, if in a 40 hour week 5 hours are spent on indirect work, the charge for this must be divided between the balance of 35 hours when assessing the hourly charge for a job. Over a year, failure to do this will amount to four or five weeks unpaid work. The student should keep accurate time sheets during the later part of training. A detailed breakdown of the time taken on every stage of each job should be recorded, not forgetting time spent in research. This will ensure that once sufficient experience has been gained to undertake commissions it will be possible to estimate accurately the time needed to complete most assignments.

Overheads
These are the costs of maintaining a workshop or business and might include:

rent;
depreciation and replacement of equipment;
interest on capital;
heating, lighting and power;
telephone, postage, stationery;
packing;
delivery or motoring expenses;
insurance; and books, catalogues, subscriptions.

The total of all these must be allocated proportionally to the jobs done. The annual total of the estimated cost of these items is divided by the number of hours worked. This will establish the cost of overheads per hour. The chargeable hourly rate for a job is obtained by adding together the cost of labour and the cost of overheads. The standard charge for materials is added to the total of the chargeable hourly rate for the job.

Records
Unless trading as a limited company there is no legal obligation to keep accounts. However, everyone engaged in business must make an annual return to the Inspector of Taxes. In the absence of adequate records the inspector makes an assessment on his conception of a fair sum. It is therefore in the interest of the restorer to keep a record of the incoming and outgoing monies if only, on some occasions, to prove how little tax is payable.

Accepting commissions

The terms on which china is accepted for restoration must be clearly understood by both parties. It is wise to seek legal advice on a suitable form of receipt. Keep a record of all china accepted stating client's name and address with an identifiable description of the goods. China which is not claimed after repair is subject to the Disposal of Uncollected Goods Act 1952.

Using a dwelling house for business purposes or storing flammables could invalidate existing insurances and contravene tax or local planning laws. It is worth checking these points with the appropriate authority.

There is a lot of help and advice available on starting and running a small business, much of it obtainable free of charge. Bank managers are usually helpful on accounting matters. Leaflets on tax and insurance are available from the Inland Revenue and insurance offices. Some useful addresses for this information are given at the end of this chapter.

Reference library

The owner of the china to be mended frequently supplies sufficient information for any missing parts to be remodelled and this of course is to everyone's advantage. Visiting libraries and museums for research is not always possible and takes time. It is necessary to have a least a small library always at hand. A very useful and inexpensive reference file can be built up from illustrations cut from magazines specialising in antiques. The catalogues issued by the larger auctioneers are also invaluable, as are illustrated museum catalogues and books. Museums in areas where the pottery trade is established have published excellent books, for example, Worcester and Derby.

As well as illustrations of china, pictures to help when replacing missing limbs and accessories will be needed. Advertisements can be most useful here. Very few illustrated magazines will not yield a few useful pictures of hands and feet in various positions which can be very helpful when modelling, especially when the limbs are shown from the side or rear. When choosing books make sure the pictures show clearly the parts of the article most likely to need repairing. So often the illustration is of the decoration, not the knob or handle, which is of course the part most vulnerable to damage. Do not choose books showing

Fig. 142 Oriental cup handle shapes

Fig. 143 Different types of ring handles. A good reference
library is essential to help with making the correct
replacements

Fig. 144 Cup handles based on the question mark shape

Fig. 145 Examples of useful knob shapes

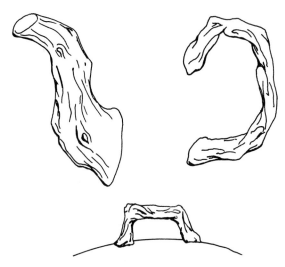

Diagram 74 Crabstock spout, handle and knob

Diagram 72 Shell spout with appropriate handle and knob

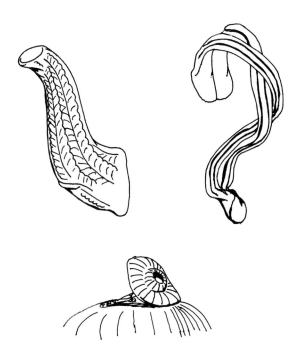

Diagram 73 Fern-leaf spout with appropriate handle and knob

only unique museum pieces; these articles are in protective custody and will not often come into the commercial restorer's workshop.

A suggested list for the nucleus of a library is given. This includes books on antique china, anatomy and accessories as well as further reading on techiques and general management.

Training

Finding good tuition is always a problem for the student wishing to learn china restoration. The large museums do train a small number of people but the intake is limited. The Craft Council, London, the Victoria and Albert Museum, London, and the magazine *Antique Dealer and Collectors Guide* all hold lists of establishments offering tuition, although this does not imply any recommendation on their part. The Antiques Year Book contains a list of restorers, some of whom offer tuition. A copy will be found in the reference section of most public libraries. The County Further Education Officer should also know of available classes in their respective areas and should be able to advise. As far as is known at present the only full time training available, apart from a very few apprenticeships, is a one year course at West Dean College of Crafts, Chichester, Sussex.

It cannot be stressed too strongly that there is no substitute for good training and practice under the guidance of an expert. This book is intended as an aid and reference, not as an alternative to a tutor.

Bibliography

Ceramics

CUSHION, J., *Animals in Pottery and Porcelain*, Studio Vista, London 1974.

FISHER, S., *Fine Porcelain and Pottery*, Octopus, London, 1974.

GODDEN, G., *An Illustrated Encyclopaedia of British Pottery and Porcelain*, Barrie and Jenkins, London, 1980.

GODDEN, G., *Jewitts Ceramic Art of Gt Britain 1800–1900*, Barrie and Jenkins, London, 1972.

HARRIS, N., *Porcelain Figurines*, Studio Vista, London, 1975.

REILLY, R., and SAVAGE, G., *Dictionary of Wedgwood*, Antique Collectors' Club, Woodbridge, Suffolk, 1980.

WHITER, L., *Spode*, Barrie and Jenkins, London, 1978.

General

BEECROFT, G., *Casting Techniques for Sculpture*, Batsford, London, 1978. Instructions on mould making.

CRAFTS COUNCIL, *Setting Up a Workshop*, The Crafts Council, London, 1975. Advice on starting a small business.

GAMMON, P., *Musical Instruments in Colour*, Blandford, Poole, 1975. Useful illustrations for repairs to figure groups.

GORDON, L., *Anatomy and Figure Drawing*, Batsford, London, 1979. Useful illustrations for modelling limbs.

LARNEY, J., *Restoring Ceramics*, Barrie and Jenkins, London 1975. Dealing chiefly with museum repairs.

MARTEN, C., *The Artists' Airbrush Manual*, David and Charles, Newton Abbot, 1980. Instructions on airbrushing, intended chiefly for illustration and retouching work.

SICHEL, M., *Costume Reference Series*, Roman to Present Day, Batsford, London, 1977–79. Contemporary accessories illustrated; useful for figure groups.

WILKINSON-LATHAM, R., *Antique Guns in Colour*, Blandford, Poole, 1977. Useful illustrations for repairs to figure groups.

Periodicals

Antique Dealer and Collector's Guide

Model engineering. Carries advertisements for airbrushing equipment and occasional articles on equipment.

Graphics World. Advertisements for airbrushing equipment.

Drawing Office Paper. Occasional articles, reviews and advertisements for airbrushing equipment.

Museums and Galleries in Gt Britain and Northern Ireland, ABC Travel Guides Ltd. Annual publication listing museums and their contents.

Sources of Useful Information

Antique Dealer and Collector's Guide, The Editor, City Magazines Ltd, Park House, 165–177 The Broadway, London SW19 1NE. Advice on tuition.

Ciba Geigy, Plastics Division, Duxford, Cambridge, CB2 4QA. Leaflets on handling epoxy resins.

Crafts Council, The, 12 Waterloo Place, London SW1Y 4AU. Advice on tuition.

Fire Prevention Information and Publicity Centre, The, Fire Prevention Association, Aldermary House, Queen St, London EC4N 1TJ. Advice on fire precautions.

Health and Safety Executive, Baynards House, 1 Chepstow Place, London w2. Advice on handling materials.

Health and Social Security, Dept of (Address in local telephone directory). Leaflet NI41, *National Insurfance for the Self-employed.*

Industry, Dept of, Small Firms Division, Abell House, John Islip St, London sw1 4LN. Free booklets and advice.

Inland Revenue, Inspector of Taxes (address in local telephone directory). Booklet IR28, *Starting in Business.* Information on tax for the self-employed.

Victoria and Albert Museum, The, London sw7 2RL. Advice on tuition.

West Dean College of Crafts, The Principal, Chichester, Sussex, PO18 0QZ. Advice on tuition.

Professional Organisation

International Institute for the Conservation of Historic and Artistic Works, The, 6, Buckingham Street, London wc2n 6ba. Affiliated regional groups worldwide.

Sources of Supply

Artists' Suppliers

Artists' oil colours
Brushes
Dividers
Gum strip
Large modelling tools
Paint dippers
Pencils
Plasticine
Spatulas
Spring clips
Tracing paper

Graphic Arts Shops

Clutch lead holders
Glass fibre erasers
Polymer drawing leads

Hardware Stores

Abrasive papers
Adhesive
Biological bleach
Chlorine bleach
Dismantling lubricant
File card
Liquid latex
Methylated spirit
Needle files
Paint stripper
Pliers
PTFE tape
Rust remover
Soldering irons
Spring clips
Tension files

Pharmacists

Acetone
Barrier Cream
Cleaning brushes
Dental plaster
Dental steriliser
Hydrogen Peroxide 100 volume
Lissapol
Methylated spirit
Oxalic acid crystals
Protective gloves
Resin removing cream
Scalpels

Specialist Suppliers in the UK

Airbrush and Compressor manufacturers or importers

De Vilbiss, Ringwood Road, Bournemouth, Hants. and provincial branches: airbrush model E63.

Frisk Products Ltd, 4, Franthorne Way, Randlesdown Road, London se6 3bt: E.F.B.E. airbrush model B1.

Microflame (uk) Ltd, Abbots Hall, Rickinghall, Diss, Norfolk ip22 ils: Paasche airbrush model H.

Morris and Ingram 156, Stanley Green Road, Poole, Dorset bh15 3be: Badger airbrush model GXF.

Sim-Air Compressors, 16 Woodsley Road, Leeds ls3 idt: noiseless compressors.

Airbrush mechanics and suppliers

Allen, J. W., 103 Palace Road, Bromley, Kent.
Dell, F., 50 Syon Park Gardens, Isleworth tw7 5nd.

General

Chintex, Wraxall, Bristol, Avon: clear glaze and thinners. Strictly mail order only. Worldwide distribution.

Claudius Ashe, Summit House, Moon Lane, Barnet, Herts en5 5ua, and provincial branches: Stents composition and de Treys Universal Wax.

Copydex Ltd, Penfold House, Brent St, London nw4 2eu. Direct worldwide distribution.

Frank W. Joel Ltd, Oldmedow Road, Hardwick Industrial Estate, Kings Lynn, Norfolk, Sepiolite, titanium oxide; many restoration materials available. Worldwide distribution.

Fulham Pottery and Cheavin Filter Co, 210 New Kings Rd, London sw6: Titanium oxide, best quality china clay, talc. Counter sales and mail order.

Geo Whiley, The Runway, Off Station Approach, South Ruislip ha4 6sq: bronze powder, gold leaf and sable paint brushes. Worldwide distribution.

Protective Polymers Ltd, Rhee Valley Works, Barrington Road, Shepreth, Royston, Herts: Propol Clear Glaze. Direct distribution worldwide.

Signs and Labels Ltd, Kenyon House, Moor Top Place, Heaton Moor, Stockport, Cheshire sk4 4jb: Makers of approved health and safety labels.

Tiranti, 70, High St, Theale, Berkshire: manufacturers of small modelling tools, suppliers of moulding rubber, respirators, fine bronze powders, files and most sculpture requirements.

Turnbridges Ltd. London sw17: manufacturers of Joy Thinners.

Winsor and Newton, 51–52, Rathbone Place, London wip iab: artists' dry ground colours and all artists' supplies. Direct distribution worldwide except usa and Australia, where they have agents.

Specialists Suppliers in Australia

(*see also worldwide distributors in main list.*)

Ciba-Geigy Australia Ltd, Orion Road, PO BOX 76, Lane Cove, Sydney, NSW 2066: Araldite adhesive. Main distributor.

DeVilbiss (Australasia) Pty Ltd, 55, Capella Crescent, Moorabbin, PO BOX 247 Victoria 3189, and at PO BOX 7, Coorparoo, Queensland 4151: airbrush model E63.

Harrison Mayer Craft and Education, 33, Adron St, Welshpool, Western Aus 6106: China clay.

Toltoys Pty Ltd, 157, Fitzroy St, St Kilda, Victoria 3182 Aust.: plasticine.

Winsor and Newton Pty Ltd, 102–104, Reserve Rd, Artarmon, NSW 2064: artists' suppliers.

Crafts Council of Australia, 27, King St, Sydney 2000. General information.

Specialist Suppliers in the USA

(*See also worldwide distributors in main list.*)

Colourforms Ltd, Walnut St, Norwood, New Jersey 07648. Plasticine.

Faber Castell Corp, 41, Dickerson St, Newark, NJ 07107: glass fibre erasers, drawing leads and holders.

Marx Brush Mfg Co Inc, 400, Commercial Ave, Palisades Park, NJ 07650: brushes.

Paasche Airbrush Co, 1909, Diversey Parkway, Chicago, Illinois 60614: Airbrush model H.

Ren Plastics Inc, 5656 South Cedar St, Lansing, Michigan 48909: Araldite adhesive, main distributors.

The DeVilbiss Company, 300, Phillips Ave, Toledo, Ohio 43692: airbrush model E63.

Winsor and Newton Inc, 555, Winsor Drive, Secaucus, NJ 07094: Artists' supplies.

American Crafts Council, 29, West 53rd Street, New York 10019. General information.

Details of Pigments

T = transparent   **P** = poisonous

Pigment	Composition of pigment	T/P
Aureolin (*English*) Aureoline (*French*) Aureolin (*German*)	Double nitrate of cobalt and potassium	
Burnt Sienna Terre de Sienne Brûlée Gebrannte Sienna	Calcined raw sienna	T
Burnt Umber Terre d'Ombre Brûlée Gebrannte Umbra	Calcined raw umber	

Cadmium Red Rouge de Cadmium Kadmiumrot	Complex cadmium sulpho-selenides	**P**
Cerulean Blue Bleu Caeruleum Conlinblau	Stannate of cobalt	
Chrome Yellow Jaune de Chrome Chromgelb	Normal chromate of lead	
Cobalt Blue Bleu de Cobalt Kobalt Blau	Cobalt aluminate or phosphate, some alumina	**T**
Cobalt Violet Dark Violet de Cobalt Kobalt Violett	Phosphate of cobalt	**P**
French Ultramarine Outremer Français Französiches Ultramarin	Combination of silica, alumina, soda and sulphur	**T**
Lamp Black Noir de Bougie Lampenschwarz	Carbon black	**T**
Paynes Grey Gris de Payne Paynes Grau	Preparation of slate, lamp black, iron oxide and ultramarine	
Prussian Blue Blue de Prusse Preussischblau	Potassium ferric-ferrocyanide	
Raw Sienna Terre de Sienne Naturelle Terra di Sienna	Native earth containing hydrated ferric oxide	**T**
Raw Umber Terre d'ombre Naturelle Umbra	Native earth containing ferric oxides and manganese dioxide.	
Rose Madder Garance Rose Rosa Krapplack	Preparation of madder root	**T**
Sap Green Vert de Vessie Saftgrün	Mixture of organic pigments	**T**
Titanium White Blanc de Titane Titanweiss	Titanium oxide	
Viridian Vert Emeraude Chromoxydgrün Feurig	Chromium sesquioxide	**T**

Details of Materials

Material	Shelf life	Storage conditions	Hazards
Acetone	Indefinitely, rapid evaporation unless sealed	Cool, secure, fireproof	Flammable, skin degreaser
Artists' pigments	Indefinitely	Cool, in tightly sealed containers	Some pigments toxic (see list of pigments)
Biological bleach	Indefinitely	Dry	Skin degreaser
China clay	Indefinitely	Dry, airtight container	Dust
Chintex glaze	Six months	Cool, dark, tightly sealed	Flammable, fumes
Chlorine bleach	Indefinitely	Airtight labelled container, secure place	Poison, do not mix with other chemicals
Copydex	Indefinitely	Keep cool and securely capped	
Dental composition	Indefinitely		
Dental Plaster	Indefinitely	Dry, airtight container	Dust
Dental wax	Indefinitely	Cool	Flammable if overheated
Epoxy resin	Indefinitely	Cool, dry	Fumes and dust, can cause dermatitis.
Lissapol	Indefinitely		Skin degreaser
Methylated spirit	Indefinitely	Cool, labelled tin, secure place, fireproof	Flammable, skin degreaser
Paint Stripper	Indefinitely	Cool, secure place	Caustic, toxic
Oxalic acid Crystals	Indefinitely	Cool, dry, secure place	Toxic, do not mix with other chemicals
Peroxide 100 volumes	Indefinitely	Cool, dark, labelled container	Explosive, harmful to skin
Plasticine	Reusable but dries out with use	Airtight containers	
Propol cold setting resin	Indefinitely	Cool, do not mix until required for use	Fumes; toxic through skin absorption
Rust remover	Indefinitely	Cool, secure place	Toxic, caustic
Sepiolite	Indefinitely	Dry	Fibrous dust**
Talc	Indefinitely	Dry	Dust
Thinners	Indefinitely; rapid evaporation	Cool, dark, labelled well sealed tin	Flammable, toxic
Titanium oxide	Indefinitely	Dry, dust proof container	Dust

**Note: Research into the dust hazards of sepiolite is at present incomplete. Until data is available the use of a respirator is advised.

Index